WORSHIP
Old and New

WORSHIP
Old and New

Robert E. Webber

ZONDERVAN
PUBLISHING HOUSE   OF THE ZONDERVAN CORPORATION
GRAND RAPIDS, MICHIGAN 49506

WORSHIP OLD AND NEW
Copyright © 1982 by The Zondervan Corporation
Grand Rapids, Michigan

First printing, August 1982

Library of Congress Cataloging in Publication Data
Webber, Robert.
   Worship, old and new.

   Bibliography: p.
   Includes indexes.
   1. Public worship.   I. Title.
BV15.W4   264   82-1969
ISBN 0-310-36650-X   AACR2

Unless otherwise indicated, Scripture quotations are from the New International Version © 1978 by New York International Bible Society. Used by permission.

Early-church design on title page and pages 21, 57, 85, 149, and 191 are from Ernst Lehner, "Symbols, Signs and Signets," Dover Publications, Inc.

Edited by Maureen LeLacheur and Gerard Terpstra
Designed by Louise Bauer

Printed in the United States of America

83 84 85 86 87 88   9 8 7 6 5 4 3 2

Dedicated to my sister and her husband

Eleanor and Nelson Entwistle

*in appreciation for the warm hospitality
they have shown to many people and
especially for the love and tender
care given to our parents in their
maturing years.*

Contents

Preface

This is a book about public worship—what the church does on Sunday morning (or at another time designated for worship). The topic itself has imposed certain limitations on the book. Occasions such as baptisms, weddings, and funerals, that are properly part of the worship of the church are not discussed.

The main purpose of the book is to examine the biblical roots, the historical development, and the theological meaning of worship. A secondary purpose, but one that is not worked out extensively, is to probe ways in which the old practices can be applied to worship in the twentieth century, especially among evangelical Christians. Each church will have to work this out for its particular situation.

The primary value of the book is as a classroom text in seminary and college courses on worship. However, it should also be of interest to pastors, Christian-education directors, worship committees, and laypersons who wish to be more informed on the subject.

I wish to acknowledge the helpful criticisms of Dr. Warren Wiersbe; Dr. Ralph Martin; Dr. James White; and my editor, Dr. Stanley Gundry. I also wish to express my appreciation to my secretary, Amy Richards, who has typed and retyped this manuscript in its several stages, and to Howard Fowler for the preparation of the indexes.

Chapter 1

Introduction

We are living in a time when almost every major denomination has been affected by renewed interest in the history, theology, and practice of worship. Landmark books published by liturgical scholars have effected renewal in the Roman Catholic, Episcopal, Presbyterian, Lutheran, Methodist, and Congregational churches, to name a few.[1] In the meantime many evangelical churches have remained virtually untouched by this vast amount of research and the application of it to worship renewal in the local congregations.

It is the purpose of this book to introduce the primary sources of worship literature that has recently become available and to challenge the church to renew worship through understanding the history and theology of the practice of worship. The argument is that the old forms of worship have not lost their value for worship today. Forms must be contextualized to meet the cultural situation of each worshiping congregation, but contemporary worship should not be drastically out of step with the worship heritage handed down by generations of Christians guided by the Holy Spirit.

We will begin by defining worship in its broadest sense as a "meeting between God and His people." In this meeting God becomes present to His people, who respond with praise and thanksgiving. Thus, the worshiper is brought into personal contact with the one who gives meaning and purpose to life; from this encounter the worshiper receives strength and courage to live with hope in a fallen world. To introduce this vast and complicated subject we will consider three preliminary concerns: (1) the need for worship renewal among Evangelicals; (2) the sources for worship renewal; and (3) basic principles of worship.

THE NEED FOR WORSHIP RENEWAL

A common complaint of a growing number of Protestant evangelical Christians is that public worship has little meaning. There is a boredom with sameness; an increasing discontent with the attempt to entertain; a concern over the packaging of worship; and a restlessness with an overemphasis on an appeal either to the mind or the feelings.[2] There are three sources from which these problems arise.

First, the antihistorical bias of many Evangelicals has led to a prideful rejection of the past among some pastors and leaders.[3] The problem with this attitude is that the rejection of historical perspective imprisons a movement within its present culture.[4] This imprisonment results in the uninformed normalizing of the present moment in history, together with all its aberrations and shortcomings, and leads to a suspicious attitude toward the legitimate use of historical insights. One by-product of recent liturgical scholarship is the discovery of those documents that provide insight into the meaning and practice of worship in the early church. We can now reconstruct the development of Christian worship from its sources in Judaism through the New Testament into the fully developed form of the early church. Studying the origins of Christian worship supplies the key to overcoming the negative results of historical amnesia. Anyone who desires to achieve worship renewal must pay attention to the sources and development of Christian worship.

Second, the imbalance of worship lies in its overidentification with rationalism, emotionalism, or entertainment. Worship in some quarters is characterized by an emphasis on the rational element. The emphasis is on the mind—on a thoughtful, reflective, cognitive approach to worshiping God. This approach usually emphasizes the understanding of the Word. Scripture reading is sometimes accompanied by explanation. Sermons are almost always exegetical, emphasizing the meaning of the text, sometimes without application to the hearer. Other congregations display a tendency to overemphasize the emotional element. This approach to worship focuses on the feelings—the immediate experience of God that results in feeling good about being in church. Still others place too much emphasis on entertainment. In this instance the worship of the church is oriented toward showing the people a good time. The chancel becomes the stage, and musicians and speakers work up the audience to provide them with a happy experience. The element of production and show in this approach to worship tends to call attention to itself and to the beauty, brilliance, and talent of the performers. True worship does stimulate the mind, move the emotions, and produce a sense of fun, as will be shown. But worship ought not to be reduced to a lecture hall, a psychiatric couch, or a stage.[5]

A third reason for the loss of worship is the loss of balance—a failure to give adequate attention to each aspect of the life of the church in the world. The church is to be involved in worship, teaching, mission, fellowship, healing, and service. However, churches often overemphasize one or another of these functions to the neglect of the others. For example, Roman Catholic, Orthodox, and Anglican communities place their emphasis on the worship of the church; Evangelicals tend to emphasize the teaching and mission functions of the church; Anabaptists stress the fellowship of the Christian community; the Charismatics place a strong accent on the church as a healing community; Liberals elevate the social side of the gospel. What is at stake is a matter of balance. All the churches mentioned above function to one degree or another in all six areas of church life. But there is a degree of imbalance in practically every major Christian community. Because evangelical Christianity suffers from a case of imbalance in worship, it is imperative to recover a proper view of worship for the sake of the spiritual health of the evangelical Christian community.

The diagnosis then is this: We have lost the art of worship as a result of historical amnesia; the infiltration of rationalism, emotionalism, or entertainment; and the failure to keep balance in all aspects of church life.

SOURCES FOR WORSHIP RENEWAL

A major problem for pastors and congregations is finding adequate sources of information for worship renewal. Gimmicks and so-called innovative approaches to worship become threadbare all too quickly. So where should they turn? My argument is that the most powerful sources of worship renewal are found first in the Scripture and second in the history of the church.

First, a hallmark of evangelical Christianity is the recognition that the authoritative source for Christian faith and practice is the Scripture. Building on this conviction, we should keep three guidelines in mind as we explore the Scripture for teaching on worship. (1) *Principles of worship may be drawn from both the Old and the New Testament.* In the Old Testament, descriptions of worship are much more common than they are in the New Testament. In the Old Testament God gives His people specific directions regarding the how, when, and wherefore of meeting Him in worship. These directions contain principles that were not abrogated for the Christian church. (2) *Old Testament forms are fulfilled in Christ.* Hebrews clearly sets forth the thesis that the ritualistic forms of Old Testament worship are fulfilled in Christ. The death of Christ is the ultimate sacrifice for sin in which all the Old Testament sacrifices, as well as the temple, are fulfilled and made no longer necessary. The same is true of the feasts—especially the Passover, which is fulfilled in the Last Supper. (3) *New Testament worship is also characterized by form.* The argument of some for a worship that is purely spiritual cannot be maintained on the basis of the New Testament testimony. The content of early Christian worship was rooted in the event of Christ celebrated in the forms of coming together, interpreting the Scripture, celebrating the Lord's Supper, and praying. These forms were more simple and informal than those in the Old Testament, but they were forms, nevertheless.

A second source for worship renewal can be found in the practice of the church as it has interpreted and applied biblical principles of worship throughout its history. Inasmuch as the Holy Spirit has been given to the church, we must acknowledge the illumination of the Holy Spirit in the life of the whole church. If contemporary Christians acknowledge this work of the Spirit, they will not assume an antihistorical stance that rejects what the Spirit has given to the church in the past. Neither will they act as though the Spirit first came to the sixteenth-century Reformers and discount all that precedes them as apostate. Instead, they will affirm the whole church and seek to draw on the resources that have been handed down from every generation of Christian people. Second, the most formative period of the church is the first six centuries. It is a basic principle of New Testament studies that one can understand the New Testament better if it is studied within the context of the first six centuries. There is a direct link between the apostolic witness to Christ and the formation of the canon, the creeds, and worship that were taking shape at the same time. This does not mean that the interpretation of the Fathers or the practices of the early church are placed on the same level as the Scripture. Rather, the early sources are important because the church was committed to the apostolic tradition and sought to understand and practice Christianity in continuity with the apostles. Third, the most important re-formative period of worship is the sixteenth-century Reformation. The Reformers reacted against the corruptions that had entered the church during the late medieval period and sought to reform the worship along the lines of Scripture and classical practice. The most significant resources for worship renewal in the church, then, are found in the Scripture and in the ancient and Reformation periods. This does not mean that other periods of history do not offer valuable resource material, nor does it mean that new insights are not being achieved today.

The burden of this book is to show how the resources from the past can be applied to the present, but such application must be based on several premises. First, worship has fixed parts. Worship renewal that is entirely dependent on new sources of worship is doomed to failue. The meeting that takes place between God and persons is always based on the Word, prayer, and sacrament through which God speaks and people respond. Second, customs of worship will vary from place to place. Some communities will opt for a very simple, perhaps informal approach to worship while others will insist on ceremonies that give worship a more formal character. Nevertheless, customs established in antiquity and used by the church universally ought to be given serious consideration by congregations desiring to achieve a renewal of worship. Third, worship renewal cannot occur without an understanding of the meaning of worship. Congregations ought to commit themselves to the study of worship—its origins, development, and meaning. Fourth, worship renewal cannot occur without faith. Worshipers must examine their own personal faith and trust in the gospel and exercise that faith through an intentional worship. Worship does not just happen; it comes as the result of knowing what to do and doing it purposefully.[6]

BASIC PRINCIPLES OF WORSHIP

It is my purpose to lead the reader into a knowledgeable appreciation of worship so that intentional worship may occur. To begin, here are four statements of the basic principles involved in meeting God. These principles will be more fully developed in part 3 and particular attention will be given to their application to worship in the evangelical community today in part 5.

The Theocentric Character of Worship

Worship is a personal meeting with God in which we hymn, magnify, and glorify Him for His person and actions.

The reasons for worship are basic. We worship God simply because He is God. There is none other besides Him. He is high, holy, and lifted up.[7] He alone is God, the Almighty, the King of the universe, the Lord of all. We also worship God because of His gracious actions toward us.[8] In creation He has given us all that we have or expect to have. We are completely dependent on Him. And even though we have fallen away from Him because of sin, He has entered history and acted in history to redeem and save us. And more, He has constituted us His people. He has entered into a covenantal agreement with us, promising us His faithfulness and love. In this context we, His "chosen people, a royal priesthood, a holy nation, a people belonging to God," are called to "declare the praises of him who called [us] out of darkness into his wonderful light" (1 Peter 2:9). From this it seems clear that the church is primarily a worshiping community—a community called to proclaim and enact the wonderful deeds of its Savior to the praise of the Father.

The Christocentric Character of Worship

Worship takes place in and through Jesus Christ, who is the eternal praise of the Father because of His work of redemption.

The worship of the church always has to do with the central conviction of the Christian faith enunciated throughout the Scripture: *God comes to humanity in order that humanity may be brought to God.* It is a primary axiom of Christianity that it is God who saves (John 3:16; Eph. 2:8–10). The descending line is that

God has come in Jesus Christ; the ascending line is that humanity is brought to God by Jesus Christ. Nowhere is this descending and ascending line more clearly visible than in the worship of the church as it celebrates the redemption of the world in Jesus Christ. Consequently, worship is christocentric.[9] Because the perfect work that Christ accomplished is the true worship of the Father, it is only in and through Jesus Christ that we may offer our worship. We praise the Father for giving His Son for the redemption of the world. Because the work of the Son is the once-for-all offering to the Father, our worship is an offering of praise and thanksgiving through the Son who gave Himself for our salvation. For this reason the prayers of the early church were always offered in the name of Jesus Christ, the only begotten Son, "Through whom and with whom be glory and power to thee, in thy most holy, good, and life-giving Spirit, now, henceforth, and for ever more."[10]

There is another side to the place of Christ in Christian worship. Not only does He mediate our worship to the Father, but He also mediates the blessings and grace of the Father to us (Eph. 1:13–14: 1 Peter 1:3). For this reason the early church saw Christ as the principal minister of all the sacraments. It is Christ who baptizes and it is Christ who gives Himself to His church in the Eucharist.

The principal function of Christ, therefore, in worship is that of a mediator. He mediates our worship to the Father and mediates salvation and all other blessings from the Father to the worshiper.[11]

The Ecclesial, Pneumatological, and Sign Character of Worship

The public worship of God takes place in the community of the church, the body of Christ, by the power of the Holy Spirit, in the proclamation and enactment of the work of salvaton, through visible and tangible signs.

Worship is ecclesial;[12] that is, worship is an activity that belongs to the church, the body of Christ. Because Christ is the worship of the Father and because the church is the bride of Christ, it follows that the recital of those deeds of Christ by which the church is redeemed rightfully occurs in the church. The church proclaims, recites, recounts, recreates the deeds of Christ through which its redemption was accomplished.

The community character of worship is particularly emphasized in the Eucharist. Here the whole church comes together (see 1 Cor. 11:18, 33; 14:23; Ignatius, *Letter to the Ephesians* 13:1; *Didache* 14:1; Justin, 1 *Apol.* 67). The term *comes together (synaxis)* was used as a technical word in the early church to describe the gathering of Christians for worship. It pointed to the indisputable character of public worship as something that the church does in community. The public worship of the church occurs only when "two or three come together in [Jesus'] name" (Matt. 18:20).

Furthermore, worship is pneumatological. That is, worship occurs by the power of the Holy Spirit. But how does this take place? What does the Holy Spirit do? A New Testament theology of the Holy Spirit seems to suggest an actual interaction between the Spirit of God and the spirit of man—a kind of meeting that takes place between the two. St. Paul uses the poetic image of the Spirit of God joining with our spirit to help us in our worship: "For you did not receive a spirit that makes you a slave again to fear, but you received the Spirit of sonship. And by him we cry, 'Abba, Father'" (Rom. 8:15, 26–27). The essential function of the Spirit in worship is to *enable* us to worship. Thus the "by" in Philippians 3:3 is properly construed as a dative instrument: "We who worship by the Spirit of God."[13]

In the power of the Holy Spirit the worshiping community reenacts the content of the gospel story. It proclaims and acts out the great themes of the story that interprets and gives meaning to the world and our life in it. In this sense worship is a sacred drama through which we act out the meaning of existence and enter into the storm center of existence itself, the death and resurrection of Jesus Christ for our salvation.

The "sign character" of worship has particularly to do with the sacraments, especially baptism and the Eucharist.[14] Here the water of baptism and the bread and wine of the Eucharist carry the signs, or the "pledges" as John Calvin called them, of God's saving purpose toward his people. These signs put us in contact with the archetypical story of the universe. They rehearse the original saving event both of God's work for us and of our incorporation into that saving work. Consequently, worship is a proclamation to the ecclesial community: a renewal of God's revelation of Himself in which He becomes uniquely and savingly present to His people.

It is important for Evangelicals to rediscover the place of the outward expression in worship as a corrective to the erroneous and somewhat gnostic tendency to deny the role of the physical. We must keep in mind that the work of Christ for the Father is communicated to us through physical means (the preaching of the Word and the reenactment of the Lord's Supper) and that our response of hearing, seeing, handling, and tasting is physical. For this reason we need to pay closer attention to the physical side of worship.[15]

The Pistical, Missiological, and Eschatological Character of Worship

In the physical actions that are the expession of personal faith the church prepares to serve the world in anticipation of the return of Christ.

It is unthinkable that worship can actually occur without faith and obedience. In trusting totally and completely in the work of Christ for our salvation, we allow Christ to represent us to the Father. In this way our worship is offered to the Father in and through Jesus Christ. Christ, therefore, presents to the Father not only His finished work on Calvary but also the church, his body, that He has won for His glory.

Worship entails the personal offering of one's entire life to the Father through Jesus Christ. Worship occurs not only with our lips but also with our lives. Therefore, our worship is to be expressed through service to the world.[16] The church acts as a sign of Christ in the world when it proclaims Christ. The church also acts as a sign of Christ in the world when it serves the world in the name of Christ. As the writer of Hebrews said, "Let us consider how we may spur one another on toward love and good deeds" (Heb. 10:24). We dare not ignore the social ramifications of the death and resurrection of our Lord. His redemption extends to the entire created order; thus our participation in worship of Him can do no less.

Finally, worship looks beyond the present world and anticipates the eschatological hope of God's people. In particular, the Eucharist is a sign of His coming, the consummation of the age, and the new heavens and the new earth. For this reason true worship always meets the existential needs of the worshiper. It provides a constant source of strength to live with faith and courage in the face of a fallen and corrupt world system.

Conclusion

There is a cancer at the heart of many churches—*the failure to understand and practice public worship*. There is only one remedy. It is not an easy one and may therefore be shunned by those who are caught up in the instant gratification cult of our modern age. The remedy consists of repentance, a *metanoia*, a turning away from all shallow and uninformed approaches to worship. It means we must renew our understanding and practice of worship. In the following pages we will deal with the content of this kind of worship renewal.

UNUS DEUS, VNUS CONCILIATOR DEI ET HOMINV̄, HOMO CHRISTVS IESVS,
QVI DEDIT SEMETIPSVM PRECIVM REDEMPTIONIS PRO OMNIBVS

Part I

THE
BIBLICAL
BACKGROUND

ITE IN MVNDVM VNIVERSVM, ET PRÆDICATE EVANGELIVM OMNI CREATVRÆ.

Chapter 2

Old Testament Sources

The purpose of this chapter is to discover the sources of Christian worship in the Old Testament. Because Christianity originated within the Hebraic culture the most powerful influence that gave shape to the Christian faith was Hebraic.[1]

Although the Old Testament sources of Christian worship are rich with descriptions of worship and contain a voluminous amount of material, we will limit our study to four Old Testament sources that influenced New Testament worship. They are the Sinai event, the temple, the synagogue, and the festivals.[2]

THE SINAI-EVENT

In the Exodus God brought the people of Israel up out of Egypt, across the Red Sea, and to Mount Sinai, where He entered into a covenant relationship with them. A striking feature of this covenant is not only the content of the agreement but the *context* in which the agreement was made.

The full context of the Sinai-event is described in chapters 19–24 of the Book of Exodus. The most pertinent part of this material is the public meeting that took place between God and Israel at the foot of Mount Sinai. Here is the full text of that meeting:

Then he said to Moses, "Come up to the LORD, you and Aaron, Nadab and Abihu, and seventy of the elders of Israel. You are to worship at a distance, but Moses alone is to approach the LORD; the others must not come near. And the people may not come up with him."

When Moses went and told the people all the LORD's words and laws, they responded with one voice, "Everything the LORD has said we will do." Moses then wrote down everything the LORD had said.

He got up early the next morning and built an altar at the foot of the mountain and set up twelve stone pillars representing the twelve tribes of Israel. Then he sent young Israelite men, and they offered burnt offerings to the LORD. Moses took half of the blood and put it in bowls, and the other half he sprinkled on the altar. Then he took the Book of the Covenant and read it to the people. They responded, "We will do everything the LORD has said; we will obey."

Moses then took the blood, sprinkled it on the people and said, "This is the blood of the covenant that the LORD has made with you in accordance with all these words."

Exodus 24:1–8

This meeting between God and Israel is important because *it contains the most basic structural elements for a meeting between God and His people.*[3] These elements, the very substance of public worship, are found later in the more detailed descriptions of Judaic and Christian worship. They are five:

First, the meeting was convoked by God. It was God who called the people out of Egypt and brought them to Mount Sinai. Now God called His people to meet with Him at the foot of the mountain where they became the *Q'hal Yahweh,* the "assembly of God." In this is seen the prerequisite of true worship—that God calls His people to meet with Him.

Second, the people were arranged in a structure of responsibility. Although the role of leadership was given to Moses, other parts of the drama were to be played by Aaron, Nadab, Abihu, the seventy elders of Israel, the young Israelite men, and the people. The picture is not that of leaders and an audience, but full participation of those congregated. Each had his or her own part to play. The full orchestration brought every person together in a harmonious whole. This points to *participation* as a fundamental aspect of worship.

Third, the meeting between God and Israel was characterized by the *proclamation of the Word*. God spoke to His people and made His will known to them. In this it is shown that worship is not complete without hearing from the Lord.

Fourth, in the assent the people acknowledged their acceptance of the conditions of the covenant, thus signifying a subjective commitment to hear and to obey the Word. An essential aspect of worship in both the Judaic and Christian traditions is *the continuous renewal of personal commitment*. In worship the community is engaged in the renewal of the covenant that exists between God and itself.

Finally, the meeting was climaxed by a *dramatic symbol* of ratification, a sealing of the agreement. In the Old Testament God always used a blood sacrifice to demonstrate the sealing of His relationship with man. These sacrifices pointed to the once-for-all sacrifice of Jesus Christ. After His sacrifice the Lord's Supper is the sign of the relationship that the church sustains with God.

THE TEMPLE

The second Old Testament source of Christian worship is the sanctuary and the temple. Although this is a highly complex subject, we can give it only minimal attention, pointing to its most basic features.[4]

First, the tabernacle and the temple emphasized the presence of God in the midst of Israel. For example, God spoke to Moses, saying, "Then have them make a sanctuary for me, and I will dwell among them" (Exod. 25:8; see also 2 Chron. 6:7; Ezek. 43:7). Furthermore, the sacrifices were a constant reminder of the ratification of God's covenant with Israel at Mount Sinai (see Exod. 24). Also, the temple was seen as an expression of the antithesis between Israel and the surrounding culture. Worship set the Israelites apart from the worship conducted by the pagans and accented their relationship to Yahweh (see Deut. 12). Thus, the tabernacle and the temple became the visible and tangible signs of Israel's relationship to God.

A second feature of the tabernacle and the temple was its symbolic character. It was characterized by a sacred sense of space, sacred rituals, and sacred ministers.[5] A striking feature of these sacred symbols is that *they were ordained by God.* In the account of David's giving Solomon the plans for the temple, the writer explicitly tells us that "he gave him the plans of all that the Spirit had put in his mind for the courts of the temple of the LORD" (1 Chron. 28:12). "'All this is in writing,' David said, 'because the hand of the LORD was upon me, and he gave me understanding in all the details of the plan'" (28:19). The implication is that the pattern of the temple itself was a symbolic communication of the relationship Israel sustained with God (see also Exod. 25:9).

The temple was characterized by a symbolic use of space. The arrangement of the outer court, the inner court, and the Most Holy Place communicates the distance between the worshiper and God who dwells in the Most Holy Place. All of the pieces of furniture such as the altar, the laver, the golden lampstands, the table with the bread of the Presence, the altar of incense and the ark were laden with symbolic meaning as they depicted an encounter with God. Nothing in the temple furniture or layout was randomly selected or haphazardly placed.

Furthermore, the temple was characterized by a number of sacred rituals.[6] In addition to the general rules for making a sacrifice (presentation of the victim; placing hands on the victim; slaying the victim; sprinkling the blood; and burning the sacrifice) there were sacrifices for various occasions. For example, the burnt offering (the daily offering of a lamb, entirely consumed to indicate complete consecration to God), the fellowship offering (a voluntary offering symbolizing communion and fellowship between persons and God), the sin offering (offered for sins of omission among other things), and the trespass offering (offered for sins of commission). The important feature of these sacrifices is that they are visible and tangible expressions of the relationship of God's people with Himself. They grow out of the act of ratification at Sinai, and they anticipate the sacrifice of Christ (Heb. 10).

Finally, the temple was characterized by a sacred ministry. These ministers of the sacred ritual represented the entire nation. They were the mediators between Israel and God. Not just anyone could be a priest, only the Levites. They were called by God and consecrated to His service in an elaborate ceremony (Exod. 29); they wore garments fitting to their service (Exod. 28:40–43; 39:1–31); and they were given stringent requirements for holy living (Lev. 21:1–22:10).

In the New Testament the temple was fulfilled in Jesus Christ (Mark 14:58; 15:29, 38; John 2:19–21), and the church, His body, becomes the temple, the dwelling place of God (1 Cor. 3:16–17; 6:19; 2 Cor. 6:16; Eph. 2:21–22). Nevertheless the sense that *there is a physical side to spiritual life and activity,* a sense that came from the temple, continued in New Testament worship. New Testament Christians rejected the nonphysical spirituality of the Gnostics and continued to express their spirituality through physical means. For that reason the sense of sacred place (church buildings), sacred rituals (the Eucharist), and sacred ministers (ordained persons) all have a vital connection with the impact made by temple worship on the development of Christian worship.

THE SYNAGOGUE

The synagogue probably originated as a result of the destruction of Jerusalem and the temple and the subsequent dispersion of the Jewish people during the Exile.[7] Thus it is an intertestamental phenomenon and not strictly an institution of the Old Testament. A motivating concern was the preservation and propagation of the Word of the Lord in the context of the Jewish community. Thus the synagogue became the religious, educational, and social center of Jewish village life. Through it the traditions of ancient Jewish religion were preserved and passed down from generation to generation.

Worship in the synagogue was strikingly different from that in the temple. It had no sacred rituals and did not support a sacred ministry. Its focus was on reading and understanding the Word of God.[8]

Synagogue worship consisted of an affirmation of faith, prayer, and the Scriptures. The affirmation of faith is expressed in the *shema,* which is divided into three different sections. The first section (Deut. 6:4–9) proclaims the unity of God as a central confession and sets forth the primary duty of Jewish people to "love the Lord your God with all your heart and with all your soul and with all your strength" (Deut. 6:5). The second emphasizes the doctrine of rewards and punishment (Deut. 11:13–21). The third stresses the duty of each person to strive for holiness because the essential nature of God is to be emulated. In this way Jews could become a holy nation (Deut. 28:1–11).

Next, synagogue worship stressed prayer. The tefillah, a series of prayers divided into three sets, was recited in a standing posture. The first set is a series of three prayers concentrating on the praise of God by paying homage to the God of Abraham, Isaac, and Jacob and revering God as the one "who nourishes the living, quickens the dead, and is the Holy One of Israel."[9] The next series are thirteen "congregational petitions for such boons as wisdom and understanding, forgiveness of sins, restoration of Israel, good health, and sustenance."[10] Specifically, the prayers concerned repentance, forgiveness of sins, ability to study the Torah, deliverance from misfortunes such as persecution, famine, and sickness. They also mention the coming of the Messiah and ask for God's acceptance of the prayers of Israel. The three concluding prayers of the final series emphasize personal thanksgiving to God, concluding with a prayer for peace.

The third element of synagogue worship was the Torah.[11] A thoroughgoing reverence was given to the Scriptures because they embodied the traditions of ancient Israel. A primary duty of every Jew was to study the Torah and to pass on its teachings to the next generation: "Impress them on your children. Talk about them when you sit at home and when you walk along the road, when you lie down and when you get up" (Deut. 6:7). This notion that common people could understand and learn the tradition was a revolutionary concept. In other religions the tradition was secret, known only to the priestly class. But in Judaism, the tradition of Israel and her relationship with God was not only public but also a requirement for every Jew to know and teach to the family.

The reading of the Torah was followed by a sermon (see Luke 4:16–30). Usually the reading of the Torah was done verse by verse accompanied by a translation. (The translation was necessary because many Jewish people spoke the language of the culture where they resided.) Here is a tenth-century description of the reading that had remained unchanged for centuries:

> The one called to the Torah reads and another translates, verse by verse . . . and a third person stands between the reader and the translator . . . to help the reader and the translator, and to prompt them before they read or translate. . . . If there is one who does not know how to read well, or is shy, then the third one helps him. But if he doesn't know at all how to read, he may not be called to read or to translate. . . . And if the reader

erred, the translator may not correct him. Similarly if the translator erred, the reader may not correct him. Only the third one may correct the reading or the translating.[12]

The sermon interpreted and applied the Scripture reading to the daily life of the people. It was known as the *derashah*, an act of "searching" in the Torah for its teachings. The preacher was called *darshan,* or one who "searched." The objective of the preachers was moral and theological instruction. They offered the people comfort and hope as they taught the doctrines and laws by which the people were to live.[13]

The influence of the synagogue on Christian worship, as we shall see in chapter 4, was remarkable. The whole sense of affirming faith, of offering prayer for specific concerns, and reading and preaching from the sacred writings was easily transferred from the synagogue to the Christian assembly as Christians began to form their own separate worshiping communities.

THE FESTIVALS

The festivals of ancient Israel were the fourth source of Old Testament influence on early Christian worship.[14] Major and minor festivals, centered around the temple and the home, were celebrated annually to commemorate special occasions in the life of Israel. Through these feasts Israel marked time (giving them a sacred sense of time). The worship connected with these feasts resulted in a sense of the continuity of the work of God in the history of Israel and in a keen awareness of God's continued presence.

Of the three major festivals—Passover, Pentecost, and Tabernacles—two play a major role in the worship of the early church.

The Passover is associated with the release of the people of Israel from Egyptian bondage. The word derives from the Lord's "passing over" the families where the blood had been smeared on the doorpost of the house to protect the first-born.

The Passover was a festival of redemption attesting to God's gracious acts in bringing His people out of Egypt with "a mighty hand and an outstretched arm" (Deut. 26:8). For this reason the Old Testament sets forth an elaborate set of guidelines defining the manner of celebration in detail including the date, the time, and the manner of eating (Exod. 12; Num. 9; Deut. 16; 2 Chron. 35).[15]

The meaning of the Passover was to be taught in the context of the family meal. The father was to recall history, to lead his family through the meal, to explain the meaning of all the symbols "because of what the LORD did for [him] when he came out of Egypt" (Exod. 13:8).

Christians see significance in the fact that Jesus introduced the Lord's Supper during the celebration of the Passover. It not only puts emphasis on Jesus as the Passover lamb (1 Cor. 5:7), it also accents the Lord's Supper as the central rite of the New Covenant.

The second important festival that influenced Christian worship was Pentecost, also known as the "feast of weeks." Pentecost (which means fifty) concluded the cycle of time that began at Passover. It was a feast of joy and thanksgiving for the completion of the harvest season bringing people from all over to Jerusalem to celebrate (Deut. 16; Acts 2:5). After the coming of the Holy Spirit (see Acts 1–2) Christians marked the beginning of the church as an institution at Pentecost.

Conclusion

In this chapter we have considered the worship of the Old Testament for the purpose of discovering the cultural context in which primitive Christian worship was born. It must be remembered, however, that there is a distinct difference between the Old and New Testament approaches to worship. This difference lies in the historical events that inform and give meaning to worship. Old Testament worship is rooted in the cluster of events surrounding the Exodus. New Testament worship is rooted in the cluster of events surrounding the birth, life, death, and resurrection of Jesus Christ, the incarnate Son of God.

In summary, we can note the following Old Testament elements that have affected the development of Christian worship:

1. The Sinai-event sets forth the common structure of a meeting with God: it is convoked by God; the people are arranged in a structure of responsibility; the Word of God is proclaimed; the people give their assent; the meeting is sealed by an act of ratification.
2. The temple emphasizes the presence of God and the sacred sense of space, rituals, and ministers.

3. The synagogue emphasizes a confession of faith, prayer, and the Word.
4. The festivals recall history and set the stage for a sacred sense of time.

As the event of Christ fulfilled and thus superseded the Old Testament, the *content* of Old Testament worship that foreshadowed the coming of the Messiah was abolished. Some Christians contrast Old and New Testament worship as though the former were physical and the latter spiritual. This is a false dichotomy that fails to recognize the contrast between the content of the Old Testament (the Sinai-event) and the content of the New Testament (the Christ-event). Worship in both the Old and the New Testament has both spiritual and physical aspects. As we develop the physical side of Christian worship, we will see how Old Testament principles are still found in Christian worship. The radical difference is that they are informed by the event of Jesus Christ, the main content of the Christian faith.

Chapter 3

New Testament Developments

The study of the development of worship in the New Testament is more difficult and complex than a study of the development of worship in the Old Testament because of the fragmentary nature of the sources. There is no single highly developed statement on worship in the New Testament. Rather, brief descriptions provided by hymns, confessions, benedictions, doxologies, and subtle hints in words descriptive of worship are scattered throughout the New Testament documents. Changing and somewhat confusing patterns force us to remember the simple, but necessary, principle of *the process of development.* Thus, allowance must be made for a certain degree of flexibility and inability to pull all the loose ends together into a coherent whole.[1]

However, it is certain that *the worship of the New Testament was born in the crucible of those events surrounding Jesus* that were recognized as the fulfillment of the Old Testament prophecies to Israel. At first there was no hint that a new people of God, one including the Gentiles, was being formed as a result of these events. Therefore, early Christians worshiped in continuity with the past, until, because of the growing conflict between those who accepted Jesus as the Messiah and those who did not, a gradual separation occurred. In this context Christian worship developed characteristics that were distinct from Jewish worship.[2]

In this chapter we will reflect in a systematic way on the beginnings of Christian worship in the first century by concentrating on two questions: (1) What is the basis of New Testament worship? and (2) What descriptions of worship emerge? Other issues such as New Testament prayer, hymns, confessions, and the like will be treated elsewhere.

THE BASIS OF NEW TESTAMENT WORSHIP

The basis of New Testament worship may be discovered by examining the attitude of Jesus toward worship and the meaning of the Christ-event.

Jesus' Attitude Toward Worship

First, *Jesus supported Old Testament worship.* An examination of His relationship to the temple, the synagogue, and the Jewish feasts affirms this conclusion. The Gospels record Jesus' presence in the temple (see Luke 2:21–51; John 7:14–49; 10:22–23). But there is no suggestion that Jesus offered an animal sacrifice or approved of the sacrificial system. Nevertheless, His respect for the temple and its proper use as a place of worship is evidenced by the anger that the misuse of the temple provoked in Him at the time of the cleansing of the temple (Luke 19:45–48).[3] According to Luke, Jesus went regularly to the synagogue on the Sabbath (see Luke 4:16: "he went into the synagogue, *as was his custom*").[4] Jesus also attended the feasts of Israel (John 7:2; 10:22). The detail with which He celebrated the Passover before the Last Supper is evidence of His knowledge and appreciation of the major feast of Israel (Matt. 26:1–30; Mark 14:1–26; Luke 22:1–23; John 13:1–30).

Second, *Jesus viewed Old Testament institutions of worship as pointing toward Himself.* For example, the cleansing of the temple had to do with Jesus' view of the end of temple sacrifice. So, the real significance of His action is to make the traditional sacrificial ritual or cult impossible. By putting a stop to the sacrificial cult, He pointed to Himself as the fulfillment of the cult; as later Christianity understood, He made sacrifices obsolete.

The sentiment of Jesus Himself that "one greater than the temple is here" (Matt. 12:6) clearly laid the groundwork for the attitude developed by the Hellenistic Christians and articulated by

Stephen who was accused of saying "that this Jesus of Nazareth will destroy this place" (Acts. 6:14). In this it appears clear that Jesus proclaimed the end of the temple cult.

Although Jesus did not proclaim the end of the synagogue or the feasts, He did see the central reason for the existence of each as pointing to Himself. For example, He applied the Old Testament Scripture, which is central to the worship of the synagogue, to Himself. This is the case in the only recorded sermon of Jesus at a synagogue (see Luke 4:16–30) where He pointedly interpreted the Old Testament lesson as pertaining to Himself, saying, "Today this scripture is fulfilled in your hearing" (Luke 4:21; see also Luke 24:25–27, 44–47). The same principle is true of the Passover. When Jesus said, "This is my body" (Matt. 26:26), and, "This is my blood of the covenant, which is poured out for many for the forgiveness of sins" (Matt. 26:28), He fulfilled the eschatological meaning of the Passover and filled the rite with new meaning. Thus, Jesus viewed Old Testament institutions of worship in relationship to His life, death, and resurrection.

This understanding of Jesus brings into focus a third principle: *Jesus assumed the right to reinterpret the customs of Jewish worship.* For example, in the confrontations Jesus had with the Pharisees over the Sabbath, Jesus asserted, "The Sabbath was made for man, not man for the Sabbath. So the Son of Man is Lord even of the Sabbath" (Mark 2:27–28). Jesus' willingness to break the rules of the Sabbath carried over into His attitude toward the regulations that governed cleanness and uncleanness (Mark 7:1–23), as well as the rules regarding fasting and prayer (Matt. 6:5–8, 16–18). The point in each of these cases is that Jesus is proclaiming Himself—His lordship, His place in the kingdom, His place in the revelation of God in history. In this manner Jesus prepared the way for the significant changes that occurred in worship as the new people of God gradually developed a worship depicting the fulfillment of the Old Testament in Jesus Christ.

The Christ-event

In the same way that Old Testament worship celebrates the Sinai-event, New Testament worship proclaims the story of the second Exodus—the entrance of Christ into the world for the purpose of redeeming His people from bondage to sin. [5]

The birth of Christ resulted in a significant amount of worship literature praising God for fulfilling the Old Testament prophecies.[6] The keynote of the birth narratives is struck by Mary in the *Magnificat,* "My soul praises the Lord" (Luke 1:46–55). This note of worship is recognized as one of the earliest hymns of the church. The event of Jesus' death and resurrection produced a worship response that stressed the destruction of the powers of sin and death. This theme is the focus of early preaching and the Lord's Supper as well. Jesus Christ, as Paul stated to the Colossians, has "disarmed the powers and authorities" and has "made a public spectacle of them, triumphing over them by the cross" (2:15). This power of God demonstrated in the Cross has, since the Ascension and Pentecost, been evident in the church. The outpouring of the Spirit is manifested in the lives of God's new people who by the Spirit act in His name and worship Him. The fact that Jesus is now seated at the right hand of the Father and will return in judgment focuses worship not only on past events but also on the completion of those events in the consummation. In this way the events associated with Christ have informed and shaped the content of Christian worship.

These themes are so pervasive in the literature of the New Testament that some scholars view portions of the New Testament as products of early worship.[7] Some scholars think that "at an early date liturgical and catechetical forms began to be developed for the worship and teaching of various churches and soon spread widely among the rest."[8] Although there is no absolute proof that elements of Old Testament worship are incorporated in the New Testament documents, the idea itself is fascinating and has provoked scholarly inquiry that demands attention.

For example, these scholars make a case that the *Magnificat* (Luke 1:46–55), the *Benedictus* (Luke 1:68–79), the *Gloria in Excelsis* (Luke 2:14), and the *Nunc Dimittis* (Luke 2:29–32) were all hymns of the church, known and used by the church before their incorporation in the gospel text. The same has been said for the Christ-hymns such as John 1:1–18, Philippians 2:6–11, and Colossians 1:15–20, and the many psalms and doxologies such as those found in Revelation (4:8, 11; 7:12; 11:17–18; 15:3–4). It seems reasonable to assume that worship traditions would have developed and spread rapidly among the various Christian communities. Since the Gospels were not written for a number of years after

Pentecost, the development of hymns and doxologies predating the literature of the New Testament was natural.

EMERGING DESCRIPTIONS OF WORSHIP

Christianity began among the Aramaic-speaking Jews and then spread to the Hellenistic Jewish community and eventually to the Gentiles. These three groups as well as the developments in subapostolic Christianity provide chronological and cultural insights into the development of New Testament worship.

Aramaic Christian Worship

Aramaic Christians were characterized by both identification with and differentiation from Jewish worship. They worshiped "in the temple courts" and "in their homes" (Acts 2:46). [9]

First, *Aramaic Christian worship was characterized by a continuity with temple worship.* Although the New Testament texts provide little detail about the Christians' relationship with the temple, it is clear that they continued to observe the temple hours of prayer (Acts 3:1) and used the temple as a place to proclaim the gospel (see Acts 3:11–26; 4:12–13, 19–26, 42).[10]

A more controversial issue is the early Christian relationship to the sacrificial cult.[11] According to Luke there were "many thousands of Jews" who were "zealous for the law" and sought to "live according to [Jewish] customs" (Acts 21:20–21). Furthermore, Paul was admonished to join in the purification rites and he did, although it turned out to his own disadvantage. This suggests a close alliance between Jewish and Christian worship. The danger was a return to a Jewish law and ritualism. But the resistance of Aramaic Christianity against the Judaizers in the Jerusalem Council (Acts 15) indicates that Aramaic Christians were alert to the difference between Christianity and Judaism.[12]

Second, *that Jewish Christians were caught in the tension between being Jewish and Christian is suggested by their additional worship in houses.*[13] Here their differentiation with Jewish worship became obvious. According to Luke, "They devoted themselves to the apostles' teaching and to the fellowship, to the breaking of bread and to prayer" (Acts 2:42). In these activities the Christ-centered content of Christian worship is clear. It was the Hellenistic Christian who would carry this difference into a more radical break with Judaism.

Hellenistic Christian Worship

The Hellenists, unlike the Aramaic Christians, were not steeped in the temple and cultic practices of the Hebraic heritage. They had adopted the practice of the prevailing Hellenistic culture in language and customs. Therefore, they had much less interest in preserving continuity with Hebraic religious practices than did the Aramaic Jews.[14]

The evidence of two Jewish Christian communities emerges very early in the development of Christianity. Luke made no effort to hide the differences between them. These differences necessitated the appointment of seven Hellenists by the apostles to serve the special needs of the Hellenistic community (Acts 6:1–6). The city of Antioch later became the center of Hellenistic Christianity and a strong and vital link was maintained with Jewish Christianity in Jerusalem, especially through Barnabas. An examination of the literature pertaining to the Hellenists suggests two predominant characteristics of their worship: a renunciation of Jewish rituals and an emphasis on the fulfilled meaning of these rituals. In this the Hellenists appear closer than the Aramaic Christians to the attitude of Jesus toward the temple and the cultic practices.

First, *Hellenistic worship was characterized by the renunciation of Jewish ritualism.* Members of the synagogue falsely accused Stephen before the Sanhedrin saying, "This fellow never stops speaking against the holy place and against the law. For we have heard him say that this Jesus of Nazareth will destroy this place and change the customs Moses handed down to us" (Acts 6:13–14). The contest between Stephen and his opponents became more severe and soon erupted in the confrontation recorded in Acts 7. The inflammatory portion of this sermon was Stephen's rejection of the temple expressed in the following quote from Isaiah: "Heaven is my throne, and the earth is my footstool. What kind of house will you build for me? says the Lord. Or where will my resting place be? Has not my hand made all these things?" (vv. 49–50). Here Stephen struck a predominant note of the Hellenists: The temple had been superseded by the work of Christ. Because the Old Testament was fulfilled in Christ the cult was no longer needed.

This view set the stage for the second characteristic of Hellenistic worship: *Jewish rituals were reinterpreted as having been fulfilled in Christ.* For example, Christ was seen as the Passover lamb who had been sacrificed (1 Cor. 5:7; see also Rom. 3:25; Eph.

5:2; 1 Peter 1:19); the temple was replaced by the body of Christ: "Don't you know that you yourselves are God's temple and that God's spirit lives in you? If anyone destroys God's temple, God will destroy him; for God's temple is sacred, and you are that temple" (1 Cor. 3:16–17; see also Eph. 2:19–22; 1 Peter 2:4–5); the people who constitute the church, the new temple, were designated a "royal priesthood" (1 Peter 2:9). The reinterpretation of the temple, the sacrifices, the Passover lamb, and the priesthood and their application to the emerging church were radical and new. They reached into the very essence of Judaism and struck at the heart of Jewish worship. For the Hellenist, Jewish and Christian worship did not mix.

Christian differentiation with Jewish worship was clearly set forth in Hebrews. The keynote was struck in 7:18 in the discussion of the priesthood. "The former regulation," insisted the writer, "is set aside because it was weak and useless." This strong rejection of Jewish regulations was exhibited against all Jewish cultic practices. They had been fulfilled and were no longer needed. They had served their purpose, and now that a new and better way had come, they were obsolete (see Heb. 7–10). These notions paved the way for the developments that were to occur in the worship of the gentile Christian community.

Gentile Christian Worship

The idea that Christianity would extend to the Gentiles was at first unthinkable. Christ was the Jewish Messiah, the fulfillment of Jewish longings. There had been no hint among the Jews that their Messiah and His kingdom were to be universalized. Thus, the notion that Gentiles were to be included was resisted by the early Christians until God spoke to Peter in a vision and showed him they were to be included (Acts 10–11).[15]

The most extensive example of early gentile Christian worship is found in the Corinthian correspondence that occurred in the middle fifties, some twenty-six or twenty-seven years after Pentecost. The study of Christian worship at this time must be made against the background of two concerns: on the one hand the Gentiles were highly interested in maintaining their freedom in worship, and on the other it had become obvious that the Gentiles needed to be taught how to worship.

The desire for freedom was expressed in the ecstatic phenom-

ena common to the Gentiles. A number of Christians were expressing enthusiastic utterances in worship in the church to the point of
disorder and the disruption of worship. Paul urged them to use this
gift in an orderly and proper manner (1 Cor. 14:40).

Some scholars have argued that Paul intended the letter of
1 Corinthians to be read to the Christians just before celebrating
the Lord's Supper. Whether this can be proven or not, it at least
points to a major feature of 1 Corinthians; namely, that it contains
an immense amount of teaching on the subject of worship. However, the worship material does not appear in an organized and
systematic fashion. Rather, it is scattered throughout the letter.
Some of it is indirect, and other is more direct.

Some of the indirect allusions to worship suggest what may
have been included in a service of worship. The material, verified
by other liturgical sources of the period, include such things as the
forms of blessing (1:3; 16:23), worship on Sunday (16:1–2), possible
celebration of Pentecost (16:8), and Passover (5:7), the use of the
holy kiss (16:20), and church discipline with an emphasis on ex-
communication (5:5; 16:22).

More helpful for our purposes are the didactic statements
about worship. First, *Paul emphasized the necessity of order.* Because gentile freedom had gotten out of hand, there was a need to
do things "in a fitting and orderly way" (14:40). This emphasis first
appeared in reference to the gifts. Apparently worship was at times
a chaotic mass of confusion: "If the whole church comes together
and everyone speaks in tongues, and some who do not understand,
or some unbelievers come in, will they not say that you are out of
your mind?" (14:23). Paul did not tell them to stop speaking in
tongues. He simply asked that the proper place of tongues be seen
in worship and that all tongues speaking and interpretations should
proceed in an orderly manner.

Order was also a matter of concern in regard to the Lord's
Supper. Paul commented on Corinthian practice in the following
words: "When you come together, it is not the Lord's Supper you
eat, for as you eat, each of you goes ahead without waiting for
anybody else. One remains hungry, another gets drunk"
(11:20–21). Even in this central rite of the Christian faith, the
Corinthians had to be taught how to come to the table.

Second, *Paul's teaching about worship had to do with content.*
Unfortunately he does not give us an order of service, but he does

mention many of the major aspects of Christian worship, especially in 1 Corinthians 12 and 14. They are:

Revelation, knowledge, prophecy, word of instruction (14:6).

A hymn, a word of instruction, a revelation, a tongue or an interpretation (14:26).

The role of response is also clearly stated in this chapter:

Pray, sing, say "Amen," give thanks (14:13–17).

Furthermore, Paul clearly indicates the role of the Spirit "for the common good" in 1 Corinthians 12:

Wisdom, knowledge, faith, gifts of healing, miraculous powers, prophecy, ability to distinguish between spirits, ability to speak in different kinds of tongues, and the interpretation of tongues (12:7–11).

This material reveals an outstanding variety in the worship of the gentile community. To it must be added preaching and the Lord's Supper, which Paul emphasized as key factors in Christian worship. In regard to both preaching and the Lord's Supper, the Corinthians appear to have had some misunderstandings. Correction was in order. In the celebration of the Lord's Supper Paul introduced a note of sobriety, accenting the death of our Lord as the focus of Communion (11:23–26) and the need of personal examination before partaking (vv. 27–30).

In preaching, Paul reminded them of the *kerygma* that had been handed down in the church. Some did not believe in the resurrection of the dead (15:12–58). So Paul reminded them of the tradition of the church that he had received and passed on to them. He gave this tradition to them in a confessional form: "Christ died for our sins according to the Scriptures, . . . he was buried, . . . he was raised on the third day according to the Scriptures, and . . . he appeared to Peter and then to the Twelve" (15:3–5). This confession lies at the heart of the kerygma, it is a basic confession for all Christians, and it must be at the center of Christian preaching.

The Subapostolic Period

The period A.D. 60 to 100 is frequently designated as the subapostolic period. It is imperative to keep in mind that this was a highly formative period in the life of the early church as shown through signs of *maturation in the increased organization of the church*.[16]

By now the mission of the church had extended throughout most of the Roman Empire and beyond. Concomitant with this spread was the challenge posed by the rise of heretical groups. Consequently, the church was put under an external pressure to define itself more clearly. This it did through a growing literature (the Gospels and Epistles), a more fixed and precise organization of the church (see 1 Tim. 3:1–13), the emergence of creedal statements (see 1 Tim. 3:16; 1 Cor. 15:3–5), and a more highly developed liturgical consciousness.

An increasing number of scholars recognize the presence of worship materials in the literature of the apostolic and subapostolic period. The argument presupposes the incorporation of the church's hymns, baptismal catechetical literature, creedal statements, confessions, doxologies, and benedictions in the writings of the apostles. For example, it is thought that hymns of the church are sometimes used as arguments to make a particular doctrinal point or that large sections of the Epistles are elaborations on existing worship materials already known to the church. Even the Gospels do not escape the setting of worship. Oscar Cullmann has attempted to set forth "the connexion between the contemporary Christian worship and the historical life of Jesus" in the gospel of John.[17] And others, like Massey Shepherd, have argued for the structure of a Christian worship service as the organizing principle for the revelation of the apostle John in the Apocalypse.[18]

An examination of this vast amount of material leads to the conclusion that *the subapostolic period was characterized by an increasing emphasis on the ordered approach to worship.* For example, the Pastoral Epistles emphasize the role of the office of ministry in the worship of the church. At the same time the church attempted to find a balance between Corinthian enthusiasm and Jewish forms and concern for order. Thus, in the subapostolic period worship became more fixed. That this seems to be the case is suggested by the study of the worship forms known to us from the second century, the subject of the next chapter.

Conclusion

The purpose of this chapter has been to trace the *development* of New Testament worship. Although there are many gaps in the

fragmentary documents on worship, it is evident that we are deal-
ing with a *process* and with a *variety* in the earliest Christian
communities.

However, three summary statements can be made with a degree of certainty:

1. Christ proclaimed the end of the Jewish ritual or cult.
2. The common source of Christian worship is rooted in the
   Christ-event.
3. There is no single complete picture of worship in the New
   Testament.

Because the New Testament does not provide a systematic
picture of Christian worship, guidance may be sought regarding
worship from the practice of the early church.

On the conviction that God is the Lord of the church, that He
has given His Spirit to guide the church into all truth, and that the
immediate successors to the apostles were careful to maintain apostolic practice, we turn in the next chapter to observe the relationship of the earliest noncanonical descriptions of worship to the New
Testament sources.

Chapter 4

Early
Christian Worship

T he time lapse between the letters of Paul and Justin Martyr's description of worship in the second century may be filled in with references to Peter, the Book of Hebrews, and the Apocalypse as well as several noncanonical writings. In this chapter we will examine worship practices seen in Pliny and Justin and then consider their New Testament origins as we observe the normative picture of Christian worship emerging in the second century.

DESCRIPTIONS OF SECOND-CENTURY WORSHIP

Elaborate descriptions of worship are not found in either the New Testament or the second-century church. A superficial observation may suggest that little is said about worship because worship was not important to the early church. However, the contrary is true. Worship was of such vital importance to the early Christians that they *consciously withheld information* lest they cast their pearls before the swine. The Lord's Supper in particular was deliberately protected from pagans.[1]

The Letter of Pliny

The secrecy of worship in the second century provided an inquiry on the part of Pliny, the governor of Bithynia (A.D. 111–

113). He wanted to know what Christians did when they gathered together for worship. In a letter addressed to the Emperor Trajan, Pliny described his findings. From this report we gain some small insight into worship, especially the secrecy surrounding Christian worship. He informed the emperor that "the substance of their fault or error was that they were in the habit of meeting on a fixed day before daylight and reciting responsively among themselves a hymn to Christ as a god."[2] Some think that the word translated "hymn" means "religious formula" and may refer to the Lord's Supper.

Pliny also told the emperor that Christians "bound themselves by an oath not to commit any crime but to abstain from theft, robbery and adultery, that they should not break their word or deny a deposit when called upon to pay it." While it is not absolutely clear how this oath was expressed, it is generally believed to be what liturgical scholar Joseph Jungmann describes as "a distant parallel to the Sunday confession of sins,"[3] perhaps the recital of the Decalogue.

A third part of Pliny's statement reported that "when they had performed this it was their custom to depart and to meet together again for a meal, but of a common and harmless kind. They said they had even given up doing this since the promulgation of my edict, by which, in accordance with your commands, I had forbidden the existence of clubs." The reference to this meal as "common" and "harmless" indicates a fair amount of knowledge on Pliny's part about the meal. That it was probably not the Lord's Supper is suggested by the fact that it was held separately from the "hymn" and that the Christians "gave it up" as a concession to Pliny. More than likely it was the *agape* feast, a common meal eaten together by the church, but set apart from the Lord's Supper.[4]

The Didache

A second document coming from the same period of time is the *Didache* (A.D. 100). This short document, an early church manual, contains among other things instructional material for the early Christian church. For our purposes the most striking feature of the *Didache* is the full text of an early *agape* feast!

Regarding the Eucharist. Give thanks as follows:

First concerning the cup:

"We give Thee thanks, our Father, for the Holy Vine of David Thy servant, which Thou hast made known to us through Jesus, Thy Servant."
"To Thee be the glory forevermore."

Next, concerning the broken bread:
"We give Thee thanks, our Father, for the life and knowledge which Thou hast made known to us through Jesus, Thy Servant."
"To Thee be the glory forevermore."

"As this broken bread was scattered over the hills and then, when gathered, became one mass, so may Thy Church be gathered from the ends of the earth into Thy Kingdom."

"For Thine is the glory and the power through Jesus Christ forevermore."

Let no one eat and drink of your Eucharist but those baptized in the name of the Lord; to this, too, the saying of the Lord is applicable: Do not give to dogs what is sacred.

After you have taken your fill of food, give thanks as follows:
"We give Thee thanks, O Holy Father, for Thy holy name which Thou hast enshrined in our hearts, and for the knowledge and faith and immortality which Thou hast made known to us through Jesus, Thy Servant."
"To Thee be the glory forevermore."

"Thou, Lord Almighty, hast created all things for the sake of Thy name and hast given food and drink for men to enjoy, that they may give thanks to Thee; but to us Thou hast vouchsafed spiritual food and drink and eternal life through (Jesus,) Thy Servant."

"Above all, we give Thee thanks because Thou art might."
"To Thee be the glory forevermore."

"Remember, O Lord, Thy Church: deliver her from all evil, perfect her in Thy love, and from the four winds assemble her, the sanctified, in Thy kingdom which Thou hast prepared for her."

"For Thine is the power and the glory forevermore."

"May grace come, and this world pass away!"

"Hosanna to the God of David!"

"If anyone is holy, let him advance; if anyone is not, let him be converted. Maranatha!" "Amen."

But permit the prophets to give thanks as much as they desire.[5]

The *agape* feast was a Christian communal meal having its origin in the earliest worship experiences of the church. Luke recorded this meal in Acts 2:46: "They broke bread in their homes and ate together with glad and sincere hearts." Originally the Lord's Supper was celebrated in the context of the *agape* meal. However, the Lord's Supper and the common meal gradually became separated (reasons for this will be given later in this chapter.) The *Didache* provides an example of the common meal and the prayers of the *agape* that preceded the Lord's Supper.[6]

The *agape* feast was a carry-over from the Jewish table fellowship. It was a common practice among Jewish people to repeat blessings at the meal over the cup and the bread. Thus, it was natural for the early Christians, who were also Jewish, to change these prayers slightly for use in the Christian communal meal. Compare, for example, the following prayers over the cup and bread.

JEWISH	CHRISTIAN
The blessing over the cup: Blessed art Thou, O Lord our God, King Eternal, who createst the fruit of the vine.	We thank thee, our Father, for the holy vine of David, thy servant which thou hast made known to us through Jesus Christ, thy Servant; to thee be glory forever.
The words said over the bread: Blessed art thou, O Lord our God, King Eternal, who bringest forth the bread from the earth.	We thank thee our Father, for the life and knowledge which thou hast made known to us through Jesus thy servant: to thee be glory forever.[7]

The table prayers are beautiful in content, expressive of the theology of creation, the church, and the coming again of Christ. But they have no *direct* relationship with the prayers of the institution of the Lord's Supper. Consequently, the *agape* feast of the *Didache* should be regarded as a common meal similar to the one mentioned by Pliny. Although it was an enjoyable experience of fellowship, it was not central to worship and therefore, as in the case of the Christians investigated by Pliny, it could be dropped without compromise.

Justin Martyr

The next document, *The First Apology*, comes to us from the middle of the second century. It was written by the apologist Justin[8] to the Emperor Antoninus Pius. This work provides a considerable amount of information about the structure and meaning of Christian worship. Here is Justin's most important statement regarding the structure of Christian worship:

> And on the day called Sunday there is a meeting in one place of those who live in cities or the country, and the memoirs of the apostles or the writings of the prophets are read as long as time permits. When the reader has finished, the president in a discourse urges and invites [us] to the imitation of these noble things. Then we all stand up together and offer prayers. And, as said before, when we have finished the prayer, bread is brought, and wine and water, and the president similarly sends up prayers and thanksgivings to the best of his ability, and the congregation assents, saying the Amen; the distribution, and reception of the consecrated [elements] by each one, takes place and they are sent to the absent by the deacons.[9]

An important feature of this worship service is the two-part structure of the Word and the Lord's Supper. By including information about worship from other sources in Justin's writings the following outline appears as the normative structure of early Christian worship:

THE SERVICE OF THE WORD

Readings from the memoirs of the Apostles (Gospels)
Sermon by the President
Prayers by all the people, said standing

THE SERVICE OF THE LORD'S SUPPER

The Kiss of Peace (mentioned elsewhere)
Presentation of bread and a cup of wine and water to the President
The Eucharistic Prayer (prayers of praise and thanksgiving offered by the President in an extempore manner)

Response (the people say "Amen")
Reception (the bread and wine is distributed and then taken by
    the deacons to the absent)
Collection (alms are received and distributed to the needy)

These descriptions of worship provide insight into the accepted structure and content of Christian worship by the middle of
the second century. We are now in a position to trace worship
patterns that developed into this normative two-part structure.

THE NEW TESTAMENT ORIGINS OF THE
TWO-PART STRUCTURE OF CHRISTIAN WORSHIP

The concern of this section is to discuss the *origins* of the
two-part structure of Christian worship. (In part 3 of this book, "A
Theology of Worship," the *meaning* of the various parts of these
two aspects of Christian worship will be discussed.) Two lines of
development informed and shaped early Christian worship. They
grew out of the practices of the synagogue with its emphasis on the
Word and out of the Last Supper. Although these two institutions
can be traced separately, it is significant that they have a common
basis in the earliest worship experience of the church. It is to this
experience that we turn first.

Earliest Christian Worship

The earliest description of Christian worship is found in Acts
2:42:

> They devoted themselves
> to the apostles' teaching
> and to the fellowship,
> to the breaking of bread
> and to prayer.

Some scholars have argued for a twofold sequence of Word
and sacrament in this text.[10] But there is no universal agreement on
this matter, and the text itself can stand as no better than a proba-
ble twofold sequence. However, the sequence of Word and sacrament is more firmly based on 1 Corinthians 16:20–24. The conclusions about this passage reached by J. A. T. Robinson and the
suggestions of H. Lietzmann and G. Bornkamm are now generally
accepted. They are (1) that in 1 Corinthians 16:20–24 the language

is "not merely of epistolary convention, but of one worshiping community to another, the converse of the saints assembled for Eucharist," and (2) that in this pericope there can be traced "the remains of the earliest Christian liturgical sequence which we possess, and which is pre-Pauline in origin."[11] The basic structure of worship from the early New Testament church appears to be a twofold emphasis on Word and the Lord's Supper attended by prayer and praise. First Corinthians was to be read in the service of the Word, and immediately after that the service of the Lord's Supper was to be celebrated, as indicated by the allusions in 1 Corinthians 16:20–24.[12]

We now need to turn to the connecting lines between the twofold sequence of worship in the New Testament to that expressed by Justin in A.D. 150 by tracing both the influence of the synagogue on early worship and the development of the Lord's Supper as the background factors in the sequence of Word and sacrament.

The Influence of the Synagogue

It was always Paul's practice to go directly to the synagogue to preach Christ (as in Acts 13:5).[13] Those who became Christians remained in the synagogue at first and gradually formed worshiping communities of their own. At the death of Paul in the mid-sixties Christianity was still a Jewish sect but by the middle of the second century it clearly stood on its own. Thus, the official break between the two groups took place within that period of time. Contributing factors to this break include the differing opinions over the literal observance of the law and the Christian view of Jesus as the Messiah.[14]

In spite of the antagonism between Jews and Christians at the end of the first century, there is considerable evidence that the relationship that existed between them before their break was of sufficient duration to influence Christian worship significantly. The evidence suggests that the first part of Christian worship, the liturgy of the Word, was directly influenced by the synagogue.

First, Christian worship, like that of the synagogue, holds to *the centrality of Scripture.* It was the Jewish custom to read and comment on the Scriptures.[15] Portions from the Pentateuch and the prophets were read regularly. Likewise, the Christian practice of reading and expounding Scripture was attested to by Luke who

described Paul as one who "reasoned with them from the Scriptures, explaining and proving that the Christ had to suffer and rise
from the dead" (Acts 17:2–3). Soon the writings of the apostles
were read in worship along with the Old Testament. Early evidence of this practice is found in Colossians 4:16: "After this letter
has been read to you, see that it is also read in the church of the
Laodiceans and that you in turn read the letter from Laodicea" (see
also 2 Peter 3:16). The earliest noncanonical evidence of the reading of Scripture is found in the *Apology* of Justin quoted earlier:
"The memoirs of the apostles or the writings of the prophets are
read as long as time permits. When the reader has finished, the
president in a discourse urges and invites [us] to the imitation of
these noble things." The dependence here on the form of the
synagogue is hardly coincidental.[16]

Second, the church, like the synagogue (which followed the
temple practice), emphasized *prayer*.[17] There is a correspondence
in the time of prayer. The first Christians observed the daily hours of
prayer practiced in the synagogue: the third hour (Acts 2:15), the
sixth hour (Acts 10:9), and the ninth hour (Acts 3:1). These times of
prayer were continued in the early church as evidenced by Tertullian and Hippolythus in the early third century. There also seems to
be a correspondence in the use of the *shemoneh 'esreh* (the Eighteen
Benedictions) and of the Lord's Prayer. In the synagogues the
shemoneh 'esreh was read at each of the services (it is the prayer *par
excellence* of the synagogue).[18] Likewise, the Lord's Prayer was said
three times daily, according to the *Didache*.[19]

More striking, however, is the correspondence between the
language and the content of the prayers. The matters of concern
articulated in the *shemoneh 'esreh* appear to have had a strong
influence on the prayers of the early church, which bear a striking
resemblance to the Jewish Benedictions. A comparison with an
early Christian prayer found in the letter of Clement to the Corinthians bears this out:

SHEMONEH 'ESREH	CLEMENT
(Grant us) to hope in Thy Name, the first source of all creation; open the eyes of our heart to know Thee, that Thou alone art the Highest among the highest, and remainest Holy among the holy ones.	Thou art holy, and holy is Thy Name; and holy ones praise Thee every day. Blessed art Thou, O Lord, the Holy God.[20]

Clement's prayer, which is much longer than the above quotation, strongly influenced the development of Christian prayer in the early church. The central emphasis on the holiness of God and the praise given Him by the highest is frequently found in the liturgical prayers of the early church. Other traces of the Eighteen Benedictions can be found in early Christian prayer. Examples of such prayers include prayers for spiritual enlightenment, the *agape* prayer over the bread, prayers regarding the creation, intercessory prayers, prayers of confession, prayers for the forgiveness of sin, and the doxology. Such other aspects as the central emphasis on redemption, the sanctification of the Name ("Holy, Holy, Holy is the LORD Almighty; the whole earth is full of his glory," Isa. 6:3), the saying of the Amen, the use of the Psalms in recitation and singing, the confession of faith, the reading of the Decalogue, and using the Lord's Prayer are all traceable to the influence of the synagogue. Even the inclusion of extempore prayers as indicated by Justin has its roots in the prayer life of the synagogue.[21]

Because Christian liturgy was in the process of development, we cannot expect to find exact nor complete parallels between the Eighteen Benedictions and Christian prayer. Nevertheless, the sheer number of parallelisms and the similarity of the language offer weight to the argument that the entire liturgy of the Word in the early church owes its structural origin to the practices that had developed in the synagogue in the pre-Christian era and had served as the matrix out of which the early Christians' experience of worship was initially formed.

The Development of the Lord's Supper

The origin of the Lord's Supper lies in the institution of the supper on the night before the crucifixion.[22] Aside from Jesus' statements, the first mention of the words of institution is made by Paul in A.D. 57 in the first letter to the Corinthians (11:17–34). This has raised some questions about the origin and development of the Lord's Supper. These questions focus in part on the interpretation of "the breaking of bread" mentioned in Acts 2:42, 46; 20:7. Are we to assume that this term refers to the Lord's Supper?

We have already noticed that the worship of the early church recorded in Acts 2:42 occurs in the context of a meal. The question is this: Was "the breaking of the bread" part of the common meal itself (as in a Jewish meal) or does it designate an act apart from the meal (although in the context of the meal)? If "the breaking of the bread" was a self-contained act, then a case can be made that this expression is an early reference to the Lord's Supper. Because the act of breaking bread is structurally separated from fellowship and the term "breaking bread" was used for Jewish meals, one could suggest that Christians used the term to refer to the Holy Bread of the Christian Communion. Although this argument is not indisputable, two other considerations also favor this interpretation.

First, in the postresurrection appearances of Jesus the disciples always *ate* with him as they had done at the Last Supper (see Luke 24:13–43; John 21:1–14). In Emmaus Jesus went through the same fourfold action as at the Last Supper. He "took bread, gave thanks, broke it and began to give it to them" (Luke 24:30; compare Matt. 26:26). When the disciples returned to Jerusalem to tell the other disciples what had happened, they told "how Jesus was recognized by them when he broke the bread" Luke 24:35). On the shore of the Sea of Galilee they "knew it was the Lord" and "Jesus came, took the bread and gave it to them" (John 21:12–13). The "breaking of the bread" in the early Christian community may have been a means of recalling the presence of Jesus who was made known in "the breaking of the bread."

Second, it should be noted that "the breaking of the bread" was always in the context of a meal. Not only does the breaking of the bread evoke the memory of Christ, but the meal also serves the same purpose. For the meal goes back to that last meal and is a reminder of the promise of future meals (Matt. 26:29). Both the meal and "the breaking of the bread" of the early Christian community stem from the postresurrection appearances and beyond that from the Last Supper. Now, in this new meal of the kingdom, the resurrected and now-ascended Christ is made especially present in the meal and in "the breaking of the bread." For this reason the worship of the early church was characterized by a tremendous sense of joy and gladness (Acts 2:46, 47).

The relationship between the meal and the Lord's Supper is seen in Paul's letter to the Corinthians (1 Cor. 11:17–34). Here it is unquestionable that the Corinthians "really connected the holy celebration with a great banquet."[23] It is equally clear that certain abuses had crept into this resurrection celebration, at least at Corinth. Paul chastized the Christians for their poor conduct:

When you come together, it is not the Lord's Supper you eat,
for as you eat, each of you goes ahead without waiting for
anybody else. One remains hungry, another gets drunk. Don't
you have homes to eat and drink in? Or do you despise the
church of God and humiliate those who have nothing? What
shall I say to you? Shall I praise you for this? Certainly not!

1 Cor. 11:20–22

It appears that the banqueting aspect of the communal meal had
got out of hand.

Because of the overemphasis on the party aspect of the
Corinthian meal, Paul emphasized the element of the death of
Christ by reminding the Corinthians of the Last Supper and the
accent on death in the words of Jesus. That he was not introducing
a *new* element is evident in the words "I received from the Lord
what I also passed on to you" (1 Cor. 11:23). The words of institution were known in the tradition of the church and had been passed
down in the practice of the church.[24] Apparently the procedure
was to have the meal first, followed by the Lord's Supper.[25] The
Corinthians had so abused the joy of the meal that they were too
drunk to take the Lord's Supper in appropriate seriousness. Consequently, Paul urged them to eat at home: "If anyone is hungry,
he should eat at home, so that when you meet together it may not
result in judgment" (1 Cor. 11:34).

The Pauline emphasis on the Lord's Supper as a remembrance
of Christ's death and the stress to eat at home provides an example
of the forthcoming separation of the celebration of the Lord's Supper from the meal.[26] The *agape* meal in the *Didache* may therefore
be viewed as introductory to the following Eucharist. However, by
the middle of the second century the meal had been dropped
altogether from the service of worship. It was replaced by the ritual
of bread and wine, which remained the essential feature of the
second half of the liturgy.

No documents available from this period provide clear insight
into the reasons why the meal was separated from the Lord's Supper. The earliest explanation is the account provided by Paul in
1 Corinthians. Here the reason is clear. The Corinthians were
abusing the meal. The letter of Pliny as well as the *Didache* seem
to assume the separation between the meal and the Supper. In the
time of Pliny the meal was omitted because of persecution. In

other cases the meal may have been omitted for practical reasons. It may have become burdensome for the growing church to accommodate increasing numbers of people at the common meal. Consequently, the many tables were replaced by one—the table of the Lord on which the elements of bread and wine were placed. In this way the concept of the meal and the Lord's Supper were fused into the single ritual action that we find by A.D. 150 in the description provided by Justin.

Conclusion

Both the Old and New Testament contributed to the worship patterns of the early church. The normative pattern that emerged included the following essential features of Christian worship:

1. The *content* of Christian worship is Jesus Christ—His fulfillment of the Old Testament, His birth, life, death, resurrection, ascension, and coming again.
2. The *structure* of Christian worship is Word and sacrament including prayers, hymns, doxologies, benedictions, and responses.
3. The *context* in which worship takes place is in the Christian church called by God to worship, in which each member plays his or her part and in which God speaks and the worshiper responds. The meeting is sealed by the Lord's Supper, through which Christ is presented under the symbols of bread and wine.

UNUS DEUS, UNUS CONCILIATOR DEI ET HOMINU, HOMO CHRISTUS IESUS, QUI DEDIT SEMETIPSUM PRECIUM REDEMPTIONIS PRO OMNIBUS

Part II

THE HISTORICAL DEVELOPMENT

ITE IN MUNDUM UNIVERSUM, ET PRÆDICATE EVANGELIUM OMNI CREATURÆ

Chapter 5

Ancient and Medieval Worship

We turn now to an outworking of the biblical principles of worship in the history of the church from the third century to the Reformation. Although the limitations of this work preclude an exhaustive study, it is still possible to determine the broad strokes of historical development in order to gain insight into the various ways these principles of worship have been developed or disregarded.[1] This survey will provide a helpful background from which we may examine evangelical worship.

THIRD-CENTURY WORSHIP

The third-century sources of worship are few in number, the most important being *The Apostolic Tradition* of Hippolytus of Rome (about 220) and the *Didascalia* of the apostles (from northern Syria in the first half of the third century). Information is also given in the writings of Clement of Alexandria (d. 220) and Origen (d. 251). These sources provide a smattering of information from the three major centers of Christianity.[2] A worship service dating from the end of the third century may have looked something like the liturgies on the following page.[3]

THE LITURGY OF THE WORD

Lections: Law, Prophets, Epistles, Acts, Gospels, Letters
from bishops

Psalms sung by cantors between the lections

Alleluias

Sermon or sermons

Deacon's litany for catechumens and penitents

Dismissal of all but the faithful

THE LITURGY OF THE UPPER ROOM

Deacon's litany for the faithful, with diptychs (lists of names) of
living and dead

Kiss of peace

Offertory: Collection of alms

           Presentation of elements

           Preparation of elements and admixture of water to
wine

Sursum corda [Lift up your hearts]

Consecration Prayer:

     Preface: Thanksgiving and adoration for creation, holiness of God, etc.

     Sanctus [Holy, Holy, Holy]

     Thanksgiving for redemption [a prayer]

     Words of Institution

     Anamnesis [remembrance]

     Epiclesis [invocation of the Holy Spirit]

     Great Intercession for living and dead

Lord's Prayer

Fraction [breaking of the bread]

Elevation—'Holy things to the holy'—and Delivery

Communion of all in both kinds, each communicant replying
"Amen"; during reception Psalms xliii and xxxiv were
sung by cantors

Post-communion Thanksgiving

Deacon's litany and celebrant's brief Intercession

Reservation of bread only, for sick and absent

Dismissal

A comparison of the above service of worship with that provided by Justin one hundred years earlier shows no essential change in the structure of Word and sacrament, in the Christ-centered nature of worship, or in the sense of enactment. However, some ceremonial additions had also been made. Let us look at these:

Salutation

Minister: The Lord be with you.
    or, Peace be with you.
    or, The grace of the Lord Jesus Christ, the love of God, and the communion of the Holy Ghost be with you all.
People: And with thy spirit.

The salutation had its origin in ancient Israel as a greeting exchanged between people. For example, when Boaz arrived from Bethlehem he greeted the harvesters with "The LORD be with you," and they called back, "The LORD bless you" (Ruth 2:4). This same kind of greeting, which was common among Christians, soon became the greeting that signaled the beginning of Christian worship and preceded the prayers of the church. Its usage in the third-century liturgies testifies to its common acceptance in the church by the end of the second century, although the actual origin of its usage is unknown.

Sursum Corda

Minister: Lift up your hearts.
People: We lift them up to the Lord.
Minister: Let us give thanks to the Lord.
People: It is meet and right to so do.

Cyprian is the first to give us evidence of the use of the *Sursum corda* although the exact origin of it is not known. It was developed, however, as a preface to the Lord's Supper to accent the spirit of thanksgiving. It is found everywhere in all the liturgies after Cyprian.

Sanctus

  Holy, Holy, Holy, Lord God Almighty,
  Heaven and earth are full of thy glory;
  Glory be to thee, O Lord.

The biblical origin for the use of the *Sanctus* in worship is found in the heavenly visions of Isaiah (6:3) and John (Rev. 4:8).

The first allusion to its use in Christian worship is made by Clement (A.D. 96) in his letter to the Corinthians. Although it is not possible to trace its development, it was in wide usage by the third century. It was used during the Lord's Supper and marks the beginning of the special prayer of thanksgiving (the eucharistic prayer).

Ancient sources also mention the use of the *Kyrie eleison* (Lord, have mercy) as well as the "thanks be to God" after Scripture readings and the "Amen" after prayers. The Lord's Prayer was also frequently used after the prayer of consecration (of the bread and wine).[4]

Prayers were probably said while people stood with their arms stretched heavenward or folded on the breast as in ancient Jewish worship. The Scriptures were read from a rostrum. It was the custom to stand during the reading of the Gospels to accentuate the fact that these books are the most precious of the New Testament because they speak directly of the Savior. Gradually signs of respect accompanied the reading of the Gospel and the bringing forth of the elements of bread and wine. These two acts were among the most significant actions of the worshiping community because they were the chief points of proclamation.

The chief officiant of worship was either the bishop or the minister or ministers, depending on the size of the congregation. The deacons were also highly involved in worship. They directed the people, read the Scriptures, led in prayer, guarded the doors, maintained order, presented the elements, and helped to distribute them. The people were also involved. They assisted in the readings and played their part in the drama with responses, prayers, and alms.[5]

It is generally recognized that while certain parts of the service were fixed (i.e., the use of Scripture, prayers, salutation, *Sursum corda* and *Sanctus*), there was nevertheless a great deal of freedom. The prayers were not yet fixed and the liturgy was not so completely structured that free worship could not be contained within the generally accepted order. The statement that Justin had written, "The president similarly sends up prayers and thanksgivings to the best of his ability," appears to have been true in the third century as well. Nevertheless, the increasingly strict attention given to the content of the eucharistic prayer in the third century is evidenced by *The Apostolic Tradition* of Hippolytus.

FOURTH- AND FIFTH-CENTURY WORSHIP

In the fourth and fifth centuries the status of the church changed dramatically following the conversion of Constantine. In this favored context the church grew rapidly, formulated its theology in various creeds, and developed a more fixed form in its worship. This era is known as the period of classical Christianity, the golden age of the Fathers, and the most creative and formative time in the history of the church. While there is warrant for criticism of worship in this era, it still remains the most important historical period for the thoughtful working out of the rituals that have characterized Christian worship through the centuries. Therefore, an understanding of this period is highly important if we would know how to worship today.[6]

One important factor was the emergence of ecclesiastical centers in the influential cities of the Roman Empire. These centers gradually developed a particular style that was reflected in theology and worship. Each area assumed, as it were, a special stamp. In basic structure all the liturgies are the same, retaining the two foci of Word and sacrament. The difference arises in the ceremony and style that reflect the local culture.

The Eastern Liturgy

Worship in the fourth century began to reflect the culture of which it was a part. This is particularly true of Eastern Christian worship. The Eastern world view was informed by the Hellenistic love for the aesthetic. The great contributions of this culture were poetry, literature, art, and philosophy. All of these interests aided the development of a poetic mind and a sense of imagery and artistic expression. That worship was shaped by the Hellenistic imagination is evident in the extensive use of ceremonial signs and symbols in Eastern worship. Byzantine worship was highly ceremonial, gloriously beautiful, and deeply mystical.[7]

Ceremony in the St. John Chrysostom liturgy is most clearly seen in the Little Entrance and the Great Entrance. The Little Entrance centers around the reading of the Gospel and intends to accent the significance of the Word of God. In a rich ceremony intending to invoke awe and reverence for the Word of God, the Book is carried by a deacon accompanied by a procession of ministers and acolytes who bear crosses, candles, and incense. They proceed through the north door of the iconastasis screen, a screen on which the icons are arranged, dividing the altar area from the sanctuary. They walk down the center aisle of the church where the Book is ceremonially blessed and kissed. They then return through the Royal Door to the Holy Table where the Gospel lesson is sung or read.

The Great Entrance centers around the bread and wine and intends to accent the death and resurrection of Jesus Christ. It is even richer in ceremony than the Little Entrance to emphasize its importance in the work of redemption. This procession includes all the ministers, with the acolytes carrying lights, the thurifers swinging the incense, and others carrying signs of the Passion such as the cross, the spear, the scourge, and the thorns. They pass through the North Door of the iconostasis returning again through the Royal Door. The celebrant bears the cup and the deacon carries the paten on his head for all to see the veiled symbols of bread and wine. The doors are shut while the ministers receive the elements and then are flung open for the people to come and communicate.[8]

These rich ceremonies are carried out in the context of glorious beauty. The Eastern church has been strongly influenced by the images of heavenly worship described by the apostle John in Revelation 4 and 5. The opening lines of John's vision provide a glimpse of this beauty: "I was in the Spirit, and there before me was a throne in heaven with someone sitting on it. And the one who sat there had the appearance of jasper and carnelian. A rainbow, resembling an emerald, encircled the throne" (Rev. 4:2–3). This vision combined with the natural Hellenistic propensity toward beauty has given shape to the rich colors of the fresco painted walls, the simple beauty of the icons, and the colorful vestments of the clergy. The concern of Eastern worship is to bring heaven down to earth and transport earth to heaven. It is born of the conviction that we earthlings join in that heavenly assembly. No beauty can surpass the beauty of God on His throne encircled by His creation and His creatures worshiping Him.

A story in the *Russian Primary Chronicle* relates how Vladimir, the Prince of Kiev, chose to adopt the Orthodox form of Christianity. He sent emissaries to search for the true religion. They visited the Muslim Bulgars of the Volga, the German and the Roman Christians, and finally traveled to Constantinople where they found the true religion as a result of attending the liturgy of the church of the Holy Wisdom. In their report to Vladimir they wrote: "We knew not whether we were in heaven or on earth, for surely there is no such splendor or beauty anywhere upon earth. We cannot describe it to you; only this we know, that God dwells there among men, and that their service surpasses the worship of all other places. For we cannot forget that beauty."[9]

The rich ceremony combined with this glorious beauty intends to convey the sense of the mystical. Since earthly worship joins heavenly worship, God is present. For this reason care is taken to communicate the mystical presence of God in the ceremony and beauty of the liturgy. This sense of the mystical is communicated especially in the development of the sanctuary screen. Behind the screen the great mystery of Christ's death and resurrection is enacted in the drama of the Eucharist.[10]

The Western Liturgy

The information about the development of Western liturgy is scanty and late by comparison with the sources available from the East. Early sources are found in Justin Martyr and Hippolytus, but between 220 and 500 we have no adequate sources of information regarding the Western liturgy.[11]

After A.D. 500 two rites, the Gallican and the Roman, appear to exist side by side in the West. The Roman rite was used principally in Rome, whereas the Gallican rite was used throughout Europe and varied considerably according to local custom. There is evidence that both these rites influenced each other until the ninth century when the Gallican rites were suppressed under Pepin and Charlemagne. Thereafter, the Roman rite was the standard approach to worship in the West. From the tenth to the sixteenth century the Roman rite underwent numerous minor changes in ceremony and emphasis until 1570 when it became fixed in form.

The Gallican rite, originating from the primitive worship of the early church, reflects customs that are more colorful, sensuous, symbolic, and dramatic than does the Roman liturgy. It is longer and more flexible than the Roman rite as well.[12]

The origins of the Roman rite are equally unclear. The earliest liturgies, in Greek, were gradually translated into Latin in the fourth century. The only document of importance from this period is the *de Sacramentis* that provides insight into the developing customs of worship. More helpful is the *Gelasian Sacramentary,* from Pope Gelasius (492–496), and the *Gregorian Sacramentary*, named after Gregory the Great, pope from 590 to 604. The texts between the ninth and fifteenth centuries, contained in *Ordines Romani*, are more helpful because they give detailed descriptions of the Mass.

Like the Eastern church the Western church also reflected the culture of which it was a part. The Roman mind set is considerably different from that of the Greak East. The Romans were characterized by a spirit of pragmatism. This is evident in their buildings and in the development of Roman laws. This spirit is reflected in early Roman worship. It is not ostentatious or highly ceremonial. Rather, Roman worship is characterized by soberness and simplicity.

The tendency toward simplicity is obvious in both the order and symbols of worship. A brief comparison of the Roman rite with the Byzantine rite clearly indicates the uncluttered nature of Roman worship. It moved simply without much ceremony from part to part. It had not developed much beyond the simple movement of a third-century liturgy. The character of simplicity was equally true in Roman ceremony. Ceremonies including the elevation of the host, the ringing of bells, the use of lights, censing and genuflections were not in use in the fifth century. In the Roman rite they came into use much later. Nevertheless, there was great beauty, a sense of God's presence, a feeling of awe and reverence provoked by the simple majesty of the Roman rite.[13]

It is clear that the early church did not have an absolutely fixed order or use of symbolic communication. Rather, these aspects of worship developed in respect to the cultural context in which worship was being formed. This contextual principle is important to keep in mind when translating the principles of worship into American evangelical churches or the churches of developing countries.

There are other developments during this period that we will examine in part 4, "The Context of Worship." They include the emergence of church buildings, the development of the church year, and the development of church music.

MEDIEVAL WORSHIP

The medieval period was characterized by a shift in the meaning of worship. We can trace the beginning of this change from the fourth and fifth centuries to the early medieval period, the time when two distinct lines of development become discernible. On the one hand the established church increasingly emphasized worship as a mystery, while on the other hand the monastic movement stressed the devotional character of worship.

Worship as Mystery

The idea of worship as mystery has its origin in the mistaken use of ceremonial forms. Forms in and of themselves are not wrong. They are the means through which worship is conducted, the signs and symbols of the reality they bear. However, when ceremonial forms become an end rather than a means they assume a cultic character and tend to replace the message they bear.[14]

The change that occurred in medieval worship was not in the form of worship, but in the understanding, the meaning, and the experience of forms. The ceremonial forms (hereafter referred to as the cult) became

> more and more a sacred action in itself, a mystery performed for the sanctification of those participating. This is most noticeable in the evolution of the external organization of the cult: in the gradually increasing separation of the clergy (who "perform the mystery") from the people; in the emphasis by means of ceremony on the mysterious, dreadful and sacred character of the celebrant; in the stress which is laid henceforth on ritual purity, the state of untouchableness, the "sacred" versus the "profane."[15]

There are a number of reasons why this change of understanding occurred. First, during the Constantinian era the church converted many pagan festivals and customs and invested them with Christian meaning. This missiological strategy had its definite advantages in Christianizing the Empire but also suffered the disadvantage of an unhealthy influence from the mystery cults (although it is now recognized that the influence was much less than previously assumed). The major problem in the mystery cult is that the cultic action is regarded as an end in itself. This notion influenced the church, making the action of worship a mystery.[16]

The idea that the church's worship was a mystery was augmented by several other developments. The change in language, for example, was a factor. Although the church spread into German, French, and English-speaking areas it retained Latin as the language of the Mass. This surrounded the Mass and the clergy with an aura of mystery since most of the people did not understand what was happening. Furthermore, the church distanced itself from the people even more as it increasingly viewed itself as a hierarchical institution rather than a body. The church dispensed salvation. The liturgy, especially the Eucharist, became the means of receiving this salvation. This view of the church was enhanced by the developments in Eucharistic theology. In the ninth century Paschasius Radbertus proposed a view of the presence of Jesus in the Mass by virtue of the miraculous change that occurred in the bread and wine. This view laid the groundwork for the doctrine of transubstantiation that became dogma at the Fourth Lateran Council in 1215.[17]

A major result of the mystical view of worship is that the Mass became an epiphany of God. An overemphasis on the *action of God* in the Mass tended to overshadow the corporate action of the people in worship. The Mass assumed the character of a sacred drama that was played out by the clergy while the people watched. Furthermore, the Mass itself assumed an allegorical character. This sacred drama of the life, death, and resurrection of Jesus was perceptible to the eye. Each part of the liturgy and the vestments, the utensils, and the motions of the clergy were invested with meaning from the life of Christ. A typical example of this approach is found in the writings of Amalor in the ninth century:

> The *introit* alludes to the choir of the Prophets (who announced the advent of Christ just as the singers announce the advent of the bishop) . . . ' the *Kyrie eleison* alludes to the Prophets at the time of Christ's coming, Zachary and his son John among them; the *Gloria in excelsis Deo*, points to the throng of angels who proclaimed to the shepherds the joyous tidings of our Lord's birth (and indeed in this manner, that first one spoke and the others joined in, just as in the Mass the bishop intones and the whole church joins in); the (first collect) refers to what our Lord did in His twelfth year . . . ; the Epistle alludes to the preaching of John, the *responsorium* to the readiness of the Apostles when our Lord called them and they followed Him; the Alleluia to their joy of heart when they heard His promises or saw the miracles He wrought . . . , the Gospel to His

preaching. . . . The rest of what happens in the Mass refers to the time from Sunday on, when the disciples drew close to Him (along with the multitude—making their gift-offerings), up to His Ascension or to Pentecost. The prayer which the priest says from the *secreta* to the *Nobis quoque peccatoribus* signifies the prayer of Jesus on Mount Olivet. What occurs later signifies the time during which Christ lay in the grave. When the bread is immersed in the wine, this means the return of Christ's soul to His body. The next action signifies the greetings offered by Christ to His Apostles. And the breaking of the offerings signifies the breaking of bread performed by the Lord before the two at Emmaus.[18]

Another example of the mysteriological view of worship is the notion that the Mass is a sacrifice offered to God for the benefit of the living and the dead. This resulted in an extreme reverence for the handling of the host (no lay hand was to touch it) and outlandish claims for the efficacy of the Mass. For example, it was argued that food tastes better after hearing a Mass, that one will not die a sudden death, and that the souls in purgatory will not suffer while a Mass is being said for them. This view led to a multiplicity of masses and the practice of "saying mass" for the benefit of someone (living, sick, or dead) for a stipend. More altars were needed for this purpose (a requirement that affected architecture in the medieval period), and the Mass became more firmly entrenched as something belonging to the clergy. In many instances the mystery was turned into a superstition and the real meaning of worship was lost to both clergy and the people alike.[19]

Worship as Devotion

The second strand of development in the medieval period occurred within the monastic movement. Originally the monastics began as a protest against the growing worldliness of the church, but gradually they became a formative and influential movement within the church, though they maintained a prophetic stance.

At first the worship of the monastic orders was no different from that of the church. They celebrated the Eucharist on Saturday and Sunday even though they had to walk long distances to do so. However, the monastics developed their own approach to prayer. Prayer had always been important in the Christian tradition, but the new attitude saw prayer as the sole content of life. The difference was not that the monks did not work (though some did spend their entire time in prayer), but that everything in life became subordinated to prayer. Prayer became the chief work of the monks.[20]

This attitude of monasticism came into sharp contrast with the growing institutionalism and "this-worldliness" of the medieval church. The emphasis of the established church shifted from the eschatological kingdom of God to the kingdom of God on earth. The church became, therefore, the protector and the sanctifier of the world. Monasticism, as it continued to emphasize the kingdom to come, reacted against the secularization of the church and continued to emphasize the otherworldly character of the Christian faith.

The continuing eschatological concern of monasticism was reflected in an approach to worship that became increasingly pietistic or devotional. For example, the Eucharist became an instrument of piety. Participation in the Eucharist was a means of becoming more holy, a means of sanctification and growth in Christ. The early church's emphasis on the Eucharist as the actualization of the church and an anticipation of the future feast of the kingdom was not denied. The newer view considered the Communion as an act of spiritual benefit, a means of receiving spiritual nourishment.

A similar case may be made for the emergence of the rules of prayer, the devotional manuals developed for the various times of daily prayer. These times of prayer remained consistent with the times set aside in the church and the devotions retained the same content of Psalms, prayers, Scripture, and chants. In addition, a private rule of prayer developed among the monastics, having a strong emphasis on personal prayer and the Psalms. Originally, the church's prayers were offered for their content and the set times were intended to demonstrate that all time from morning to night belonged to God. Those prayers were a proclamation of the meaning of time and life and, although devotional, did not have as their prime intent the development of personal piety. In the medieval period, however, the personal pietistic concern of the monastic life of prayer influenced the prayer of the church toward a personal devotional meaning. As a result prayer became a means to increase piety.

Conclusion

In this chapter we have seen an outline of the development of worship from the third century to the dawn of the Reformation. Although space has not permitted a detailed discussion of this development, the lines along which worship was passed down in history are clear.

In brief the norm of Christian worship is both Word and sacrament that proclaim the death and resurrection of Jesus Christ for the salvation of the world. Around these two foci are gathered the prayers of the church and words of acclamation and praise. In these actions of the church, the church as the people of God is actualized and the kingdom is anticipated.

Gradually, however, beginning with the Constantinian era, worship changed by the increasing addition of ceremony and the subtle influence of the mystery religions that were being replaced by Christianity in the Roman Empire. These new emphases became more extreme in the medieval period. Although the basic structure and content of worship remained continuous with the past, the meaning of worship for both the clergy and the laity underwent some major changes. Worship became a "mystery" in which God was made present (an epiphany). This was accomplished through an allegorical view of the Mass and the doctrine of the bodily presence of Jesus in the bread and wine. In this way the Mass assumed the character of a sacrifice and was celebrated for the benefit of both the living and the dead (creating a multiplicity of masses and other abuses).

Thus, the principle to keep in mind in constructing a worship for today is that we ought not allow worship to be accommodated to current cultural norms to such an extent that worship loses its meaning.

Chapter 6

Reformation and Modern Protestant Worship

It is the purpose of this chapter to introduce classical Protestant worship as we consider areas of agreement and disagreement among the early Reformers on the subject of worship. We will also illustrate two changes that took place in succeeding centuries as the focus of worship changed from mystery and devotion to understanding and experience. Both of these changes have affected contemporary evangelical worship.*

CLASSICAL PROTESTANT WORSHIP

Although the Reformation was principally a reform of theology, it was inevitable that a reform of worship should result from it.[1] How worship was conceived at the beginning of the Reformation is aptly summarized in the following words of William D. Maxwell in his book *An Outline of Christian Worship:*

> We have seen that, at the beginning of the sixteenth century, the celebration of the Lord's Supper in the Western Church had become a dramatic spectacle, culminating not in communion but in the miracle of transubstantiation, and

---

*Since this work is intended for Protestants, I have not included comments on the current changes in worship among the Catholics. Insight into these changes is best found in "The Liturgical Constitution," documents of Vatican II.

marked by adoration, not unmixed with superstition, at the elevation. Said inaudibly in an unknown tongue, and surrounded with ornate ceremonial and, if a sung mass, with elaborate musical accompaniment, the rite presented only meagre opportunity for popular participation. The people were not encouraged to communicate more often than once a year. The sermon had fallen into a grave decline, most parish priests being too illiterate to preach; and the place of the Scripture lections had been usurped on a great many days by passages from the lives and legends of the saints. The Scriptures were not fully accessible in the vernacular, and paid masses and indulgences were a source of simoniacal exploitation. Reformation was an urgent necessity.[2]

In spite of the similarities among reforming groups, the reform of worship was not uniform. Some groups retained continuity with the past, while others completely broke with tradition to forge new styles of worship. In order to understand these trends we will look at the common concerns of Reformation worship and the differences between Reformers that account for the various styles of worship in the Reformation churches.

The Common Concerns of the Reformers

First, Protestants rejected the Mass because of the medieval view of it as a repetition of the sacrifice of Christ. Luther, in "The Babylonian Captivity of the Church," called the Mass an "abuse" that brought

an endless host of others in its train, so that the faith of this sacrament has become utterly extinct and the holy sacrament has been turned into a veritable fair, tavern, and place of merchandise. Hence participants, brotherhoods, intercessions, merits, anniversaries, memorial days, and the like wares are bought and sold, traded and bartered in the church, and from this priests and monks derive their whole living.[3]

Luther's most direct criticisms were aimed at the Roman prayers of the eucharistic canon. The Mass, Luther charged, had lost its original focus as a *thanksgiving* and had become a propitiation to please God. For Luther, this notion was incompatible with the Scriptures. It stood against the gospel and had, therefore, to be excised from worship. Furthermore, the theology of sacrifice in the Mass created a host of other problems. People expected all sorts of benefits and advantages from hearing Mass, including healings, the release of souls from purgatory, and other magical results. The Mass had even lost the idea of communion, because people did not have to be present at the Mass—it could be said on their behalf. Consequently, the priest *saying* the Mass took the place of worship by the people and became a legalistic means of buying salvation. This view struck at the heart of the Christian message and perverted the essential nature of the Christian faith as a religion of *grace*. The overthrow of the Mass as a sacrifice was necessary. In this all the Protestants concurred.

Second, the Reformers rejected the doctrine of transubstantiation. Underlying transubstantiation was the Roman notion of *opus operatum*, the belief that the mere performance of the Mass effected the presence of Christ automatically. In this view the performance of the rite imparted a blessing without the faith of the recipient, even without the elements of the Mass being distributed to the congregation. Transubstantiation explained the means by which Christ became present in the sacrifice. The *substance* of bread and wine changed into the body and blood of Christ and was offered to the Father as a sacrifice for salvation. The connection between the Mass as a sacrifice and transubstantiation naturally led the Reformers, who rejected the one, to reject the other as well.

Next, the Reformers insisted on the restoration of the Word to its ancient and proper place in worship. The imbalance between Word and sacrament that led to the falling away of preaching and teaching the Word of God was regarded as a one-sided approach to worship. In the spring of 1523 Luther issued instructions in a pamphlet entitled *Concerning the Ordering of Divine Worship in the Congregation* in which he concluded with these words:

> This is the sum of the matter: that everything shall be done so that the Word prevails. . . . We can spare everything except the Word. We profit by nothing so much as by the Word. For the whole Scripture shows that the Word should have free course among Christians. And in Luke 10, Christ himself says: "One thing is needful"—that Mary sit at the feet of Christ and daily hear his Word. . . .[4]

Zwingli went even farther than Luther in insisting that the people were to give ear to the Word of God *alone*. Consequently, he abolished organs as well as other music, vestments, pictures, and anything else that would detract from the centrality of the Word.

Finally, the Reformers agreed on two other matters: (1) that worship should be in the vernacular and (2) that the twofold structure of Word and sacrament be maintained. Zwingli was the only Reformer who disagreed with the desire to return to the ancient structure of Word and sacrament. His emphasis was on the Word only. This position remained the most influential in the circles of Calvinism, and, to the distress of John Calvin, quarterly communion, rather than weekly communion, became standard in the churches most influenced by Calvinism. This influence extended through the English Puritans to the Baptists, Presbyterians, Congregationalists, and independents and spread through them to most of American Protestant Christianity.

The Differences Among the Reformers

In spite of unity on the above matters, distinct differences regarding worship existed among the Reformers. The fundamental disagreement occurred over continuity with the Roman Catholic heritage. The Lutheran and Anglican traditions retained much of ancient worship; the Zwinglian and Anabaptists made a radical break with the past; and the Reformed church maintained a middle position.[5]

For example, the Lutheran Augsburg Confession states:

> Our churches are falsely accused of abolishing the mass. Actually, the mass is retained among us and is celebrated with the greatest reverence. *Almost all the customary ceremonies are also retained* [emphasis added]. . . . The mass among us is supported by the example of the church as seen from the scriptures and the fathers.[6]

The Anglicans also retained much of the past. After the break with Rome the Mass remained essentially the same throughout the reign of Henry VIII. Not until the reign of Edward VI were strong Protestant notions asserted in the Mass. These were contained in Cranmer's *Order of the Communion* and included such things as the deletion of the word *mass*, the abolishing of vestments and the replacement of altars by communion tables. Other changes were made in the order of worship including the deletion of the *introit*, the *Glory be to thee, O Lord* at the Gospel reading, and the prayers for the dead. These changes, however, were short lived because of the accession of the Roman Catholic Mary to the throne. Her short reign was followed by the lengthy reign of Elizabeth, under whom the *Book of Common Prayer* as revised in 1559 was established by law. In the *Book of Common Prayer* and in the tract entitled *Of Ceremonies* the Anglican church reaffirmed continuity with the ancient rite with few changes.[7]

A more drastic approach was taken by Zwingli and the Anabaptists. Zwingli repudiated all ceremonies as pagan and commenced to rid the church of traditions and many worship rubrics regardless of their possible value to the church. He was convinced that faith came through the Holy Spirit alone apart from physical channels or external means.

The Anabaptists not only rejected ceremonies in worship, but also the necessity of formal public worship. It was their conviction that the true church was an obedient and suffering people whose daily walk with God was of utmost importance. This walk climaxed in the gathering of Christians together for prayer, Bible reading, admonition, and the Lord's Supper in the informal atmosphere of the home. They thus refused to attend the worship of the state church and met in secret at various times in an unscheduled and impromptu manner. The time and place of other scheduled meetings were communicated by word of mouth to those who belonged to the closely knit community.[8]

The Reformed community forged out a mediating approach to worship. Calvin's major source was the work of Martin Bucer of Strasbourg, who combined a Zwinglian emphasis with Lutheranism and developed *The Strasbourg Liturgy*.[9] Before Bucer the worship at Strasbourg retained ceremonial aspects such as vestments, elevation, washing of the celebrant's hands, and genuflection but omitted all indications of a doctrine of sacrifice. Bucer reduced the worship to its most simple forms. Most of the versicles and responses disappeared with the resulting loss of the antiphonal character of worship. Proses such as the *Gloria in excelsis* and the *Kyries* were replaced by metrical psalms and hymns. Even the *Sursum corda* and the prefaces such as the *Sanctus* and the *Benedictus* disappeared, being substituted by a general prayer of thanksgiving for Christ's work. The lections also disappeared, allowing the minister to "pick his text," and sermons became an hour in length. In general, it may be said that an impoverishment of the historic substance of worship was replaced by forms less aesthetic and graceful. A more rational approach to worship had set in.

Calvin came to Strasbourg and ministered to a small group of French exiles between 1538 and 1541. It was here in this context that his views on worship, influenced by Bucer and the *Strasbourg Liturgy*, began to take shape. His standard was the corporate worship of the early church, which he thought was best represented in the rites of Strasbourg. His writing on worship, *The Form of Prayers and Manner of Ministering the Sacraments According to the Use of the Ancient Church*, shows where his sympathies lie.[10] Calvin made some changes in the *Strasbourg Liturgy* in the variants, the confession, the Lord's Prayer, the reading of the Decalogue, and the singing of psalms. But none of this changed the essential character of Bucer's synthesis between the Lutheran and Zwinglian approach to worship. Calvin's liturgy, following Bucer's synthesis, became the major approach to worship in the Reformed churches.[11]

One further matter should be noted about Calvin. It was his intent, in keeping with his appreciation of the worship of the early church, to maintain the ancient structure of worship proclaiming Christ's death, resurrection, and return in *both Word and sacrament*. The fact that most Reformed churches today follow the Zwinglian practice of quarterly communion is no fault of Calvin. The magistrates who were influenced by Zwingli in this matter did not allow Calvin to celebrate Holy Communion weekly as he wished. This attitude is seen in a letter Calvin wrote to the magistrates of Berne in 1555:

> There is another matter, though not a new one [to which I would call your attention], namely, that we celebrate the Lord's Supper four times a year, and you three times. Please God, gentlemen, that both you and we may be able to establish a more frequent usage. For it is evident from St. Luke in the Book of Acts that communion was much more frequently celebrated in the primitive Church; and that continued for a long time in the ancient Church, until this abomination of the mass was set up by Satan, who so caused it that people received

communion only once or twice a year. Wherefore, we must acknowledge that it is a defect in us that we do not follow the example of the Apostles.[12]

MODERN PROTESTANT WORSHIP

The development of Protestant worship from the seventeenth through the twentieth century could be traced only in a history of each denomination. Since such a task is beyond the scope of this work it will be sufficient to state three trends in Protestant worship and provide illustrations from various denominations. These trends include an antiliturgical stance, an emphasis on understanding the Word of God, and an emphasis on experiencing God in worship.

The Antiliturgical Stance

The antiliturgical movement among mainline Christians originated with the Puritans in England.[13] The emphasis shifted away from the use of a prayer book to spiritual worship. Three examples from the early Baptists, the Congregationalists, and the Quakers will suffice to illustrate the point.

John Smyth, an early Baptist, wrote:

We hold that the worship of the New Testament properly so called is spiritual proceeding originally from the heart: and that reading out of a book (though it is a lawful ecclesiastical action) is no part of spiritual worship, but rather the invention of the man of sin, it being substituted for a part of spiritual worship.

We hold that seeing prophesying is a part of spiritual worship: therefore in time of prophesying it is unlawful to have the book (i.e., the Bible) as a help before the eye.

We hold that seeing singing a psalm is a part of spiritual worship: therefore it is unlawful to have the book before the eye in time of singing a psalm.[14]

The Congregationalists rejected the use of written prayers, insisting that prayer should be from the heart, directed by the Spirit of God. In support of this view they set forth six arguments:

1. Written prayers deprive the person of his or her own thoughts and words.
2. Set forms could not meet the variety of needs in a particular congregation.

3. Set forms are idolatrous as they equate the liturgy with the Bible.
4. Set forms lead to overfamiliarity and lack of interest.
5. Imposing set forms is a manner of persecution. [We may note that this argument was set forth in the contest for each congregation to be "free" to follow its own desires and is not as applicable today.]
6. Set prayers oppose the appropriate approach to the Father. [15]

Quaker worship is characterized by its abandonment of the ordained ministry and the sacraments in favor of a personal "waiting upon the Spirit" by every member of the congregation. The central concern of Quaker worship is the simple intention of the people of God to open themselves to the presence of Christ in the meeting ("where two or three come together in my name, there am I with them") and to wait upon Him to speak through the Spirit. This view rejects any dependence on external aids or rites such as the sacraments (in extreme groups the Spirit's revelation was more important than the Bible). It argues that all ceremonies and forms have been abolished by the New Covenant and that the offices of Christ as prophet, priest, and king are exercised in the worshiping community as they silently wait upon Him. Worship is supremely *inward.* Water baptism has been made unnecessary by Spirit baptism, and the Eucharist is an inward spiritual reception of Jesus that has no need of an external rite. [16]

The Emphasis on Understanding

A second trend in Protestant worship stressed the need for understanding the Word of God. Examples may be drawn from the early Congregationalists and Presbyterians.

Congregationalists developed a commentary approach to the reading of Scripture that opposed what they called "dumb reading." The reader, usually the minister or one trained in the Scripture, always made comments on the meaning and interpretation of the text as it was being read. After the "commentary reading" people from the congregation were encouraged to make prophetic statements or ask questions. The reading was followed by the sermon, which ran for two or three hours with a pause in the middle to allow the people to stretch. [17]

Presbyterians placed a strong emphasis on the use of Scripture in worship. The greatest grievance of the Puritans against the Anglican *Book of Common Prayer* was that it limited the use of Scripture. Later the *Westminster Directory* stipulated the reading of two full chapters (from both the Old and the New Testament) along with the Psalms as responsive reading. Presbyterians also practiced "lecturing," the habit of making comments on the Scripture as it was being read, and emphasized expository preaching. The minister was encouraged to seek the illumination of God's Spirit through prayer and a humble heart. His sermon was to consist of three parts: the doctrinal content of the text, a development of the argument and reasons for the doctrine in the text, and the application of the text to the hearer. For this reason ministers were to be highly trained in the use of the original languages and theology. They were cautioned, however, against using the original languages in the pulpit. Although the *Directory* recommended "frequent" communion, Presbyterians adopted the practice of quarterly communion. Thus the Scripture and its exposition became the dominant and most central factor in Presbyterian worship. Finally, Presbyterianism rejected the use of all "ceremonial" in worship unless it was prescribed in the New Testament.[18] For this reason worship remained simple and appealed to the mind alone, not to sight, smell, taste, and hearing (other than the Word of God).

The Emphasis on Experience

A third trend in Protestant worship emphasized personal experience. This can be illustrated from Pietism, Moravianism, Revivalism, and the contemporary charismatic movement.

Pietism was a movement against dead orthodoxy. It began in Lutheranism in the seventeenth century and spread into pockets of both Protestant and Roman Catholic Christianity. Its major concern was to effect a personal reform of faith over against a mere formal doctrinal or external adherence to the Christian faith. Consequently, Pietists rebelled against established Protestant worship as too dependent on external form. Externalism, it was believed, prevented personal involvement motivated by an openness to the Spirit.[19]

Jean de Labadie of Middleburg was one who emphasized informal worship to more ordered practice. Ordered worship was for the nominal Christian, but free worship was for the truly converted person. Converted Christians frequently met in homes, where they prayed from the heart and where a free exposition of Scripture by all was predominant. The key to Pietist worship is found in the stress on *conversion*. In conversion, worship centered no longer on the objective and corporate action of the church, but on the personal experience of the worshiper in worship and was followed by a rigorous ethical walk in personal life. In effect, those who were truly converted needed less structure and were less dependent on others for worship. In this way the corporate worship of the congregation and systematic order of congregational action were gradually replaced by the stress on individual experience in worship and a personal walk with the Lord.

One of the most prominent contributions of *Moravianism* to personal experiential worship is in hymnody. Hymn singing among the Moravians dates all the way back to their beginnings in pre-Reformation days. The special feature of Moravian hymns is the concern to create a subjective experience of the Savior's suffering. These hymns are "emotional, imaginative, sensuous, with a minimum of intellectual structure."[20] The concern of the worshiper was to feel the pain of the Savior and to cause, therefore, a turning to Him in love and adoration. One such favorite hymn written by Zinzendorf is "Jesus Thy Blood and Righteousness." In time the extreme preoccupation to "the bloody sweat, the nail prints, the side's cleft opened wide for the faithful" were replaced by less exotic symbolism.

The most famous *Revivalist* of the eighteenth century was John Wesley. His approach to worship represented a blend of classical Protestant forms with the personal element of Pietism. He was strongly influenced by the Moravians and through them learned to stress the importance of conversion and personal experience.[21]

Like the Moravians, the Revivalists made significant contributions in hymnody. Their hymns stress conversion and a personal experience of the Savior. The use of hymns in mainline Protestant worship was greeted with a great deal of skepticism. The classical Protestant and Puritan heritage prescribed only Psalms and Scripture. The notion that the church could write her own hymns of praise was an innovative suggestion met with some suspicion. It was through Wesley, however, that hymnody became a mark of Protestant worship. Many of the hymns written earlier in the century by the Congregationalist Isaac Watts stress the personal devotional element: "When I Survey The Wondrous Cross," "Alas! And Did My Saviour Bleed?"; "Come, Holy Spirit, Heavenly Dove." Many of the hymns of Charles Wesley, considered to be the greatest literary achievement of the Revivalist movement, also contain a strong emphasis on personal experience: "Jesus Lover of My Soul"; "Soldiers of Christ, Arise."

A second significant influence of Revivalism was the shift of daily worship from the church building to the home. (This shift was found in other movements as well.) Because the converted layman had gifts for praying and teaching Scripture daily, morning and evening prayer was moved from the church into the home where the father became minister to his family. In this change, the stress on personal involvement and the exercising of gifts for ministering were developed in the home and then made available in the free worship in the church meeting.

A third mark of Revivalism was the introduction of field preaching. In field preaching the services developed a style of praying, singing, and preaching of their own. The main concern was evangelism—communicating the gospel of Christ to the unconverted. Consequently, the services were designed as an appeal to the unconverted to become converted. These services were the forerunner of mass revivals. It was never the intention of the leaders that these revival services replace the worship in the church. However, the revival approach was gradually assimilated by the church and here and there replaced Sunday morning worship.

It is difficult to describe contemporary *charismatic* worship because of the widespread permeation of the charismatic movement into both the liturgical and nonliturgical churches. In the main, however, it is appropriate to point to *the full and active participation of every member* as the key to charismatic worship. This emphasis is expressed in four concerns: body ministry, spontaneity, praise and joy, and community and love.

The emphasis on body-ministry is more than a mere participation of different persons. It is rooted in the charismatic understanding of the gifts of the Spirit and their place in congregational worship. These are gifts of tongues, prophecy, interpretation, healing, teaching, and other forms of ministry that are exercised by the members of the body for the benefit of others. For this to happen there must be a degree of spontaneity in worship. Worship may be planned but must not be overplanned. A place for the free exercise of gifts as well as singing and prayer is a characteristic of open worship. Within the context of an open worship there is room for praise and joy. Frequently Charismatics become overwhelmed with love for God. They want to express this feeling in prayer, in shouts of joy, in the raising of the hands, or some other sign. Finally, the Charismatic believes the experience of joy in worship should be expressed in the community of the faithful. God's people come together in community especially to experience and share one another's joy in the Lord. Worship is, therefore, congregational and corporate as well as personal and private.

Conclusion

This brief survey of Protestant worship suggests several things. First, it shows that the Reformers desired a restoration of those biblical principles of worship that had been enunciated by the early Church Fathers and the classical liturgies. Second, the history of modern Protestant worship points to the importance of the subjective needs of the worshiper. It cannot be denied that modern Christians want to understand what they are doing when they worship and through worship desire an authentic experience of God. Thus, the urgent need to find a viable worship for contemporary Evangelicals must take into consideration both the objective content of worship and the Evangelical's need to understand and experience God. Lasting worship renewal will occur only through the combination of the substance of worship and the experience of the worshiper. One without the other will not do.

UNUS DEUS, UNUS CONCILIATOR DEI ET HOMINU, HOMO CHRISTUS IESUS,
QUI DEDIT SEMETIPSUM PRECIUM REDEMPTIONIS PRO OMNIBUS

Part III

A THEOLOGY
OF WORSHIP

ITE IN MUNDUM UNIVERSUM, ET PRAEDICATE EVANGELIUM OMNI CREATURAE.

Chapter 7

A
Christocentric
Focus

Ⓘt is the purpose of this chapter to show how the work of Christ is central to worship. The point is that when the church worships the Father through the Son, it praises the Father for the encompassing work of the Son. This work can be understood only in the context of Creation, Fall, Incarnation, Death, Resurrection, and Consummation.[1] Christocentric worship recapitulates these aspects of the Christ-event as it actualizes the church and anticipates the kingdom. These facets of worship are also explored in this chapter.

THE COSMIC WORK OF CHRIST

Christ-centered worship acknowledges the role of Christ in Creation. It affirms that God in Christ not only made the world but is present within it. Therefore, everything in creation belongs to God and may be set to His use. This is true of the physical elements of water, fire, oil, bread, and wine. It is also true of the less tangible aspects of creation such as time, space, color, sound, and smells. Those who deprecate God's physical world and deny God's freedom to be present in and through His creation espouse a dangerous and unbiblical position. They repudiate the physical side of spiritual reality.[2]

Second, Christ-centered worship recognizes the cosmic dimension of the Fall. Sin is not only a matter of moral depravity; it is much more, for it introduces the element of human rebellion that unleashed the power of Satan in the entire creation. Consequently, the entire created order, the physical and material world, became subject to the power of evil.

Evil introduced the element of chaos, discord, and disintegration that distorted the relationship of creatures and creation with the Creator. The created world became the place where Satan acted out his rebellion, the domain in which he exercised his power of distortion. He still delights to turn everything God made against God. For this reason Paul wrote that Christians should be aware that their "struggle is not against flesh and blood, but against the rulers, against the authorities, against the powers of this dark world and against the spiritual forces of evil in the heavenly realms" (Eph. 6:12).

The point is that the powers of evil are exercising a destructive influence on God's creatures and creation. Satan continually seeks to turn God's creatures and creation away from Him so that they no longer praise God as God intended. Instead, creatures and creation come under the dominion and power of the evil one, as unwilling slaves of his demands.

It is important to note that the power of Satan over creation does not make creation intrinsically evil. As God's creation it is still good. However, a change has occurred because of the Fall. It is not a change of essence, but a change having to do with power, dominion, and authority. It is now Satan's domain, and his purpose in exercising evil power is to diminish God's glory by making himself the one who is obeyed and worshiped. Spiritual wickedness expresses itself in a physical and material way.

For this reason all the physical elements of water, oil, bread, wine and the less tangible aspects of creation such as time, space, and sound now become physical means through which people express spiritual wickedness.[3] It is in this sense that the entire created order is affected by the Fall. Human beings, ruled by the powers of evil, reflect their fallen state in their use of the creation. Their sensitivity to the creation is no longer informed by an allegiance to the Creator. Consequently, they freely misuse and abuse all the elements of creation.

Creation and the Fall must be kept in mind when we introduce the third concern of Christ-centered worship, the Incarnation. The Incarnation affirms that God became flesh (John 1:14). But what does that mean? Irenaeus, a second-century theologian, used the following helpful phrase to explain the Incarnation: "born by his own created order which he bore."[4] In this phrase Irenaeus accented the physical, material, and tangible side of the Incarnation. In becoming man, the Word assumed His creation. The Creator actually received His own creation in bodily form in the womb of the Virgin Mary. What the Word assumed was not only a material body, but a body that bore the major effect of sin—death. He became subject to the disintegrating corruptibility that has characterized the created order since the Fall. Having a body was not evil. However, what He bore was the body of His own creation against which all the powers of evil had been hurled. In this body He was destined to destroy all the powers of evil and through that destruction redeem creation from the evil one. The spiritual victory over the powers was won only through a physical act. This is an extremely important point if we would understand the nature and meaning of worship. Through the physical act of one man sin and death entered into the entire created order. Now through the physical act of another man (the second Adam) the effect of sin and death in the creation will be destroyed (see Rom. 5:12–21).

But how are sin and death destroyed? The answer to this lies in the next aspect of Christ's work, His death. At first glance Christ's death appeared to be a victory of the evil powers. Satan it seems had succeeded in destroying both the creation and the Creator. What an incredible victory! Indeed it would have been so if death had held Jesus down. His resurrection from death, however, is a demonstration of the power of His death. His death is, as the great Puritan theologian John Owen wrote, the death of death. In death Jesus destroyed the "powers." *In death Jesus died the death of His entire creation in order to destroy the stranglehold of death under which His entire creation lay.* In this way He became the substitute for His entire creation. He died to set the creation free from the power of death.[5]

Paul frequently witnessed to this principle in his writings. Christ, he wrote, "disarmed the powers and authorities, he made a public spectacle of them, triumphing over them by the cross" (Col. 2:15). This was a physical act accomplished in the physical body of this creation. In this physical action Jesus triumphed over the powers of evil and reconciled man and the created order to the Father:

"But now he has reconciled you by Christ's physical body through death to present you holy in his sight, without blemish and free from accusation" (Col. 1:22).

Christ's death must of course be considered in relationship to His resurrection. In His resurrection Christ demonstrated His power over death. This is the point Paul made to the Corinthian Christians: "The perishable has been clothed with the imperishable, and the mortal with immortality, then the saying that is written will come true: 'Death has been swallowed up in victory. Where, O Death is your victory? Where, O Death, is your sting?'" (1 Cor. 15:54–55).

The Resurrection also inaugurated the new creation (the sign of which is the church). The point is this: *The creator who entered His spoiled creation destroyed the spoiler through death and began the recreation of His creation.* Paul summarized this idea in his letter to the Corinthians. "Therefore, if anyone is in Christ, he is a new creation; the old has gone, the new has come" (2 Cor. 5:17). The re-creation is true not only for persons but also for the whole creation as Paul stated to the Romans. "The creation," he wrote, "was subjected to frustration, not by its own choice, but by the will of the one who subjected it in hope that the creation itself will be liberated from its bondage to decay and brought into the glorious freedom of the children of God" (Rom. 8:21). The implication is that the entire created order that had been adversely affected by the Fall is now positively affected by the redemption. It is a beginning again not only for humanity but also for the entire created order.[6]

This beginning again must be understood in relation to the Consummation.[7] The new creation inaugurated by the death and resurrection of Jesus is not yet complete and will not be until Christ consummates His work in the Second Coming. When He comes again He will completely destroy the power of evil and establish the new heavens and the new earth (Rev. 20–22).

In the meantime creation is in a state of groaning and eager expectation. Paul wrote, "We know that the whole creation has been groaning as in the pains of childbirth right up to the present time. Not only so, but we ourselves, who have the firstfruits of the Spirit, groan inwardly as we wait eagerly for our adoption as sons, the redemption of our bodies" (Rom. 8:22–23). We groan because we (and the entire created order) are still subject to the powers.

They still hold sway in the world and exercise death throughout the creation. But we (and the entire created order) wait eagerly because we know that Christ will at some future time completely destroy the powers, releasing the creation from its bondage to decay and establishing the new heavens and the new earth.

In summary, the point of these six doctrines, as they cluster together in a single whole in Jesus Christ, is to tell the gospel story. The gospel has to do with the creation of a good world, its falling away into death through sin, the assumption of the fallen creation through the incarnation of the Creator, the triumphant destruction of the powers of sin and death through the death of Jesus, the re-creation of the creation demonstrated by His resurrection, and finally that anticipation of the consummation when the work of re-creation will be completed. In a nutshell this is the gospel of forgiveness, the message of substitution, and the hope of the world.

Worship is Christocentric in that we worship the Father, in and through the work of the Son, by the Holy Spirit in praise and thanksgiving for the work of redemption. For that reason the work of Christ is central to Christian worship.

THE MEANING OF CHRISTOCENTRIC WORSHIP

The Christ-event is not only central to Christian worship, it also gives meaning to worship. Worship is not a mere memory or a matter of looking back to a historic event (that is an Enlightenment notion). Rather, worship is the action that brings the Christ-event into the experience of the community gathered in the name of Jesus. There are three implications to this understanding of worship. They are that (1) worship recapitulates the Christ-event, (2) worship actualizes the church, and (3) worship anticipates the kingdom.

Recapitulation of the Christ-event in Worship

The word *recapitulate* simply means to "sum up" or to "repeat." In worship there is a summing up of those events in history that constitute the source of the church's salvation.[8] In worship we rehearse the gospel story. We rehearse, as it were, the Creation, Fall, Incarnation, Death, Resurrection, and Consummation. Therefore, our worship proclaims Jesus Christ and His saving reality again and again. In this action a recapitulation takes place on three levels: in the heavens, on earth, and in our hearts.

The recapitulation that takes place in the heavens occurs in the everlasting worship of the Father because of the work of the Son. Jesus served the Father by destroying the works of the devil (1 John 3:8) and thus reconciled man and creation through His death (Rom. 5:10–21). Because Jesus offered Himself once for all to save creation He has returned to God the glory of all His works. This offering is His "one sacrifice" in which "he has made perfect forever those who are being made holy" (Heb. 10:14).

For this reason the heavens ring with worship. Both Isaiah and John attest to this heavenly worship (Isa. 6 and Rev. 4 and 5). The description in the Apocalypse seems to suggest that the entire creation of God—angels, archangels, beasts and man, material and immaterial—offer incessant and unceasing praise to the Father. And here, in this heavenly worship, the central focus is on the "Lamb" standing at the "center of the throne." Everything and everyone gathers around Him in worship and sings the new song (Rev. 5:11).

Some scholars believe the structure of the Book of Revelation was based on early Christian worship.[9] Whether it was or not, it at least appears that John recognized the need to pattern earthly worship after the heavenly (Rev. 4 and 5). Our worship is like heavenly worship in that it centers around Jesus and His work through which sin and death have been destroyed. In worship we "sum up" or "recapitulate" the work of Christ. That one unrepeatable event in history is made real again and again through the power of proclamation (by the Holy Spirit) that confronts us with the reality of new life in Jesus Christ.

This is not, as late medieval theology suggested, a resacrifice of Christ. It is instead the continual recognition of the once-for-all offering of Jesus Christ to the Father that was historically accomplished in a particular time and place. In worship we recall the Christ-event that accomplished our redemption and we offer our praise and adoration to the Father through the accomplished work of the Son. Thus, the character of Christian worship is informed and shaped by retelling the Christ-event.

The third aspect of recapitulation is this: what happens in heaven and what happens in the earthly form of worship must happen in the heart. The relationship between the external and the internal must never be neglected in worship. What we do externally should signify what is happening internally. In worship we offer ourselves as Paul admonished: "Offer your bodies as living sacrifices, holy and pleasing to God—which is your spiritual worship" (Rom. 12:1).

The experience of worship as a recapitulation of the Christ-event brings heaven and earth and the believer together in a single whole. The church joins in that great chorus of voices to offer praise to the Father through the Son by the Spirit, and in this action the church is actualized.

Actualization of the Church in Worship

The image that best describes what happens when the church comes together for worship is taken from the congregation of Israel at Mount Sinai. Here Israel through the covenant became the people of God. The technical term used to describe these people is the Q'hal Yahweh. They are the assembly saved from Egypt, thus they become as this term implies "the assembly of God." The special character of this assembly is worship. Thus, the five elements of worship discussed in chapter 2—divine initiative, the structure of responsibility, the proclamation of the Word, the assent of the people, and the act of ratification— characterized this assembly. These elements define the nature of the gathering in which Israel as God's special people became actualized.

In this same way the church is an assembly gathered for worship. The church is the people of God on earth assembled in the name of Jesus. Like the nature of the people of Israel, the nature of this assembly is defined by an event. In this sense the church may be defined as the "people of the Christ-event." Thus, when believers come together, the church as the people of the Christ-event becomes a reality. One can say, "Here is the church," or, "Here are the people who belong to God" as a result of the Christ-event. In this way the church is actualized.[10]

The view that worship actualizes the church rests on two arguments: First, all the physical signs of Christ's presence in the church are evident and, second, these signs signify the spiritual reality they represent.

First, the physical signs of Christ are evident. What does this mean? To what does it refer? It refers to people who constitute the body of Christ and to the organic functioning of these people in the name of Christ through the variety of gifts and workings within the body. Some have been given the ministry of oversight, teaching, or service and each has his or her own gift (1 Cor. 12:28). No one person has all the offices or all the gifts, but worship brings them all together and arranges them according to their functions. These people have the Word of God through which God speaks to them. They also have the sacraments, baptism and Holy Communion, to remind them of the One for whom (and the purpose for which) they have gathered together. The point is that in these signs—people, offices, gifts, Word, sacraments—the church is made visible, concrete, real, tangible, and present.

Second, these signs communicate the spiritual reality they represent. God has made His material and visible world in such a way that it may become the vehicle through which spiritual realities are signified and realized. We see one thing, but we apprehend another. The offices and gifts are expressed through people, but through them we see the ministry of Jesus Christ who oversees the church, pastors the flock, and serves the church. In the Word we hear the voice of God. In baptism and the Eucharist we apprehend the cleansing of our sin and receive nurture to grow up in Christ.

In this way worship actualizes the church and becomes the means through which Christ, the head of the church, becomes present to His body. We dare not deny this physical side of spiritual communication that in and through the action of worship the triumphant presence of the risen Lord is actualized and through worship the expectant anticipation of His coming again is celebrated.

Anticipation of the Kingdom in Worship

Because worship has to do with the Christ-event, the eschatological note, the hope for the consummation of the work of Christ, cannot be neglected.[11] Thus, in worship the tension between the Resurrection and the Consummation is expressed. Although we celebrate the triumph of Jesus over the powers of sin and death, we acknowledge that the powers have not yet been put under the feet of Jesus completely. Therefore, in worship we raise a prophetic voice against the powers and express the future completion of the triumph of Jesus over sin and death in His second coming. This anticipatory note of worship is expressed in Word and sacrament.

In the Word the kingdom is announced and proclaimed in the preaching of Christ. The earliest preaching included the insistence that Christ will come again as Judge and Savior. This same anticipation is expressed in the prayer Jesus taught His disciples, saying, "your kingdom come, your will be done on earth as it is in heaven." The same theme is found in the institution of the Lord's Supper; Paul told the Corinthian church, "Whenever you eat this bread and drink this cup, you proclaim the Lord's death *until he comes*" (1 Cor. 11:26). In the Eucharist the church prefigures the new creation. Here the mundane elements of creation, bread and wine, become the symbols of a re-created world. When we sit at table with our Lord, the church corporately symbolizes the messianic banquet—the celebration of the new heavens and the new earth. Thus, worship transports the church from the earthly sphere to the heavens to join in that everlasting worship described by John (see Rev. 4 and 5). In this way the church at worship signals its relationship to the age to come and derives from worship the power to live in this world now—in the tension between the Resurrection and the Second Coming, in the tension between promise and fulfillment.

Conclusion

Christocentric worship is based on the idea that the focus and meaning of worship is rooted in the cosmic nature of the work of Christ. Thus, our worship to the Father is offered in and through Jesus Christ, who has accomplished all this for the sake of the Father and to His glory. Therefore worship recapitulates the work of Christ by proclaiming it through Word and rite. In this action the church, the body of Jesus, is actualized. That is, it comes together and can be seen and experienced in a visible and concrete manner. But the work of Jesus is not yet complete; so the church in worship acknowledges that it waits with anticipation for that final triumphant destruction of sin and death in the Consummation.

Thus, the first theological principle of worship is that it must be Christocentric. Worship renewal cannot occur without the recovery of this primary principle in the mind, heart, and actions of the worshiping community.

Chapter 8

A Theology
of Enactment

The purpose of this chapter is to answer the question how do
we worship God? Worship should be seen as a dramatic enactment
of the relationship that exists between ourselves and God, a relationship with its roots in historical events. Enactment may be
done by means of recitation and drama. Recitation (creeds, hymns,
and preaching) and drama (or ritual) have their basis in the Old
Testament and the New Testament, particularly in the Passover
and Eucharist.

DEFINING ENACTMENT

The principle of acting out in worship is similar to what we do
in other areas of our lives. For example, we act out greetings,
birthdays, weddings, and national holidays such as Thanksgiving
and Independence Day through organized ritual and symbolic
gestures that communicate the meaning of the event. Thus, a
handshake or a nod, a cake and candles, a turkey "with all the
trimmings," and fireworks all signify the meaning of the specific
event.[1]

In worship we retell and act out a story. The story has to do
with what God has done for us and what our response is to His
work. It is an enactment of the event that gives meaning and

purpose to life. It aligns the believer with the Christ-event and with the community of the faithful throughout history. Therefore when worship is acted out in faith, the believer experiences again the refreshment of his or her relationship to God and spontaneously experiences the joy of salvation.

The principle of enactment is rooted in the Scriptures. An examination of worship in both the Old and New Testament demonstrates that worship is not thrown together in a haphazard way. Instead, worship is carefully designed to bring the worshiper through a well-ordered experience. In this sense the organization of worship is simply the means through which the meeting between God and human beings takes place in a vital, dynamic, and living way.[2]

Because worship is the enactment of an event, the organization of worship is not left to the whim of creative people or community consensus. Rather, it is rooted in the historic meeting that has already taken place between God and man. This meeting, enacted by God's people, is the organizing principle of worship. Therefore, the overriding feature of biblical enactment is the representation of history.

A cursory examination of biblical worship makes the *historical orientation* of enactment abundantly clear. All the events around which Israel's worship was organized are the historical actions of God in history. For example, it is significant that the major institutions of worship in Israel derive foundationally from the Exodus event: the institution of public worship at Mount Sinai celebrates the covenant that God establishes with Israel; the elaborate worship of the tabernacle and the temple are a commentary on the relationship between God and His people; the synagogue accents the giving of the law; the festivals, especially the Passover, which was the central feast of Israel, commemorate the redemption from bondage. (For further discussion, see chapter 2.)

Historical orientation also underlies New Testament worship. Christian worship derives from the death and resurrection of Christ. In preaching we retell the story, in the Eucharist we dramatize the event. Even worship on Sunday has significance in terms of enactment, for that is the day of the Resurrection. Furthermore, the special emphasis we place on Christmas and Easter is for the purpose of making the meaning of those historic days come alive in our experience.

The significance of the historical orientation of biblical worship is this: *Worship re-creates and thus re-presents the historical event.* In this way worship proclaims the meaning of the original event and confronts the worshiper with the claim of God over his or her life.[3]

Therefore, the overriding concern of worship is not simply the recreation of the event, but a personal meeting with God. On one side the emphasis is on God who has acted; on the other side the emphasis is on humans responding. In this way "something happens" in worship: God and His people meet. Worship is not simply going through the motions of ceremony. It becomes the visible and tangible meeting of God through the signs and symbols of His presence.

In worship the order is set forth in such a way that the worshiper is able to enter vicariously into the original event. This enactment of past events occurs in two ways: through recitation and through drama.

ENACTMENT THROUGH RECITATION

An examination of both Old and New Testament worship shows how enactment occurs through recitation in at least three ways: creeds, hymns, and preaching.

Creeds

The purpose of a creed is to compress historical events into a summary statement. For example, study the historical dimension and the theological breadth contained in this brief Old Testament recital:

> Then you shall declare before the LORD your God: "My father was a wandering Aramean, and he went down into Egypt with a few people and lived there and became a great nation, powerful and numerous. But the Egyptians mistreated us and made us suffer, putting us to hard labor. Then we cried out to the LORD, the God of our fathers, and the LORD heard our voice and saw our misery, toil and oppression. So the LORD brought us out of Egypt with a mighty hand and an outstretched arm, with great terror and with miraculous signs and wonders. He brought us to this place and gave us this land, a land flowing with milk and honey. Deuteronomy 26:5–9

The emphasis of this statement is historical: in a few words the most formative period of Israel is summarized. The sojourn, the harsh treatment, God's remembrance, the redemption, and the Promised Land are compressed swiftly and succinctly. But equally important to this recitaiton is the meaning that stands behind it. It is not simply the recalling of a number of events, but specifically those events that had to do with the covenant. In and through these events a special relationship was established between God and Israel. Thus, the recitation of these events in faith renews the relationship of the covenant that they represent.

Similar creedal statements are found in the New Testament.[4] Consider for example, the compression of events and the meaning suggested in the following:

> Christ died for our sins
> according to the Scriptures,
> that he was buried,
> that he was raised on the third day
> according to the Scriptures.
> 1 Cor. 15:3–4

> He appeared in a body,
> was vindicated by the Spirit,
> was seen by angels,
> was preached among the nations,
> was believed on in the world,
> was taken up in glory.
> 1 Timothy 3:16

Examples are also found in later Christian worship. By the fourth century creedal affirmations were a vital part of worship. Through creedal recitation the believer witnessed in brief form the significant events of the Christian faith. Consider the vast amount of Christian teaching compressed in the brief recitation of the Apostles' Creed:

> I believe in God, the Father almighty,
>   creator of heaven and earth.

> I believe in Jesus Christ, his only Son, our Lord.
>   who was conceived by the holy Spirit
>   born of the virgin Mary,

suffered under Pontius Pilate,
>was crucified, dead, and buried.
He descended to hell.
On the third day he rose again from the dead,
ascended to heaven,
>sits at the right hand of God the Father almighty.
Thence he will come to judge the living and the dead.

I believe in the Holy Spirit,
>the holy catholic Church, the communion of saints,
>the forgiveness of sins,
>the resurrection of the body,
>and the life everlasting. Amen.

>Textus Receptus (c. 700).

Here, in a matter of a few sentences, the entire framework of Christian truth is recited. The believer witnesses to God as triune and confesses his or her personal faith in the Father as creator; in Jesus Christ incarnate, dead, buried, ascended, and coming again in judgment; and in the Holy Spirit, who creates the church, establishes community, applies the work of Christ for forgiveness, raises the body from the dead, and confirms our eternal destiny. The important feature of reciting these events is to act out the meaning that results from these events. In this confession the believer enacts a world view. The members of the congregation tell the story that brings them together and give witness to their faith in the triune God who has acted in history for their salvation.

Hymns

The same may be said for many of the psalms used in the worship of Israel and the church. While they may refer to the experience of Israel as a nation or to that of a single person, the effect of using psalms in worship is to re-create the experience of the psalmist for the worshiper. For example, to proclaim God as King (see Psalms 93, 96, 97, 99) is to experience God as King in the activity of worship and to allow life to be lived in the meaning of that experience. The same may be said for the penitential psalms or psalms of praise (see Psalm 136).

There are similar examples in the hymns of the New Testament.[5] These hymns recount the events that give shape to the Christian faith. A good example is the hymn from Philippians 2:

Who, being in very nature God,
did not consider equality with God
something to be grasped,
but made himself nothing,
taking the very nature of a servant,
being made in human likeness.
And being found in appearance as a man,
he humbled himself
and became obedient to death—
even death on a cross!
Therefore God exalted him to the highest place
and gave him the name that is above every name,
that at the name of Jesus every knee should bow,
in heaven and on earth and under the earth,
and every tongue confess that Jesus Christ is Lord,
to the glory of God the Father.

Philippians 2:6–11

The nonbiblical hymns we sing in our churches today are also intended to tell a story, to enact an event, and to make that event contemporaneous in our experience. This is the purpose of familiar hymns like "When I Survey the Wondrous Cross," "O Sacred Head Now Wounded," and countless other hymns of the church.

Preaching

The concept of recitation laid the groundwork for the development of preaching. Preaching at its best is a form of recitation because it re-creates the past and applies the past to the present.[6] The entire Book of Deuteronomy is a good example of Old Testament preaching. Consider, for example, the beginning of this sermon. It sets the tone for the entire message, a retelling of God's actions in history on behalf of the people of Israel (see Deut. 1:5–8).

The sermons of the early church are excellent examples of recitation through preaching. In each instance the preacher tells the story of God's work in history right up to the coming of Jesus and offers an interpretation of the meaning of this history. Here, for example, is a section of Peter's sermon on the day of Pentecost:

Men of Israel, listen to this: Jesus of Nazareth was a man accredited by God to you by miracles, wonders and signs, which God did among you through him, as you yourselves know. This man was handed over to you by God's set purpose and foreknowledge; and you, with the help of wicked men, put him to death by nailing him to the cross. But God raised him from the dead, freeing him from the agony of death, because it was impossible for death to keep its hold on him. . . .

Therefore let all Israel be assured of this: God has made this Jesus, whom you crucified, both Lord and Christ.

Acts 2:22-24, 36

These illustrations point out the important role of recitation in biblical worship. The implication for contemporary worship is clear: we must be concerned to recover the place and meaning of enactment through recitation in our worship.

ENACTMENT THROUGH DRAMA

While recitation compresses and conveys a historical event through the medium of language, drama reenacts and thus conveys a historical event through visual, tangible, and concrete symbols. It thus acts out a historical event in order to re-create that event and proclaim its meaning to the worshiper.[7]

Old Testament Enactment Through Dramatic Representation

The temple rituals were re-presentations through drama and thus symbolically represented the relationship between God and the worshiper, as in the act of ratification at Mount Sinai. They also looked forward to the final once-for-all sacrifice of Christ when the ultimate and eternal drama of salvation would be carried out in the death and resurrection of Christ (although this was not fully known in the Old Testament).

An excellent example of temple ritual may be taken from the enactment on the Day of Atonement. Here, after the high priest had conducted an elaborate ritual in the sanctuary and in the Most Holy Place to make atonement for the people of Israel, the high priest visually demonstrated forgiveness of sin in the act of transmitting sin to a live goat and sending it off into the desert (see Lev. 16:20-22).

The most striking example of re-presentation through drama in the Old Testament is the Passover. The purpose of the Passover Seder is to retell the historical events in which Israel's redemption was secured and from which Israel's spiritual life developed (see Deut. 6:20–23).

The dramatic re-presentation of the flight from Egypt is a highly complicated service that was first passed on by memory and later written down and preserved in the Haggadah. This document contains specific instruction for every detail of this event. The home preparations are elaborate and time consuming, requiring the involvement of the entire family.

Today the Seder is based on three pedagogical principles. First is the biblical injunction that every Jew is bound to tell his children about the redemption of their ancestors from Egypt (see Exod. 12:26–27). The parent is admonished not to be hasty but to tell the story in depth so that it is understood and grasped. For this reason the second and third principles have to do with the method of teaching.

In the second principle the child is placed in the center of the Seder ritual. In this context the child *asks* about the meaning of the unleavened bread, the parsley that was dipped in salt water, and the bitter herbs. The answer to these questions is fulfilled in an elaboration on the story of the Exodus. The children, having dramatically re-played the original situation are in a strategic position to hear and understand the meaning of the actions they have repeated.

The third principle is that each person must regard himself or herself as if personally redeemed from Egypt. This personal dimension of the original event is carried out through a series of gestures, and the eating of particular foods to memorialize the Exodus event and produce an identification with the meaning of the Exodus.[8]

Not only is the order of the service intended to enact the historic event, but even the elements of the meal serve the purpose of communicating a re-creation of the exact event. Consequently, each portion of the meal has meaning: the matzo represents the "double portion" (Exod. 16:22) and the "bread of affliction" (Deut. 16:3); the shank-bone of lamb represents the paschal lamb; the roasted egg commemorates the festival offering; the horseradish reminds one of the bitterness of Egypt; and the *haroseth* (fruits, nuts, cinnamon, and wine) symbolizes the clay in Egypt.

The meaning of this enactment for those who celebrate it is captured by the Old Testament liturgical scholar Abraham Idelsohn in his work *Jewish Liturgy:*

This memorable celebration has retained its value for our days as in days of old, and has exercised a great pedagogical influence upon the children for which purpose it was chiefly instituted. It was introduced so that the father teach his child the religio-ethical doctrines deduced from that event and from its underlying lofty ideals that the child may be permeated with them and draw strength from them to carry on the fight for justice and righteousness and spiritual liberty with firm belief of the ultimate success.

The story tells of suffering, of sorrow and pain, of struggle with the iron yoke of slavery, of afflictions which penetrate the very core of life; it also speaks of hope for deliverance and of idealistic devotion to the cause of humanity as evinced by the illustrious leader, Moses, who created a free people out of slaves and gave them laws of the highest ethical value.

On the occasion of this celebration every Jewish home receives the atmosphere of a sanctuary in which each member of the family is a priest and the house-master—the high priest—a sanctuary to serve the purest human ideals and the living God.[9]

New Testament Enactment Through Dramatic Representation

What is true of the Old Testament is also true of the New. However, it is not quite as obvious because the New Testament institution of worship is less complex. Nevertheless, one can clearly see the elements of dramatic enactment in the Eucharist, or the Lord's Supper.[10]

First, the institution of the Lord's Supper was initiated within the context of the Passover. The suggestion that Christ's death and resurrection was the Christian Passover (1 Cor. 5:7) put the celebration of the Eucharist in the larger context that it shared with the drama of the Passover. This sense of enacting the drama of the Last Supper was carried into the early church and down through history.

The sense of dramatic enactment is first expressed in the meaning of the word remembrance *(anamnesis)*. Jesus said, "Do this in remembrance of me" (Luke 22:19). The ancient meaning of *anamnesis* is not "mere memory of the mind" as we have interpreted it in our Enlightenment-conscious world. Rather, in the ancient world it carried a more active connotation. In the *anamnesis* Christ is proclaimed in word and deed.[11]

The fact that the early Christians had a sense of dramatically playing out the meaning of the Last Supper in the Eucharist is suggested by the careful re-presentation of the meaning of Christ in the earliest liturgies of the church. The emphasis is on dramatically portraying Christ in a kind of sign language, a language that is to "image" Him or make Him present through the imagination. In this action Jesus is visibly dramatized. This dramatic element, simple at first, became more elaborate in the fourth and fifth centuries, and practically lost its meaning in the medieval period when the drama took the nature of an epiphany. Unfortunately, the Protestants reacted too strongly and lost the sense of drama, allowing the Eucharist to lose its special quality of enactment.

The Nature of Worship as Dramatic Enactment

Worship is not drama in the technical sense. Nevertheless, worship is characterized by dramatic elements and has many parallels with drama. For example, the dramatic element can be clearly seen in the worship experience of bringing the Ark of the Covenant to the new temple built by Solomon:

> The priests then withdrew from the Holy Place. All the priests who were there had consecrated themselves, regardless of their divisions. All the Levites who were musicians—Asaph, Heman, Jeduthun and their sons and relatives—stood on the east side of the altar, dressed in fine linen and playing cymbals, harps and lyres. They were accompanied by 120 priests sounding trumpets. The trumpeters and singers joined in unison, as with one voice, to give praise and thanks to the LORD. Accompanied by trumpets, cymbals and other instruments, they raised their voices in praise to the LORD and sang:
>
> "He is good;
> his love endures forever."
>
> Then the temple of the LORD was filled with a cloud, and the priests could not perform their service because of the cloud, for the glory of the LORD filled the temple of God.
> 2 Chronicles 5:11–14

Worship contains all the *external elements* of drama: a script; the director and players; words, sound, and actions; a time to meet; and the use of space.[12]

Since worship means to enact the Christ-event, there can be only one script. The notion that there should be a new and creative worship service week after week is false. There is a basic sameness to worship because the script cannot depart from the historic event of Jesus. However, the Scripture readings, the hymns, and the prayers may vary from week to week (especially if the church year is followed (and thus address different needs.

Because worship contains the dramatic element of a director (pastor) and players (worshipers) it ought to be seen as the dramatic action of the congregation. This viewpoint escapes the false performer/audience dichotomy. In worship *everyone is part of the play;* there is no audience! The pivotal persons, of course, are the celebrants. If he does not have a sense of the dramatic and if he does not understand the play (enacting the Christ-event), there is little hope that the people who are worshiping can fulfill their own role adequately.

It is imperative that the celebrants understand the meaning of the words, sound, and actions that make up the play. They must direct worship in such a way that the actions and sounds complement the words. To do this, they must understand the meaning of every part of the drama. They must lose themselves in the action so that they play their part and lead the other players into a union with the entire enactment.

For this reason the time of meeting (the sense of Sunday resurrection and the particular emphasis of the week, whether Advent, Epiphany, Lent, Easter, or Pentecost) and the use of space (the placing of the players as well as the symbols or props of the play such as the pulpit and table) are significant. They relate to the sense of what is happening, to the feeling of what is being played out.

This leads to the second element of drama in worship, namely the notion that worship contains all the *internal elements* of drama. It has to do with tempo, emotions, and the senses.

In drama the tempo is always important. When the tempo lags, the entire play is affected. The same is true in worship. In evangelical churches a serious distraction that utterly destroys the tempo of worship is the constant interruption of announcements. The need to announce every hymn and to make remarks here and there throughout the service interrupts the flow and destroys the sense of enacting the drama of the Christ-event.

Careful attention must also be given to emotion in worship. The use of appropriate emotion is normal and good. The drama of worship calls for joy and excitement as well as quietness, sobriety, and the sense of sorrow. It is important that the emotion fit the words and the action (no one likes to hear about the love of God when the emotion of the preacher, reader, or singer is anger).

Furthermore, the senses ought also to be engaged in worship. In drama we see, hear, smell, and even taste. So it is in worship. God has given us all our senses and He does not deny our use of them in any aspect of life, especially worship. If what we see and hear and smell and taste is unpleasant to the senses, then the act of worship will be disturbed and unfulfilled.

The external and internal elements of worship must be assembled properly to give worship a sense of movement and a dynamic quality. Because the entire congregation constitutes the players in the drama of worship, it is important that all of the members know their parts, understand the meaning of what is being done, and participate purposefully. For this reason it is important to remember that worship is a *group activity* and to suggest that the meaning of worship must be *learned.*

Conclusion

In this chapter we have been concerned with the method of worship. What do we do when we come together to meet God through Jesus Christ by the Spirit? The answer is that worship is a dramatic enactment of a meeting with God. God and man encounter each other as the story of God's work in Jesus Christ is retold through recitation of the Word, the dramatization of His death, and the response of His people. This second theological principle of worship must be recaptured if worship renewal is to take place in the evangelical community.

Chapter 9

A Theology of Form and Sign

In this chapter we turn to the place of form in worship. Because worship is something done by way of enactment, it necessarily involves certain forms as we act out the Christ-event and our response to it. Forms are not mere externals but signs and symbols of a spiritual reality. Even as God who is immaterial met with humans in the material form of a human person, Jesus, so Christians meet Him in worship in the context of visible and tangible forms. These forms, however rudimentary and basic, are signs and symbols of relationship to Him.[1] We will first consider the theological basis of form—creation, revelation, and incarnation—and then discuss the kinds of signs and symbols that have been found appropriate for enacting the Christ-event.

A THEOLOGY OF FORM

The theological basis of form is found in the doctrines of creation, revelation, and incarnation.[2]

Creation

First, Christianity affirms the goodness of creation as the product of God's imagination and action, a creative work that reflects the Creator. Therefore, to reject creation is to reject the Creator.[3]

The doctrinal implications of creation became clear in the second-century battle between Christianity and Gnosticism. The Gnostics rejected creation, insisting that it was the result of the creative act of an evil god. For Gnostics there were two gods—one who was good and one who was evil. The good god was spirit and immaterial as opposed to the evil god who was fleshy and material. For the Gnostics true spirituality consisted in the denial of the material (flesh) in order that the immaterial (spirit) could eventually return to the pure spirit god from which it came. (Biblical Christianity also teaches a conflict between "flesh" and spirit. But "flesh" does not refer to material creation. Rather, it is a term used to designate powers of evil that are expressed through the material creation; e.g., Eph. 6:12.)

The outcome of the Gnostic view of creation was to deny that a spiritual reality could be made known through a material expression. The most serious implication of this viewpoint is a denial of the Incarnation. For Gnostics, Jesus was not God in the flesh. Rather, Jesus was a spirit, an apparition. They reasoned that the god of spirit could not become enfleshed in the creation of the evil god without becoming the prisoner of evil. Thus a denial of the physical stood at the center of Gnostic faith. This necessitated a rejection of all material signs of spiritual reality.

Such rejection had significant implications for church practice. For example, in Scripture, water is the symbol of God's creativity and a sign, therefore, of passing from one stage to another; the people of Israel were brought through the waters of the Red Sea to Mount Sinai and passed through the waters of Jordan to the Promised Land. In the early church water was regarded as a passage rite into the church. Consequently, when Christians were baptized into Jesus through water, this represented a spiritual passage from one condition to the other. (Salvation was not without faith. Early Christians believed in the inner experience and the outer sign. Baptism was the sign of an inner reality. In the case of infants the outer sign preceded the inner reality. In the case of adults the inner reality preceded the outer sign of water.) The Gnostics' rejection of visible forms as signs of spiritual reality led them to regard water baptism as unnecessary. Tertullian, a late-second-century theologian wrote a treatise against their viewpoint, concluding, "It is not to be doubted that God has made the material substance which governs terrestrial life act as agent likewise in the celestial."[4]

Tertullian's principle, expressing the general consensus of the early church, was based on the biblical view that God had created the physical and that He could be known in and through it.

A second example is found in the Gnostic view of the Eucharist. Since Gnostics denied that Jesus had come in the flesh, it was logical for them to deny the value of material bread and wine as a sign of Jesus' presence in the worshiping community. Ignatius, the early-second-century bishop of Antioch, warned the Smyrnaeans against the Gnostic viewpoint in these words: "They hold aloof from the Eucharist and from the services of prayer, because they refuse to admit that the Eucharist is the flesh of our saviour Jesus Christ, which suffered for our sins and which, in his goodness, the father raised (from the dead)."[5] It is not clear whether the Gnostics abandoned the Eucharist altogether or not. What is clear is that their rejection of Jesus as a physical person led them to reject the view that Jesus was signified in the forms of bread and wine.

Revelation

The second theological basis for the use of material form as a means of communicating spiritual truth is found in the doctrine of revelation. First, God communicates Himself through the natural creation. The psalmist testifies that "the heavens *declare* the glory of God, the skies *proclaim* the work of his hands" (Ps. 19:1; see also Rom. 1:19, 20). Second, God communicates knowledge of Himself through historical events. He is a God of action. Through this action He makes Himself known to His people. The central action in the Old Testament is the Exodus, and the central action in the New Testament is the Cross. These principal actions of God are replete with symbolic references.

Third, God reveals Himself through the institutions of worship. Patterns of worship in the tabernacle and later the temple are laden with symbolic language. The exact architectural floorplan, the use of gold and other precious metals, the colors, the rituals of sacrifice, the presence and organization of the priests, the sacred days and hours—all of these were physical signs of a spiritual reality.[6]

The writer to the Hebrews interpreted all of these forms as "a shadow of the good things that are coming" (Heb. 10:1; see Heb. 7–10). He recognized, as did the early church, that all of the earthly regulations of the Old Testament were fulfilled in Jesus Christ. Consequently, the Old Testament regulations were no longer needed. Nevertheless, the early Christians did not reject the principle that earthly forms were signs of eternal realities. Consequently, new forms were established by Jesus (i.e., water baptism, the Lord's Supper, laying on of hands in ministry, the twofold structure of Word and sacrament), recognized in the church, and developed in the Christian community to bespeak heavenly realities. *Thus what was abolished by the New Testament was the particular Old Testament forms—not the principle that earthly forms may communicate eternal truths.*[7]

Incarnation

The doctrine of the Incarnation is the focal point for a theology of form. In the Incarnation the eternal Word was enfleshed in a human person, as John said, "The Word became flesh and lived for a while among us" (John 1:14). This fact of history forever affirms the principle that spiritual reality may be made known through earthly form. God used creation (the body of His Son) as the instrument of salvation. Consequently, the physical creation (including the body as well) has a place in worship.

Through the proper use of creation mortal creatures may signify eternal realities. As we saw in chapter 8, the entire experience of worship is a symbolic meeting with God in which the eternal covenant established by Jesus Christ is reaffirmed in the physical action of worship. Here Christians proclaim by word and rite Christ's death and resurrection and they respond in faith with praise and thanksgiving. For this reason worship necessitates form and signs. Because humans wear a body and live in a physical world and communicate through language and symbol, there can be no such thing as a bodiless, orderless, signless worship. Nevertheless, worship acted out in the body, according to form, by sign is a spiritual worship because it signifies the eternal truth that is its ultimate point of reference. Just as in the Incarnation the immaterial Word was made present in material form, so in worship the material form is the means through which the church makes its spiritual worship present to God the Father.

The form of worship is determined by three considerations. First, because worship is a meeting between God and human beings it is bound by the rules of order. It must contain a beginning and an ending and follow a sequence of events. It is natural, there-fore, that worship should begin with a procession (going to some-thing) and end with a recession (leaving the meeting). Since it is a meeting with God, the people should first address God with an appropriate greeting and in departing receive a benediction from God.

Second, because the meeting is an enactment of the gospel story, it is appropriate that it should follow the sequence of God's work in history. For this reasion the Scripture readings and the sermon act as a sign of God speaking to His people and precede the Eucharist, a sign of God coming to His people.

Third, because worship entails response, it is appropriate that God's people praise Him in doxologies, hymns, prayers, confes-sions, creeds, and offerings. These responses may be placed throughout the ordering of the service that sequentially sets forth the gospel story. The details of the historic order of worship will be discussed more fully in the next chapter.

A THEOLOGY OF SIGN

Signs may be defined as language that communicates more than what is seen by the eye.[8] In a sign "we see one thing and understand another." For example, one may see a cross but under-stand the death and resurrection of Christ. In this way a sign is an *action:* it reveals something by putting us into contact with an invisible reality and creates within us a longing for that which cannot be seen.

It is generally recognized that there are three kinds of lan-guage.[9] First, there is the *language of everyday speech.* In this, we utilize *words* to convey meaning, to elicit thoughts and to establish feeling. Words are of course the most common form of communica-tion and are basic to all peoples. Second, there is the *language of science.* This language utilizes *concepts* that have empirical refer-ence and are capable of being tested by experience. Third, there is the *language of poetry* in which we utilize *symbols* to elicit thoughts, feelings, and intuitions. All of these kinds of language belong to the Christian religion and are employed in worship.

Evangelicals are the weakest in the third area of communica-tion, the language of symbols. We have capitulated to the En-lightenment penchant for scientific objectivity, for observation and proof, for mind-oriented communication. This has resulted in a loss of our ability to express feelings and intuition symbolically.

If we are to restore symbolism, we must distinguish between dominical and ecclesiastical symbols. The former are symbols especially designated by Jesus, while the latter are those long established by usage and tradition in the church. For example, dominical symbols include the water of baptism, the bread and wine of the Eucharist, and the laying on of hands. These are limited in number. On the other hand ecclesiastical symbols are many and varied. They include universally accepted symbols such as the Bible, the pulpit, the table, the baptismal font or pool, and the cross. Still other symbols are more local and reflect the cultural bearing of a particular congregation. These include the use of icons, vestments, candles, colors, the sign of the cross and other bodily gestures such as kneeling, bowing, genuflecting, raising hands, and the like. The ancient church (and later Roman Catholic and Orthodox Christians) was accustomed to a broader and more complete use of symbols than are Evangelicals. These symbols allow the whole person—body, mind, feelings, and the senses—to be engaged in the worship of God. The misuse of symbolic communication by the late medieval church led the Reformers, and especially the leaders after them, to opt for a more spiritual (less physical) approach to worship. Unfortunately, this led to a loss of the use of the body as well as of other legitimate physical and material signs of worship.[10]

It is particularly important to recognize the objective and subjective significance of symbols. A symbol is not an end in itself. It is a medium that relates to the object to which it refers and serves the subject who beholds it. Objectively a symbol in Christian worship signifies supernatural reality. Thus, a cross represents the event of Jesus in history. Gestures such as bowing or raising the hand signify the worthiness or greatness of God. The importance of the symbol is found, therefore, in that which it signifies. On the other hand, a symbol has significance for the person whose imagination and heart attitude are triggered by the sight of the symbol. So a cross may evoke praise, and a gesture may signify humility in the presence of God. Thus, subjectively symbols and symbolic representations deal with the language of the unconscious. They elicit an emotion, a feeling, and an intuition—all of which belong to worship.[11]

All symbols have external, internal, and spiritual qualities.

The external quality is the physical entity such as a cross or an appropriate gesture; the internal quality is the interpretation given to a symbol by the group (in this case the church); the spiritual quality is the spiritual energy released by the individual or congregation in relation to the external symbol and the internal meaning. Consequently, symbols demand faith if they are to become a means of worship. For an unbeliever a cross means little more than a historic event. But to a believer a cross evokes the energy of faith in Jesus as Savior.

Therefore, the purpose of a symbol is to function like a parable. It both reveals and conceals. It reveals its meaning to the believer but conceals its meaning to the unbeliever. Because worship is for the believer, it is important to teach the believer the meaning of the action, so that the work of worship will be done out of faith as it is directed to the glory of God.[12]

For this reason Christian congregations must learn certain premises about symbols in order to enter into a full worship of God. First, the worshiper must concentrate on the supernatural meaning of the symbol. There must be an intent to worship, a purposeful desire to offer praise from the heart. Second, the worshiper must allow himself or herself to meditate on the ultimate meaning of the symbol. This leads to the incarnation of the meaning of the symbol so that "the thing intended" by the symbol becomes a reality in the person's life.

Our worship is incarnated and enacted by the proper use of space, time, and sound. Such proper use, when accompanied by faith, incites the worshiper and the worshiping community to offer praise to the Father through the Son by the Holy Spirit. These matters will be discussed in part 4, "The Setting of Worship."

Conclusion

There are a number of implications to the theology of form and signs. The principle to keep in mind is that forms and signs constitute the tangible context in which intentional worship takes place. They are not ends in themselves; rather, they are the tangible meeting points between human beings and God in which spiritual worship takes place. This is a third theological principle of worship.

Chapter 10

A Theology of Order (The Word)

In the three preceding chapters three theological principles of worship have been set forth. They are (1) that worship is Christocentric, (2) that worship occurs through an enactment of the Christ-event, and (3) that the Christ-event is acted out through forms and signs. The purpose of this chapter and the next is to examine the traditional parts of worship in which this Christocentric enactment of worship occurs and to explain the meaning of each part. In this chapter we will discuss the service of the Word and in chapter 11, the service of the Lord's Supper.

The service of the Word encompasses three major aspects: the people's preparation, the Word from God, and the people's response. The components of these aspects have been developed through the centuries.

THE PEOPLE PREPARE THEMSELVES FOR WORSHIP

As the church begins its public worship it needs to pay attention to the manner in which it approaches God. Just as one would shrink from overfamiliarity, lightheartedness, and frivolity in meeting such a dignitary as a head of state, so one should acknowledge the worth of the Person met in worship. To meet God is not an ordinary thing. It has a transcendent quality, and to profane it is

117

to rob the worshiper of the meaning of this auspicious event.

Therefore certain rules of conduct and action have been developed to guard the beginning of this meeting. These are visible and tangible acts such as silence, the procession, the greeting, the invocation, the acknowledgment of God's glory, and the recognition of sinfulness.

Silence

Silence has to do with awe. Our experience of silence at the beginning of worship is akin to the feeling of speechlessness we experience in the midst of a heavy forest or when we sense the vastness of the ocean at night or the awesome expanse of the Grand Canyon. The prophet Habakkuk captured this feeling of the numinous when he declared, "The LORD is in his holy temple; let all the earth be silent before him" (2:20). Silence evokes feelings of transcendence and puts one in touch with the otherworldly character of reality.

Thus silence has to do with inwardness, meditation, preparation, and openness. Rudolf Otto in his classic work *The Idea of the Holy* recognizes the value given to silence by the Quakers. It is, he wrote, "not so much a dumbness in the presence of Deity, as an awaiting His coming, in expectation of the Spirit and its message." In this sense silence is a "solemn religious observance of a numinous and sacramental character . . . a communion . . . an inner straining not only 'to realize the presence of God', but to attain a degree of oneness with him."[1] Therefore, recovering silence in worship ought to be a matter of genuine concern to pastor and people alike. For in worship one stands before God—Creator, Redeemer, and Judge of all.

Procession

A procession is a part of life. It usually symbolizes going to something. For example, worship in the Old Testament was characterized by elaborate processions with singing, loud-sounding instruments, and dancing. Although there is no evidence of processions in the primitive church, we know that the church after the fourth century made much of the procession. The procession became increasingly elaborate through the medieval period but was abandoned by the Reformers because of late medieval abuses. There are, of course, two dangers here: on the one hand we can overemphasize the procession so it loses its meaning; on the other hand if we totally reject the procession, we will fail to understand the meaning of entering (or proceeding) into the very presence of God.[2]

Greeting

Next comes the greeting. The greeting marks the end of the procession (the church has arrived at its destination) and the beginning of the formal act of the meeting between God and His people. It is appropriate, therefore, that the people who have come to worship God should be greeted.

The greeting that serves as a call to worship has its roots in the synagogue. Abraham Millgram points out that "the daily morning service began with the reader's call to worship. 'Praise ye the Lord who is to be praised' to which the congregation responded: 'Praised be the Lord who is to be praised for ever and ever.'"[3]

The early church used the greeting "The Lord be with you" or "Peace be to you." These greetings from Ruth 2:4 and John 20:19 came into Christian use from the beginning and are found all over Christendom in the literature of the second century. They are used not only in the beginning of worship but also as salutations before prayer and before the Eucharist. The biblical character, antiquity, universality, and dignity of this greeting suggest its importance in worship. Some congregations have replaced the ancient greeting with the more common "hello" or "good morning." Although this exchange is technically proper, it lacks the dignity that enhances a spirit of worship.

The value of a greeting was recognized by the Reformers. For example, Calvin suggested worship begin with the words "Our help is in the name of the Lord, who made heaven and earth. Amen."[4] The *Westminster Directory*, although it studiously shied away from prescribing written prayers, recognized the significance of a prefatory prayer in these words: "The Congregation being assembled; the Minister, after solemne calling on them to the worshiping of the great name of God, is to begin with Prayer."[5] Later John Wesley prepared a list of texts (similar to the Anglican *Book of Common Prayer*) from which ministers were to choose opening sentences of worship.[6]

There is, of course, no absolute and prescribed greeting that one has to follow. It may be a brief sentence of Scripture or a longer

form containing responses or even a greeting written by the
congregation and changing from week to week.

Invocation

The word *invoke* means to call upon or to make a plea. In the
instance of Christian worship the members of the congregation
stand before God and, through the representation of the one who is
presiding, call upon God to make Himself present to them.
Theologically, the invocation claims the promise of Jesus that
"where two or three come together in my name, there am I with
them" (Matt. 18:20). The invocation is, therefore, a recognition
that Christians worship the Father through Jesus Christ by the
power of the Spirit. They do not enact worship in their own power.
The ability to enter into the heavens and join the heavenly throng
in worship around the throne is initiated and accomplished by the
Triune God. The invocation, therefore, requires thoughtful and
careful attention, for it is a passage into the very presence of God.

Acknowledgment of God's Glory

Once the congregation stands before God (by invoking His
presence) it is fitting that it should recognize God for who He is.
The Scripture that has given shape to the historic burst of praise for
God's character in the service of the Word is Luke 2:14, "Glory to
God in the highest, and on earth peace to men on whom his favor
rests."

The hymn developed from this passage has had a number of
titles, but is now universally known as the *Gloria in excelsis Deo*.[7]
It originated in the first three centuries and was used frequently in
worship until the eleventh century, when it became a fixed portion
of the church's worship. The hymn has been found in a total of 341
medieval manuscripts. Among these manuscripts there are 56
different melodies by which it was sung. It is a marvelous hymn,
not only for its style, but especially for its theology that extols and
magnifies the position of Jesus in the Godhead. The verse is reflective of a Hellenistic poetic style in its repetition of the clauses.

GLORIA	EXPLANATION
Glory to God in the highest and peace to his people on earth	This introductory phrase describes the posture of the church at worship. It bows before the Almighty.

We praise thee, we bless thee We worship thee, we glorify thee We give thanks to thee for thy great glory	These clauses indicate the purpose of worship: to glorify and magnify God.
O Lord God heavenly King, God the Father Almighty O Lord the only begotten Son, Jesus Christ O Lord God, Lamb of God, Son of the Father	These invocations extol the Son in His relationship to the Father. His *person* is glorified.
Thou that takest away the sins of the world, have mercy upon us. Thou that takest away the sins of the world, receive our prayer. Thou that sittest at the right hand of God the Father, have mercy upon us,	These relative clauses acknowledge the Son for His work of redemption.
For thou only art holy; thou only art Lord; thou only, O Christ, with the Holy Ghost, art most high In the glory of God the Father. *Book of Common Prayer*	The emphasis on the pronouns brings together the prayer and summarizes the reason for worshiping the Father through the Son and the Holy Spirit.

The *Gloria* was dropped in some Reformation churches and replaced (for the most part) with a hymn.

Recognition of Man's Sinful Condition

When Isaiah stood before God and saw Him in the majesty of His holiness, his response was one of repentance—a recognition of his sinful condition before God. He cried, "Woe to me!" . . . "I am ruined! For I am a man of unclean lips, and I live among a people of unclean lips, and my eyes have seen the King, the LORD Almighty" (Isa. 6:5). This theme of repentance was also enunciated by the tax collector who beat his breast and said, "God, have mercy on me, a sinner" (Luke 18:13).

A response called the *Kyrie eleison* (Lord, have mercy) is found in the liturgies of the fourth and fifth centuries. By the eighth century the refrain *Christe eleison* (Christ, have mercy) was added and the refrain was put forth in a triple sequence beginning with *Kyrie eleison* sung three times, followed by *Christe eleison* sung three times, and concluded with the *Kyrie eleison* three times again. This repetition, which recognizes the sinful condition of the worshiper, also attests to the threefold mystery of the Trinity. It has a beautiful quality, especially when sung in Greek, the language of early Christian worship.[8]

The *Kyrie eleison* was dropped by the Reformers in favor of a hymn or a psalm that would convey the same sense of repentance. Although the use of the *Kyrie* is a matter of taste, it does seem that the recognition of man's sinful condition in the presence of God is a matter of theology. How that is expressed may vary among Christian groups, although the *Kyrie* does have antiquity on its side as well as biblical roots and appropriateness.

GOD SPEAKS THROUGH HIS WORD

The congregation is now seated in the presence of God and eagerly awaits a word from Him. For it is in and through the Scripture and preaching that God speaks to His people. This is not a monologue. Rather, communication occurs through the reading of Scripture, the active response of the people, and the preaching of the sermon.

Reading of Scripture

The use of God's Word in worship is traced back to the beginnings of public worship at Mount Sinai. Nevertheless, it was the emphasis of Ezra the scribe that made the Scripture central to Jewish worship, especially in the synagogue. Ezra was a Babylonian Jew who went to the Holy Land as the head of the second wave of immigrants. Because he was shocked to discover the weak spiritual conditions of the people of Jerusalem, he rent his garments, fasted, and prayed for renewal. Then, under his leadership far-reaching reforms were initiated, including renewal of worship. This restoration is recorded in the Scripture in these words:

> Ezra opened the book. All the people could see him because he was standing above them; and as he opened it, the people all stood up. Ezra praised the LORD, the great God; and all the people lifted their hands and responded, "Amen! Amen!" Then they bowed down and worshiped the LORD with their faces to the ground.
>
> The Levites . . . instructed the people in the Law while the people were standing there. They read from the Book of the

Law of God, making it clear and giving the meaning so that the
people could understand what was being read.

Nehemiah 8:5–8

It is interesting to note all that is going on in this incident: the
reader standing in a place where he could be seen; the people
standing as the book was opened, lifting their hands, saying
"Amen," bowing to the ground; the Levites reading, making
it clear, giving the meaning; the people understanding. This was
no passive mumbling of Scripture, no mere preliminary to the
sermon!

This strong emphasis on Scripture was carried directly from
the temple to the synagogue and on into Christian worship.

There is little direct evidence prior to Justin Martyr (A.D. 150)
concerning the methods of reading Scripture in Christian worship.
Nevertheless the allusion to the reading and use of Scripture in the
New Testament literature (see Acts 2:42; 13:5; Col. 4:16; 2 Tim.
3:16) and in other early Fathers (Clement 13:1, 14:2; Epistle of
Barnabas 21:1, 6) leaves little doubt that the description of Chris-
tian worship in Justin Martyr refers to a well-established tradition.
He wrote:

> And on the day called Sunday there is a meeting in one place of
> those who live in cities or the country, and the memoirs of the
> Apostles or the writings of the prophets are read, as long as
> time permits; then when the reader has finished, the president
> in a discourse urges and invites [us] to the imitation of these
> noble things.[9]

By the third century the liturgy of the Word included readings
from the Law, Prophets, Epistles, Acts, and Gospels with Psalms
sung by cantors between the lections. Reading was characterized
by an active involvement on the part of the people. Special attention was given to the reading of the Gospel as indicated by the
canons of Addai: "At the conclusion of all the scriptures let the
gospel be read, as the seal of all the scriptures; and *let the people
listen to it standing up* [emphasis added] on their feet, because it is
the glad tidings of the salvation of all men."[10]

The people responded by singing psalms between Scripture
readings. There is abundant evidence of the use of psalms in the
records of the third century.[11] Eusebius (260–340), bishop of

Caesarea and author of the classic *Ecclesiastical History*, wrote, "The command to sing psalms in the name of the Lord was obeyed by everyone in every place: for the command to sing is in force in all the churches which exist among the nations."[12] Athanasius referred to the Psalms as "a book that includes the whole life of man, all conditions of the mind, and all movements of thought."[13] The Reformers, especially Calvin, advocated the increased use of psalms in worship.

Response

The church has also shown respect to Scripture through the use of a preface and a response to the reading of Scripture. This practice, attested to in the liturgies of the fourth century, intends to call attention to the importance of the reading and to engage the hearer in an attentive listening. There is no absolute fixed formula for the preface and response. Here is an example:

> Reader: A reading from the book of the prophet Isaiah.
>   Following the reading:
> Reader: The Word of the Lord.
> People: Thanks be to God.

Because the Gospel carries the special privilege of communicating the memoirs of Jesus, a different formula for introducing the Gospel reading developed. It became customary to kiss the Gospel and to have a procession accompany the reader to the place where the Gospel was to be read. This procession generally included lights (candles) held by acolytes and incense carried by a thurifer. In the introductory acclamation the reader expressed special honor to Christ Himself. Here is an example:

> Reader: The gospel of our Lord Jesus Christ as recorded
>   in . . . .
> People: Glory to Thee, O Lord.
>   (reading)
> Reader: (raising the Gospel book over his head, he may say)
>   The Gospel of our Lord.
> People: Praise to Thee, O Christ.

It is not Roman or pagan to express love for the Scriptures and to give them a place of honor in worship through the use of physical

signs. These signs are ways of expressing an inner conviction regarding the value and significance of God's Word.

The Sermon

The real meaning of preaching is set forth by the apostle Paul
in the first chapter of the First Epistle to the Corinthians. He came
to preach the gospel (1:17), which he identifies as the message of
the cross (1:8) or of Christ crucified (1:23). He assures his readers
that this message was not his own (1:17). Instead, he came in a
demonstration of the Spirit's power so that faith would be in demonstration of God's power (2:4-5). Paul's theology of preaching
sees the *kerygma*—as basic to preaching. In this sense preaching
in the context of worship reenacts the event of Christ, the event
that gives shape and meaning not only to worship but also to the
lives of the worshipers.

But Paul also speaks about *didache* (teaching) in preaching,
especially in the Pastoral Epistles. This teaching is referred to as
sound doctrine (1 Tim. 1:10) or good teaching (1 Tim. 4:6). In this
it may be seen that *didache* belongs to *kerygma* and ought not to
be separated from it. The preaching of the gospel always contains
teaching, and teaching always contains the preaching of the gospel.
They both belong to the same Word of God. One is the initial
preaching of the gospel, while the other is a more advanced teaching that conforms to the proclamation of the gospel.[14] 4

Throughout history, preaching has frequently been accommodated to the prevailing patterns of cultural rhetoric. In some
churches much of the simplicity of early preaching has been replaced by long, tedious, and sometimes complicated explanations of
the text. Other congregations, particularly those strongly influenced
by Revivalism, have swung the other way toward the simple re-
presentation of the gospel week after week. These two extremes
illustrate the tension between *kerygma* and *didache*. Having falsely
separated the two, we fail to preach in such a way that both are
present in every proclamation. Where, then, is the balance?

Primarily, preaching in the context of worship is not teaching
(there are other occasions for that in the church). Rather, it is the
time when the work of Christ (Creation, Incarnation, Death,
Resurrection, Consummation) is proclaimed and *applied* to the
lives of God's people. In this way the event from which the meaning of life is derived is actualized for the worshiper once again.

THE PEOPLE RESPOND TO GOD

In this part of worship the emphasis changes. Formerly God spoke, and His people listened and responded. Now the people speak, and God listens and responds. Thus, the dominant note is that of the people's *offering*.

The offering is one of praise, confession, and prayer that are expressed through music, giving of money, recitation of the creed, and prayer.

An Offering of Music

The music of heavenly worship so beautifully set forth in Revelation is directed toward God, not man. This is the key to an offering of music. Because Christ is worthy the heavenly throng sings "a new song" (Rev. 5:9). He is the one who "created all things" (4:11), who with His blood "purchased men for God" (5:9), and now "sits on the throne" (5:13). Thus to Him "praise and honor and glory and power" are due "for ever and ever" (5:13).

The Offering of Money

In the Old Testament, tithing is rooted in the command of God. But in the New Testament the offering of money or gifts is seen as a proper response to the self-giving of God in Jesus Christ: "For you know the grace of our Lord Jesus Christ, that though he was rich, yet for your sakes he became poor, so that you through his poverty might become rich" (2 Cor. 8:9).

Caring for the poor and needy (especially in the context of the church) has always been a major concern of the Christian church (see Matt. 6:3–4; Acts 2:44–46; 11:27–30). The earliest reference to the collection in noncanonical sources is found in Justin Martyr. He wrote:

> And they who are well to do, and willing, give what each thinks fit; and what is collected is deposited with the president, who succors the orphans and widows, and those who, through sickness or any other cause, are in want, and those who are in bonds, and the strangers sojourning among us, and in a word takes care of all who are in need.[15]

In offering money as an expression of worship we are responding to God's claim on our lives and giving Him a portion of what He has in fact given us. This is a proper act of worship, one that should be done with dignity and thankfulness of heart.

Historically, the offering gradually came to be received during the offertory of the Eucharist and was brought to the table with the elements of bread and wine, which were brought by members of the worshiping community.

An Offering of Faith

Confessional statements developed early in the Christian faith (see 1 Cor. 12:3; 15:1–3; 1 Tim. 3:16).

In the course of time it was the Nicene Creed (325) that became the standard confession of faith in the church. This creed was chosen because it was the standard statement of orthodoxy against the Arian position in the fourth century. It was inserted in the regular worship of the church as a way not only of confessing faith in the triune God but of preserving that faith against the heretical statements of the Arians.

The significance of using a confession of faith in worship is that it is another way of enacting what the Christian believes. In this way the confession is a witness to personal faith and an offering of this faith to the Father through the Son.

An Offering of Prayer

The true meaning of prayer is found in the relationship it expresses between human beings and God. In prayer the posture of dependence is assumed. Therefore in the Scriptures and in the history of Christian thought the church has recognized five kinds of prayer: adoration, confession, petition, praise, and thanksgiving. In *adoration* we worship God as He is in Himself; in *confession* we recognize that forgiveness comes from God; in *petition* we supplicate or intercede on behalf of others; in *praise* we give outward expression of worship through words, music, and ceremony; and in *thanksgiving* we give an offering of thanks for the goodness of God.[16]

In worship all of these prayers are offered to God. Adoration is specifically offered when God is recognized for who He is (i.e., the *Gloria in excelsis Deo*); confession is offered when we recognize ourselves for who we are (i.e., the *Kyrie*); praise is offered frequently throughout the service in the offering of music, the singing of the Psalms, the response of Alleluia, and the like; thanksgiving is especially fulfilled in the Eucharist, which in the early church came to be known as the Great Thanksgiving. This leaves only one aspect of prayer yet to be treated—petition.

Petition should not be treated exclusively as the prayer of a pastor, but also as the prayer of the church. The early church was extremely conscious of the responsibility the whole church bore for prayers of petition.[17] In addition, the prayer of petition was regarded as the exclusive right of believers. Unbelievers or unbaptized persons were dismissed before the prayer of petition began.

The method of prayer in the early church should also be a matter of interest. The prayer of petition was designed to be a corporate act involving the whole church. Each person—the officiant, the deacon, and the laity—had his or her part. Furthermore, the prayers (as in the synagogue) were not haphazardly voiced. The leaders announced some matters of prayer; the people prayed; and then they went on to the additional matters of prayer.

Gregory Dix, one of the foremost liturgists of the twentieth century, sets forth an example of these prayers in his classic work *The Shape of the Liturgy:*

> First a subject was announced, either by the officiant (in the West) or the chief deacon (in the East), and the congregation was bidden to pray. All prayed silently on their knees for a while; then, on the signal being given, they rose from their knees, and the officiant summed up the petitions of all in a brief collect. They knelt to pray as individuals, but the corporate prayer of the church is a priestly act, to be done in the priestly posture for prayer, standing. Therefore all, not the celebrant only, rose for the concluding collect.
>
> The following is the scheme of the old Roman intercessions still in use on Good Friday.
>
> "*Officiant:* Let us pray, my dearly beloved, for the holy church of God, that our Lord and God would be pleased to keep her in peace, unity and safety throughout the world, subjecting unto her principalities and powers, and grant us to live out the days of a peaceful and quiet life in glorifying God the Father Almighty.
>
> "*Deacon:* Let us bow the knee. *(All kneel and pray in silence for a while.)*
>
> "*Subdeacon:* Arise.

"*Officiant:* Almighty everlasting God, Who hast revealed Thy glory unto all nations in Christ, preserve the work of Thy mercy; that Thy church which is spread abroad throughout all the world may continue with a firm faith in the confession of Thy holy Name: through. . . ."

There follow prayers for the bishop, the clergy, and 'all the holy people of God'; for the government and the state; for the catechumens; for the needs of the world and all in tribulation (a particularly fine collect, which has inspired one of the best of the official Anglican prayers for use in the present war [World War II]); for heretics and schismatics; for the Jews, and for the pagans. These prayers probably date from the fourth and fifth centuries in their present form, but may well be only revisions of earlier third century forms.

Or we may take an Eastern scheme from the Alexandrian liturgy, probably of much the same date as these Roman prayers.

"*The deacon proclaims first:* Stand to pray. (All have been "standing at ease" or sitting on the ground for the sermon.)

"*Then he begins;* Pray for the living; pray for the sick; pray for all away from home.

"Let us bow the knee. *(All pray in silence.)* Let us arise. Let us bow the knee. Let us arise again. Let us bow the knee.

"*The people:* Lord have mercy."[19]

This "people's prayer" derives from the profound understanding that the early church had of the organic sense of the body of Jesus Christ. Unfortunately this approach to prayer began to fade away in the fifth century and became nonexistent in the medieval period. Prayer became increasingly clericalized, with the people having no more part than an "amen" here and there. Neither did the Reformers or Puritans recapture this sense of a "people's prayer." Rather, they kept the prayers of the church in the control of the minister by means of the pastoral prayer. This has begun to change as a result of liturgical scholarship and the renewed sense of worship as the work of the entire congregation.

The Kiss of Peace

The kiss of peace is a gesture that communicates peace with God and peace with each other.[20]

In the New Testament there are a number of references to a kiss of greeting. Paul instructs the Roman Christians to "greet one another with a holy kiss" (16:16). Peter appears to connect the kiss with the peace of God: "Greet one another with a kiss of love. Peace to all of you who are in Christ" (1 Peter 5:14).

How is this command carried out? The method depends somewhat on local custom. The officiant may say, "The peace of the Lord be with you," and to this everyone would respond, "And also with you," and then turn to those around them, grasping their hand or embracing them, saying, "The peace of the Lord be with you." If the church is small enough, everyone in the congregation may "pass the peace" to everyone else. In a large church the pastor may proceed down the center aisle, passing the peace to the person at the end of the row who in turn passes the peace to the next person.

The use of the kiss in worship appears in the writing of Justin Martyr and in other writers thereafter. However, it did fall into disuse after the ancient period and was not revived until recently. Although the position of the kiss of peace appears in various places in the liturgy, the earliest accounts place it at the end of the liturgy of the Word before the beginning of the Eucharist. So Justin wrote in the *Apology*, "on finishing the prayers we greet each other with a kiss. Then bread and a cup of water and mixed wine are brought to the president of the brethren."[21] In the Eastern church the kiss was moved to the beginning of the eucharistic prayer. In either case it is seen as transitional from the Word to the Eucharist.

Chapter 11

A Theology
of Order
(The Eucharist)

Three introductory questions need to be addressed before making an analysis of the Lord's Supper. They are (1) Should this part of the worship be called the Eucharist or the Lord's Supper? (2) What is the nature of the Eucharist? (3) What is the proper order for the Eucharist? Beyond these questions, we will further explore the way the Eucharist dramatizes the work of Christ in a fourfold action.

INTRODUCTORY QUESTIONS

Eucharist or Lord's Supper?

First, both of the terms *Eucharist* and *Lord's Supper* are used in the New Testament. Paul uses the phrase *Lord's Supper* in a technical way in 1 Corinthians 11:20: "When you come together, it is not the Lord's Supper you eat." This statement refers to the institution of the Lord's Supper at the Passover meal before the death of Jesus (Matt. 26:17–35), to the continued practice of "breaking of bread" in Jerusalem (Acts 2:42), and to the spread of this tradition (1 Corinthians 11:23 carries the weight of tradition: "I received from the Lord what I also passed on to you") to Corinth. The appropriateness of the phrase Lord's Supper rests on the conviction that the church is called to reenact as a remembrance what Jesus did on that occasion.

The word *Eucharist* (from the Greek word *eucharistein* that means "to give thanks") is used by Paul in 1 Corinthians 14:16: "If you are praising God with your spirit, how can one who finds himself among those who do not understand say 'Amen' to your *thanksgiving,* since he does not know what you are saying?" (see also Matt. 26:27). Although the context of this passage does not make a clear reference to Eucharist within the Lord's Supper, the connection of the word Eucharist with the *berakah* (the Jewish blessing over bread and wine) raises the question of the scope of these terms.

We must consider whether or not the Eucharist is part of the larger scope of the Lord's Supper. Liturgical scholarship on the early practice of the Lord's Supper suggests that it was originally a common meal in which the thanksgiving (Eucharist) over the bread and wine took place. Gradually the rite of blessing (Eucharist) was separated from the common meal (also known as *agape*). When the meal fell into disuse, the term Eucharist remained as the term that more accurately described what the church was doing. The church was not sharing a common meal as much as making Eucharist (making thanks).[1]

Nevertheless it can be argued that the bread and wine symbolize the common meal. In this case the church not only makes Eucharist but also shares in the common meal with our Lord as signified by bread and wine. Thus, the more technical distinction between Lord's Supper and Eucharist is broken down and both terms can be used to describe what the church is doing.

The Nature of the Eucharist

The three most important New Testament words that describe the Eucharist are *remembrance, communion,* and *offering.* Since the last of these words is the most controversial, we will deal with it first and discuss the concepts of remembrance and communion later in this chapter.

The notion of the Eucharist as an offering is rooted in the offering Jesus Christ made of Himself to the Father. This notion was developed by the writer of Hebrews (see chapters 7–10), specifically in Hebrews 10:11–14:

> Day after day every priest stands and performs his religious duties; again and again he offers the same sacrifices,

which can never take away sins. But when *this priest had offered for all time one sacrifice for sins*, he sat down at the right hand of God. Since that time he waits for his enemies to be made his footstool; because by *one sacrifice* he has made perfect forever those who are being made holy [emphases added].

It is clear from this passage that there is only one offering or sacrifice for sin—the offering Jesus Christ made of Himself.

Several questions concerning the relationship between this offering and what is done in the Eucharist may arise: (1) Do the elements of bread and wine symbolize the offering of Jesus Christ? (2) How may the presentation of bread and wine by the congregation through the minister be regarded as an offering? (3) What effect does this offering have on the elements of bread and wine? and (4) What effect does the notion of an offering have on the worshipers?

First, does the offering of bread and wine symbolize the offering of Jesus Christ? There is no direct answer to this question in the New Testament.[2] However, the early church fathers universally and unequivocally regarded the offering of bread and wine as symbolic of the sacrifice of Jesus Christ. Clement, the bishop of Rome in the last decade of the first century, referred to Christ as "the high priest of our oblations"[3] and described the bishop as one whose office is to "offer the gifts" (*prospherein ta dōra*).[4] Sixty years later Justin informed the emperor that after the intercessions and the kiss, bread was "offered" (*prospheretai*).[5] Another sixty years later, in the beginning of the third century, Hippolytus instructed the church to "let the deacons bring up the oblation (*prosphora*), and he with all the presbyters laying his hand on the oblation shall say. . . ."[6]

Secondly, the idea of sacrifice is clearly connected with the elements of bread and wine. In the *Didache* the writer stated:

On every Lord's Day—his special day—come together and break bread and give thanks, first confessing your sins so that your *sacrifice* may be pure. Anyone at variance with his neighbor must not join you, until they are reconciled, lest your *sacrifice* be defiled. For it was of this *sacrifice* that the Lord said, "always and everywhere offer me a *pure sacrifice* for I am a great King, says the Lord, and my name is marveled at by the nations" [emphases added].[7]

Ignatius, the bishop of Antioch in A.D. 110 referred to the eucharistic assembly of the church as *Musiasterion* "the place of sacrifice."[8]

The terms *sacrifice* and *offering* used in connection with the Eucharist are especially repugnant to Protestants. This is so because of the late medieval association of these terms with a continuing sacrifice of Christ or because of the notion that Jesus is sacrificed in an unbloody manner again and again for salvation. This medieval notion is clearly unbiblical and was rightfully rejected by the Reformers. However, it needs to be made clear that this was not the theology of the early church fathers. For them the notion of offering and sacrifice, while associated with the offering and sacrifice of Christ, contained no notion of resacrifice.

This is the case in the earliest eucharistic prayer, found in Hippolytus: "We *offer* to you the bread and cup . . . and we ask that you would send your Holy Spirit upon the *offering* of your holy church . . . *that we may praise and glorify* you through your child Jesus Christ"(emphases added).[9] In this prayer bread and wine are the temporal symbols that transcend time and find their true meaning in the atonement of Jesus Christ. This answers the second question, namely, that the presentation of bread and wine is an offering, not in the sense of a sacrifice, but in the sense of an offering of praise and thanksgiving for the sacrifice of Christ.

The third question considers what effect the offering of bread and wine has on the elements. Do they *change* into the body and blood of our Lord when they are offered to the Father?[10] This question has been a divisive issue in the church. Space does not permit a detailed examination of it here. Let it be sufficient to say that the early church knew no notion of transubstantiation as developed in the medieval church and rejected by the Reformers. On the other hand, the early church had a stronger view than the memorialism adhered to in some Protestant groups.[11]

The position of the early church may be described this way: Because the elements of bread and wine have been offered to the Father, they are no longer common bread or common drink. Instead they represent to us the death and resurrection of Christ for our salvation. Thus, they proclaim to us the saving power of Jesus Christ. When we receive them by faith, we receive not only bread and wine, but mysteriously receive the saving grace that comes from the once-for-all, unrepeatable sacrifice of Jesus Christ.[12]

This observation raises the fourth and final question: What effect does this offering have on the worshiper? The answer to this question is based on the recognition that the offering of bread and wine is also an offering of self. Bread and wine are the first fruits of creation and as such represent the fruits of man's labor, the best of creation. Thus, the offering of bread and wine represent the offering of oneself, one's labor, one's whole being. This is an offering made by the whole congregation, one body of Christ. But it is made in and through Christ and His offering to the Father. Consequently, the Eucharist, or the church's thanksgiving, includes the offering of oneself as an act of thanksgiving. This personal giving of self ought to result in the confession of Christ's lordship and the living of a Christian life of personal sacrifice. For this reason the following words of Hebrews are to be interpreted in the context of worship: "Through Jesus, therefore, let us continually offer to God a sacrifice of praise—the fruit of lips that confess his name. And do not forget to do good and to share with others, for with such sacrifices God is pleased" (13:15–16).[13]

This early conviction of the Eucharist as an "offering of praise and thanksgiving," rediscovered as a result of modern liturgical scholarship, enriches the church's understanding of worship. Nothing in this view is incompatible with the Scriptures nor with an evangelical commitment to the gospel. The restoration of this teaching will prove to be a means of recovering the joy and triumph of celebrating Christ's victory over evil.

The Order of the Eucharist

A final preliminary question has to do with the order of the Eucharist. An examination of the institution of the Lord's Supper is the source from which the original order of the Eucharist may be determined. The New Testament accounts suggest a "seven-action scheme." Jesus (1) took bread, (2) gave thanks (Eucharist) over it, (3) broke it, and (4) distributed it with certain words. Then He (5) took a cup, (6) gave thanks (Eucharist) over it, (7) and, saying certain words, handed it to His disciples.

In the extant early liturgies of the church this sevenfold action has been compressed to a fourfold action. By bringing together the "taking," the "giving thanks," and the "handing it to his disciples" the result is a fourfold action of (1) taking; (2) blessing; (3) breaking; and (4) giving.[14] This is the order followed in the table experience of the early disciples with Jesus after the Resurrection. Here "he took bread, gave thanks, broke it and began to give it to them" (Luke 24:30). Because of this action "their eyes were opened and they recognized him" (24:31). They then hurried to Jerusalem to tell the other disciples that Jesus had risen from the dead and "how Jesus was recognized by them when he broke the bread" (24:35). Perhaps the Emmaus-road experience shaped the earliest eucharistic order of the Jerusalem church (Acts 2:46) and accounts for the association of the special presence of Christ in the worshiping community through the breaking of the bread.

This fourfold sequence of the Eucharist provides the framework in which the essential prayers and actions of eucharistic worship take place. An examination of the eucharistic liturgies of the early church evidences a common basic structure of ten parts. They are (1) introductory dialogue and the prayer of thanksgiving that includes (2) the preface, (3) the *Sanctus*, and (4) the post-*Sanctus* prayers of thanksgiving. This is followed by (5) a preliminary epiclesis, (6) the narrative of institution, (7) the anamnesis (remembrance), (8) the epiclesis (an invocation of the Holy Spirit), (9) the intercessions, and (10) the concluding doxology. It should be noted that not all ten parts are found in all liturgies; the sections often omitted are the preliminary epiclesis and the intercessions, except in the East. Also, there is some variety in the sequence of these ten parts.[15]

The common structure of all the eucharistic liturgies is found in *The Apostolic Tradition* of Hippolytus. In the forthcoming examination of the order of eucharistic worship the text will be given in full because of the importance of the prayers, both in terms of their antiquity and with reference to the influence this text played in giving shape to the ancient structure of Christian worship.

We turn now to an examination of the order of the eucharistic liturgy. Although our major concern is with the primitive liturgy, it should be noted that the order of worship and the content of the prayers and actions in Reformation liturgies are not significantly different. Unfortunately, space does not permit an extensive inclusion of Reformation liturgies. However, similarities, differences, and issues will be sufficiently footnoted so that the interested reader may make comparisons.[16]

THE WORK OF CHRIST IS DRAMATIZED

He Took

The first part of eucharistic worship is primarily a wordless action. Following the kiss of peace, the celebrant *takes* the bread and wine that are to be offered. This is an important action because it signifies the involvement of the whole worshiping community.

The earliest records indicate that each person or family brought bread and wine as well as other gifts (food to be distributed to the needy) and placed them on the table. Gradually, because of the increased size of the worshiping congregation, a representative brought the bread and wine for the entire congregation.

The significance of this symbol is that the people present themselves through the offering of bread and wine. Thus the entire worshiping community is involved in the action of "bringing," "presenting," and "offering." The canons of the synod of Ancyra in A.D. 314 recognize this symbolic action prescribing that the communicant "brings," the deacon "presents," and the bishop "offers." The real significance of this action is caught by Gregory Dix in these words:

> Each communicant from the bishop to the newly confirmed gave *himself* under the forms of bread and wine to God, as God gives Himself to them under the same forms. In the united oblations of all her members the Body of Christ, the church, gave herself to *become* the Body of Christ, the sacrament, in order that receiving again the symbol of herself now transformed and hallowed, she might be truly that which by nature she is, the Body of Christ, and each of her members members of Christ.[17]

Two other actions were adopted by the ancient church to communicate the meaning of the offering. First, the washing of the hands (in keeping with Psalm 26:6: "I wash my hands in innocence, and go about your Altar, O LORD") signified the innocence of those who serve the altar. This action was first recorded by Cyril of Jerusalem in the fourth century and ought not to be regarded as a primitive custom. Second, the imposition of hands on the elements; this action may have been derived from the Old Testament practice of laying hands on the sacrificial animal (e.g., Lev. 4:13–21). It could have been used to signify the blessing conferred

or to recognize that these elements represent the people who
brought them and who, through the consuming of bread and wine,
are blessed. The first occurrence of this act is found in Hippolytus.[18]

During the Reformation era there were traces of the offertory,
but for the most part it appeared in the background and it was often
dropped. In Calvin's Strasbourg Liturgy reference is made to the
minister preparing the bread and wine.[19] Luther also makes a
similar reference in his *Formula Missae* and *Deutsche Messe*.[20] In
the *Westminster Directory* all hints of an offertory are dropped and
ministers are instructed to have "the Table . . . decently covered[11]
before the service of communion begins.[21] There is no hint of
either the washing of hands or the imposition of hands on the
elements.

The Reformers' rejection of the offertory and dropping the
symbolic action of "taking" probably stemmed from the late
medieval notion of the Eucharist as a sacrifice. Unfortunately, the
Reformers' strong reaction resulted in the continued loss of the
original notion of offering.

He Blessed

The prayer of blessing over the bread and wine was the universally accepted practice of the ancient church. Justin informs us
that "the president . . . offers prayers and thanksgivings"[22] and the
later liturgies of the church give us insight into the content of these
prayers that were offered "according to his ability." The parts that
belong to the "blessing" include the introductory dialogue, the
preface, the *Sanctus* and the main body of the prayer of thanksgiving, frequently referred to as the post-*Sanctus* prayer. Each of
these aspects will be treated briefly.

First, the *introductory dialogue* contains both the *salutation*
and the *Sursum corda*. The salutation has already been discussed
in the enactment of the Word, so we will go on to the *Sursum
corda*. This preface (in varying forms) is found in all the liturgies of
both East and West.[23] Here is the *Sursum corda* from Hippolytus,
with a few interpretive remarks:

SURSUM CORDA	EXPLANATION
Celebrant:	The purpose of this response is to em-
Up with your hearts	phasize that true worship takes place in

People:
We have them with the Lord.

Celebrant:
Let us give thanks to the Lord.

People:
It is fitting and right.[24]

the heavenlies in Jesus Christ (Eph. 2:6, 7). The bidding brings the congregations into the heavens (Rev. 4 and 5).

Because thanksgiving (Eucharist) is made by the entire congregation the response to "Let us give thanks" is the permission and command of the congregation to begin the offering of praise and thanksgiving.

Second, after the worship has begun, the assembly moves into the *preface* to the great prayer of thanksgiving. The Latin *prefatio* does not mean a preliminary, but a proclamation. The purpose of the preface is to offer a brief proclamation *why* thanksgiving and praise are being offered. In Hippolytus the preface is a very brief statement: "We render thanks to you, O God, through your beloved child Jesus Christ, whom in the last times you sent to us as saviour and redeemer and angel of your will."[25] Although this statement is terse, it goes right to the heart of the matter, indicating that worship is being offered because of redemption.

Normally the preface is concluded with the *Sanctus* (from Isa. 6:3 and Rev. 4:8), the third part of the thanksgiving. This is certainly proper, considering the image of going up into the heavens to join the worship of eternity, which is characterized by the incessant singing of "Holy, Holy, Holy is the Lord God Almighty, who was, and is, and is to come." The *Sanctus* is not found in Hippolytus, although it is found in all the later liturgies, and as early as 1 Clement. Here, for example, is the preface and *Sanctus* taken from the liturgy of John Chrysostom, A.D. 380.

PREFACE AND SANCTUS

EXPLANATION

Celebrant: (Preface)
It is fitting and right to hymn you, (to bless you, to praise you,) to give thanks, to worship you in all places of your dominion. For you are God, ineffable, inconceivable, invisible, incomprehensible, existing always and in the same way, you and your only-begotten Son and your Holy Spirit. You brought us out of not being to being; and when we had fallen, you raised us up again; and did not cease

Eastern prayers are more poetic than Western ones, which are precise and terse.

This brief prayer contains the essence of the gospel message. It is the major *reason* for giving thanks and praise.

This praise joins in the great company of heavenly worship.

to do everything until you had brought us up to heaven, and granted us the kingdom that is to come. For all these things we give thanks to you and to your only-begotten Son and to your Holy Spirit, for all that we know and do not know, your seen and unseen benefits that have come upon us. We give you thanks also for this ministry; vouchsafe to receive it from our hands, even though thousands of archangels and ten thousands of angels stand before you, cherubim and seraphim, with six wings and many eyes, flying on high (aloud) singing the triumphal hymn (proclaiming, crying, and saying:)

People: *(Sanctus)*
Holy, Holy Holy, Lord of Sabaoth; heaven and earth are full of your glory. Hosanna in the highest. Blessed is he who comes in the name of the Lord. Hosanna in the highest.[26]

The *Sanctus* of the earthly church joins the heavenly throng in singing the eternal praise.

Immediately after the *Sanctus* the congregation is led in the body of the prayer of thanksgiving. This prayer enacts the whole gospel, because that is the content of the church's praise and thanksgiving. Here is that prayer from Hippolytus. Lengthier and more flowery ones are found in other extant canons.

PRAYER OF THANKSGIVING

Who is your inseparable Word, through whom you made all things, and in whom you were well pleased.

You sent him from heaven into the Virgin's womb; and, conceived in the womb, he was made flesh and was manifested as your Son, being born of the Holy Spirit and the Virgin.

Fulfilling your will and gaining for you a holy people, he stretched out his

EXPLANATION

It is particularly instructive to note how this prayer sweeps from creation to resurrection.

He begins by stating the position of the Son with the Father; extols the Son for creation; moves on to the incarnation; then the death with special emphasis on the destruction of the powers through death; and finally to the resurrection.

hands when he should suffer, that he might release from suffering those who have believed in you.

And when he was betrayed to voluntary suffering that he might destroy death, and break the bonds of the devil, and tread down hell, and shine upon the righteous, and fix the limit, and manifest the resurrection.[27]

Most liturgies make specific reference to the fall. Here, the fall is implied by way of assumption.

Hippolytus does not have a preliminary epiclesis in his liturgy. Here is an example found in the fifth-century liturgy of Mark: "Fill, O God, this sacrifice also with a blessing from you through the descent of your (all-holy Spirit)."[28] This prayer recognizes the place of the work of the Holy Spirit in empowering the worship of the church.

The Reformers retained parts of the ancient "blessing" or prayer of thanksgiving. Luther retained the salutation, the *Sursum corda*, and the preface but dropped the *Sanctus* and even the body of the prayer of thanksgiving, as well as the preliminary epiclesis in his *Formula Missae* of 1523. Calvin, in the *Form of Church Prayers* written for the church in Geneva in 1542, dropped the entire section in favor of an exhortation after the words of institution.[29]

In Calvin the eucharistic element was rejected in favor of a personal examination of faith. This marks a significant shift in the meaning of worship. In the ancient church the emphasis had been on the objective work of Jesus Christ who by His death was the sacrifice of God for humanity (the Eucharist being the offering of praise and thanksgiving for the work of Christ). Because this original notion had been corrupted by the medieval church and turned into a resacrifice, Calvin, Zwingli, and the majority of Protestants after them dropped the entire prayer of thanksgiving. They shifted the emphasis of the Eucharist from God's objective action in Christ to man's faith, self-examination, and pursuit of good works.

In this new emphasis Calvin both lost and gained something. What he lost was the sense of praise and thanksgiving evoked by the ancient Eucharist. What he gained was the Pauline emphasis in 1 Corinthians 11:28–29: "A man ought to examine himself before he eats of the bread and drinks of the cup. For anyone who eats and drinks without recognizing the body of the Lord eats and drinks judgment on himself."

The *Westminster Directory* retained a prayer of thanksgiving and instructed the ministers "to give thanks to God for all his benefits, and especially for that great benefit of our redemption, the love of God the Father, the sufferings and merits of our Lord Jesus Christ the Son of God, by which we are delivered."[30] It is a normal practice in most evangelical churches to offer an extemporaneous prayer that covers the work of redemption. More careful attention should be given, however, to be inclusive of the entire Christian faith in this prayer: moving from the Triune God through Creation, the Fall, the Incarnation, the Death, and the Resurrection.

There is no reason why the salutation, the *Sursum corda*, the preface, and the *Sanctus* should not be restored. They are all deeply rooted in biblical truth and add a dignity to the offering of the great thanksgiving of the church. A slavish reproduction of the exact prayer of Hippolytus is not necessary. The salutation, the *Sursum corda*, and the *Sanctus* would remain the same; and the prayer of the preface and great thanksgiving would cover the same structure of faith. However, the extemporaneous approach to prayer to which Evangelicals are committed need not change.

In this way both the form and freedom that were the intent of Hippolytus would find a good balance. (His prayer was not given to be memorized. Rather it was to serve as a model. It was expected that the extemporaneous approach to prayer as in Justin's report would be continued.)

He Broke

The original breaking of bread from the Jewish background probably had no meaning other than that of distribution. However, in the course of history, the action of breaking the bread attained several meanings.

The earliest meaning concerned church unity. Paul gave it this meaning in the context of the Corinthian congregation torn by strife. He wrote, "Because there is one loaf, we, who are many, are one body, for we all partake of the one loaf" (1 Cor. 10:17). This same notion is seen in Ignatius[31] and the *Didache*.[32] By the third century this emphasis seems to have been substituted by the symbol of Christ's broken body and His death on the church's behalf. This latter notion seems to be retained among most Protestant churches today.

The breaking of bread (fraction) is the climax of the section of worship belonging to the "breaking." Other parts include the narrative, the anamnesis, the prayer of intercession, and the epiclesis.

The narrative of institution is simply the repetition of the words of Jesus. Hippolytus put this quite simply, as do the other liturgies of the ancient church:

> He took bread and gave thanks to you, saying, "Take eat; this is my body, which shall be broken for you." Likewise also the cup, saying, "This is my blood, which is shed for you; when you do this, you make my remembrance."[33]

The concept of remembrance generally contains a statement of *memorial* and a statement of the *offering*. Here is an example from *The Apostolic Constitutions* of A.D. 375.

THE APOSTOLIC CONSTITUTIONS

Remembering therefore what he endured for us, we give you thanks, almighty God, not as we ought but as we are able, and we fulfill his commands.

For in the night he was betrayed, he took bread in his holy and blameless hands and, looking up to you, his Father, he broke it and gave it to his disciples, saying, 'This is the mystery of the new covenant; take of it, eat; this is my body which is broken for many for forgiveness of sins.'

Likewise also he mixed the cup of wine and water and sanctified it and gave it to them, saying, 'Drink from this, all of you; this is my blood which is shed for many for forgiveness of sins. Do this for my remembrance; for as often as you eat this bread and drink this cup, you proclaim my death, until I come.'

Remembering then his passion and death and resurrection from the dead his return to heaven and his future sec-

EXPLANATION

In the early church the *anamnesis* is regarded as more than a memorial. It is an objective act in which the event commemorated is actually made present.

The *memorial* always mentions the passion, the resurrection, and the ascension and frequently includes the incarnation, the burial, and the mediation of the ascended Christ, and the second coming.

The *offering* explicitly offers the bread and wine in identification with the offering of Jesus and as being representative of the whole created order redeemed by Jesus.

This portion of the prayer completes the drama of the work of Jesus. The focus is on the eschatological aspect of

ond coming, in which he comes to   the Christian faith—the ascension,
judge the living and the dead, and to second coming, and judgment.
reward each according to his works, we
offer to you, King and God. . . .[34]

A word needs to be said about the *anamnesis*. We tend to
translate this word as "memory," a mental action that brings to
mind something from the past. This is questionable. The word may
also mean "'re-calling' or 're-presenting' before God an event in
the past, so that it becomes *here and now operative by its ef-
fects*."[35] In this sense the remembrance places before God the
once-for-all sacrifice of Christ that is now made real and operative
in the present to the believer who by faith receives Christ under
the signs of bread and wine. In this way the remembrance is no
empty act but a powerful proclamation in the present of the
sacrifice of Christ.

Next comes the *epiclesis*, a prayer for the coming of the Holy
Spirit on both the elements of bread and wine *and* on the people
who worship. This prayer recognizes the role of the Holy Spirit as
the agent who confirms and makes worship real, a fact evident in
the following prayer of Hippolytus:

> And we ask that you would send your Holy Spirit upon the
> offering of your holy Church; that, gathering them into one,
> you would grant to all who partake of the holy things [to par-
> take] for the fullness of the Holy Spirit for the confirmation of
> faith in truth.[36]

Then comes the *prayer of intercession*. There is a strong di-
vergence of opinion here between the East and the West. The
Eastern liturgy places the prayer of intercession at this point because the worshiping community is at the very throne of God. So
Alexander Schmemann, a contemporary Orthodox theologian,
writes, "It is the very joy of the Kingdom that makes us *remember*
the world and pray for it. It is the very communion with the Holy
Spirit that enables us to love the world with the love of Christ. . . .
Intercession begins here, in the glory of the messianic banquet,
and this is the only true beginning for the church's mission."[37]

The typical place for the intercession in the Western church
has been during the liturgy of the Word, after the sermon (see
chapter 10). While the West recognizes the theological validity of
the Eastern viewpoint, a major concern has been for the rhythm of

worship and the intercession at this point has been seen as a major distraction from the emphasis on praise and thanksgiving.

Nevertheless, the West has placed the Lord's Prayer here as a recognition of the value of intercession while before the throne and at the same time retaining the focus of the Eucharist as an act of praise and thanksgiving.[38]

Finally, the *fraction* occurs.[39] Here, the bread may be lifted up for all to see and to hear, so that worship occurs through the senses of sight and sound. The Reformers kept most of the parts of the "breaking," though their whole service was organized quite differently.[40]

He Gave

More careful attention needs to be paid to the "giving" and the receiving of the elements. In the original drama Jesus handed over the bread and the cup saying certain words: "Take and eat; this is my body. . . . Drink from it, all of you. This is my blood of the covenant, which is poured out for many for the forgiveness of sins" (Matt. 26:26–27). In the earliest liturgies we find the tradition of Jesus handed down in the church. The officiant hands the bread and the cup to each person and says either the exact words of Jesus or a paraphrase of them. Here is an example from *The Apostolic Constitutions.*

> Officiant: The body of Christ.
> Person: Amen.
> Officiant: The blood of Christ, the cup of life.
> Person: Amen.[41]

The reason for such careful attention to detail is that this is the point of *communion.* It is a sacred moment. Paul reminded the Corinthians of the meaning of communion: "Is not the cup of thanksgiving for which we give thanks a participation in the blood of Christ? And is not the bread that we break a participation in the body of Christ?" (1 Cor. 10:16). At this point in the worship the *offering* and the *remembrance* become a *communion,* a mystical communication between Christ and the believer. This is not an ordinary act to be defiled by a haughty or irreverent attitude. It is also the moment when the transcendent God who sent His Son into the world so that human beings may be saved meets with them.

For this reason the ancient church treated this moment with utmost dignity and reverence. Cyril of Jerusalem in his *Catecheses* instructed candidates for baptism to take the following care as they came to receive the elements:

After this, you hear the chanter inviting you with a divine melody to the communion of the holy mysteries, and saying, 'Taste and see that the Lord is good.'

Do not entrust judgment to your bodily palate, but to undoubting faith; for what you taste is not bread and wine, but the likeness of the body and blood of Christ.

When you approach, do not come with your hands stretched or your fingers separated; but make your left hand a throne for the right, since it is to receive a king. Then hollow your palm and receive the body of Christ, saying after it, 'Amen.' Carefully sanctify your eyes by the touch of the holy body, then partake, taking care not to lose any of it . . .

Then, after having partaken of the body of Christ, approach also the cup of his blood. Do not stretch out your hands, but, bowing and saying 'Amen' in the gesture of adoration and reverence, sanctify yourself by partaking of the blood of Christ also. While the moisture is still on your lips, touch it with your hands and sanctify your eyes and forehead and the other senses. Then wait for the prayer, and give thanks to God who has deemed you worthy of such great mysteries.[42]

Benediction

The benediction is a pronouncement of blessing. It originates with the Aaronic benediction given to Aaron and his sons. In this act they were to communicate God's name and, therefore, the blessing of His presence on the people (see Num. 6:22–27).

In the New Testament a parallel to the Aaronic blessing is found in the apostolic blessing (see 2 Cor. 13:14 and note the holy kiss in 13:12). The main difference between the Old and New Testament blessing is that it is now in the name of the Father, Son, and Holy Spirit.

In the benediction, both in the Old and the New, the blessing comes from God and is communicated through His servants. Thus the benediction has always been a part of Christian worship; it is a recognition that the one who has met with God has indeed been blessed!

Recessional Hymn

The service was concluded with a prayer, a benediction, and a recessional hymn.[43]

The recessing signifies "going out from." Because the worshipers have been with God, the recession ought to be marked by great joy, a freeing exuberant note of praise. The final hymn is important, therefore, because it is a means of expressing this irrepressible urge to shout. It ought to be, as a matter of fact, a kind of shout—a final amen and alleluia to the Lord!

The ancient church also expressed the wonder and awe of this occasion through the use of music, especially the *Agnus Dei* (Lamb of God) modeled after the phrase "the Lamb of God, who takes away the sin of the world" (John 1:29).

Conclusion

In the preceding two chapters we have examined the parts of worship that were universally accepted by the ancient church and have been used to this day with some modification by Protestants. Before we examine the value and use of these parts of worship for contemporary Evangelicals, we will look at the church's regard for time, space, and sound and the relationship of worship to social action. We will then be in a good position to ask how the fullness of worship old is related to worship new.

VNVS DEVS, VNVS CONCILIATOR DEI ET HOMINVS HOMO CHRISTVS IESVS, QVI DEDIT SEMETIPSVM PRECIVM REDEMPTIONIS PRO OMNIBVS

Part IV

THE SETTING OF WORSHIP

ITE IN MVNDVM VNIVERSVM, ET PRÆDICATE EVANGELIVM OMNI CREATVRÆ

Chapter 12

Worship
and Space

It is a fundamental axiom of Christianity that worship can be conducted at any place. This conviction derives from Jesus' statement to the Samaritan woman that "God is spirit, and his worshipers must worship in spirit and truth" (see John 4:21–24).

Throughout the history of the Christian church, believers have worshiped everywhere—in the fields, in the catacombs, by the river, in homes, in prison, on ships, and on planes. Yet, it has been normal for Christians to have a *place* of worship.[1] Consequently churches, cathedrals, and auditoriums have become particular houses of worship. However, a worship building (like everything else) is not neutral. It communicates something about the convictions of the people who worship there. Thus the church has long acknowledged that what we do in worship ought to be expressed in the use we make of worship space.[2]

In this chapter we will consider the theological basis for the use of space and survey the ways that space used for Christian worship has reflected culture and changing beliefs.

THE THEOLOGICAL BASIS FOR THE USE OF SPACE
The Redemptive Understanding of Space

Space, like any other aspect of God's created order, cannot be understood apart from the framework of Creation, Fall, Incarnation, Death, Resurrection, and Consummation. Since this framework has already been discussed in some detail, little more than a brief sketch is needed here.

Space belongs to God by virtue of creation. Furthermore, space is a vehicle through which communication may occur. Thus, God communicated Himself and His desires for man in the arrangement and use of space in the garden; the tree of life and the tree of the knowledge of good and evil were in the middle of the garden.

However, because of the Fall space became a vehicle to communicate evil (e.g., the Tower of Babel). Space, not being neutral, is a powerful means through which false ideas and ideologies may be expressed in ugliness, chaos, lack of harmony, implements of war and destruction, among others.

In worship we celebrate the victory of Christ over evil. Even though the powers still communicate their false ideologies through the use of space and materiality, Christian worship expresses hope in the final deliverance of creation from evil and the restoration of all things in the new heavens and the new earth (Rom. 8:18–25; Rev. 20–22). Because the redemption of Jesus Christ extends to the entire created order, space is a vehicle through which the Christian view of redemption may be expressed. More specifically, in worship space becomes the stage on which the redemption of the world is acted out. This truth is exhibited in the signs of redemption such as the table, the pulpit, and the baptismal font, as well as in the arrangement of space for the people, the choir, the celebrant, and others who enact the gospel. Space can symbolize the victory of Christ over evil.

Biblical Support for the Spiritual Understanding of Space

In the Old Testament there are abundant references to a particular place or object regarded as sacred space (Bethel, Mount Sinai, the burning bush, the Ark of the Covenant, the Most Holy Place, etc.).

The spiritual significance of space is emphasized by the elaborate instructions given for the building of the tabernacle (and later the temple) and by the acts of consecration.

In the instructions for the building of the tabernacle as well as the directions given for worship (see Exod. 25–40) three points about space are made. First, the elaborate materials demonstrate that material things belong to the Lord and may be used to communicate truth about God; second, the repeated emphasis that God will dwell there (25:8; 29:45) substantiates the notion that God's presence in the world may be communicated symbolically; and third, the recognition that the "glory of the LORD filled the tabernacle" (40:34–35) acknowledges God's presence in a particular space.

The act of consecration also emphasizes the importance attached to a "place."[3] Solomon's dedication of the temple (1 Kings 8:3ff.) provides the model for the consecration of space in the Scriptures. This act is not to be regarded as a kind of exercise associated with magic but as an act that sets apart a particular place as special for the community to publicly meet God (see also Exod. 40 and Lev. 8). The Christian church has continued to use the practice of consecration and to recognize that the place where people gather to worship is special.[4]

The Stewardship of Space in Worship

It is obvious that whenever a group of people gather to worship, whether in the woods or in a building, they are using space. The question is, Does the space in which we worship work for or against what we are doing?

There is such an intricate relationship between the internal and the external that one tends to shape the other. The important feature of Christian worship is that the internal experience of salvation in Jesus Christ, combined with immediate external expressions of this experience have stamped the use of space in Christian worship with a particular character. Spatial arrangements differ as a result of varying emphases on table fellowship, preaching, baptism, the orders of ministry and gifts, and the sense of body ministry.

Furthermore, thoughtful reflection by the church on the meaning of the Christian experience has found artistic expression in architecture. Unfortunately, this means that the church has also expressed theological error in her use of space (as in the medieval period) as well as theological indifference (as on the part of modern Evangelicals).[5]

THE USE OF SPACE IN THE HISTORY OF CHRISTIAN WORSHIP

The principle that space is a vehicle through which the meaning of worship is expressed can be demonstrated from examples of worship and space in history.

Synagogue

We will begin our study of the relationship between worship and space with the synagogue. Here the principle of the material as a means of communicating eternal truth was carried over from the temple. Figure 1 provides a model of an early synagogue in which the theological arrangement of space is evident.[6] The orientation of the building toward Jerusalem symbolized the hope of Israel that in that city all the promises of God to Israel were to be fulfilled.

Synagogue

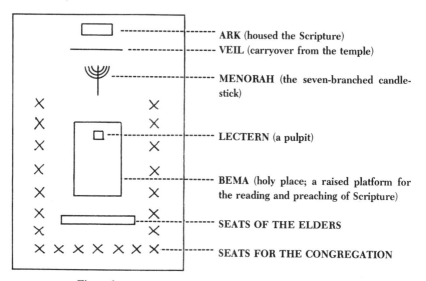

Figure 1.

The theological character of space in this synagogue can be noted in the location of the congregation and the objects of furniture around which they gathered. The congregation gathered *around* those material symbols that signify the means through which God had made Himself known in their history. For example, the meaning of "the seat of Moses" in the midst of the synagogue is captured by the liturgist Louis Bouyer in the following words: "The assembly of the People of God could meet as such only because there was always among them some one held as the authentic depository of the living Tradition of God's Word, first given to

Moses, and able to communicate it always anew, although always substantially the same."[7]

From this vantage point both the scribes and the congregation were able to *see* the symbols that communicated the meaning of their gathering. The most central symbol was the ark to remind them of the most holy object of ancient Israel, the only object allowed in the Most Holy Place. It was looked upon as an empty throne where God Himself (an invisible spirit) was present. Inside the ark, which was similar to a wooden casket, were the scrolls, the testimony to God's communication with Israel. The ark and the scrolls were protected by the veil, and in front of that burned the seven-branched candlestick. All these material objects pointed beyond themselves to the presence of God in the history of Israel and His continued presence with the people of God who had come to worship.

Another feature of the synagogue was the bema, the raised platform on which the lectern stood. It was here that the Scriptures were read and proclaimed and prayers were said. Symbolcially the bema represented the place of the Word of God in the midst of the people, and the people gathered around the Word to hear God speak and to offer Him their prayers.

This simple arrangement of the major symbols of Israel's faith allowed the worship of Israel to reenact God's action in history and His promise for the future, not only in the words that were said but in the signs and symbols that accompanied those words.

An Ancient Syrian Church

A second example may be taken from an ancient Syrian church (see Figure 2). This building appears to be a Christianized version of the Jewish synagogue.[8]

Here, as in the synagogue, the congregation gathered around the symbols of Christian worship. The presence of the symbols (ark, veil, and candlestick) that are specifically Jewish expressed the continuity between the people of God in the New Testament with those in the Old. The bishop and the presbyters were in the "seat of Moses" and continued to communicate the presence of a living tradition in the ordained ministry of expounding the Word.

There were, however, two significant and noteworthy changes. First, the apse, the central focus of the congregation, contained a table. Here the bishop went to celebrate the

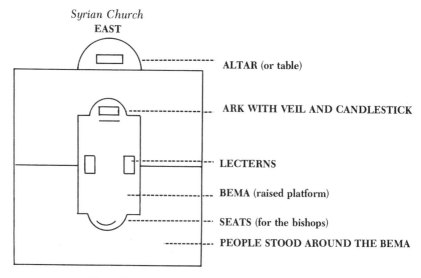

Syrian Church

EAST

ALTAR (or table)

ARK WITH VEIL AND CANDLESTICK

LECTERNS

BEMA (raised platform)

SEATS (for the bishops)

PEOPLE STOOD AROUND THE BEMA

Figure 2.

Eucharist, the supreme symbol of God's presence in the world and the climactic point of Christian worship. Second, the church no longer faced Jerusalem, but pointed toward the east. This symbolized the return of Christ in the east to gather His elect from the four corners of the world.

Here again the experience of the Christian community gave shape to the use of space. God's action in history as revealed in the Scripture, incarnated in Jesus Christ crucified and risen, and expected by the church in the second coming was expressed through the use of space, the arrangement of the people, and the symbols of God's presence.

A Roman Basilica

A third example may be drawn from the Constantinian era (see Figure 3). During this time numerous Roman basilicas were given to the church and converted into places of worship. The alteration of space to accommodate the crowds and to facilitate the growing sense of hierarchy resulted in some significant changes, not only in the use of space, but in the concept of worship.[9]

The most striking change in the use of space is the movement of the seat of the bishop from the congregation to a point behind the altar. The seat of the bishop gradually became a throne, a seat

Roman Basilica

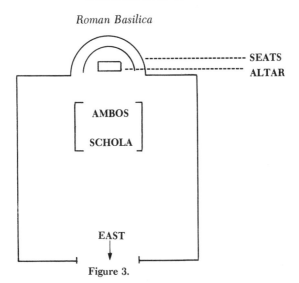

Figure 3.

of honor and power, as the church became more institutional, hierarchical, and powerful.

In this movement the initial stages of "triumphalism" are seen. The church is now an institution of power. The bishop gradually assumed more power as the people raised him to a status far beyond that of a servant of the church. Gradually the bishop became an authority outside of the collective body of the people, lost his link with the people, and became a lord over them. While this movement took some time to be completed, it also in a slow and imperceptible manner began to reshape Christian worship. What was once the collective work of the people gradually became the privilege of the clergy and the use of space symbolized that shift.

A second spatial change is found in the modification of the bema. The ark was omitted, the raised platform removed, and the ends were opened so that the procession could walk through it to the altar. In addition, the bema became the place where the ministers of the lower ranks, together with readers and singers, stood. Pulpits were added on both sides and the sevenfold candlestick was replaced by a single large candle.

This spatial change signaled a shift in worship. First, the bishop and the clergy were separated from the congregation. Second, the ministers, the singers, and the readers became a congregation within the congregation. Thus worship was gradually removed from the people and became a function of the clergy. Eventually the role of the worshipers was to watch the drama of worship conducted before them as an epiphany of the gospel. This was a dramatic step away from the earlier and more biblical approach to worship regarded as the work of the congregation. The biblical approach had demanded full participation by all, each playing his or her part in the drama of enacting the gospel.

A final alteration that sealed the move toward the clericalization of worship was to change the structure of the apse that housed the altar. In the West it became separated by rows of columns and set away from the people, against the wall where the priest said mass with his back to the people. In the East, the altar became hidden by an iconastasis screen that held the icons.[10] While the purpose was to accent the mystery of the gospel, the effect was to remove the action from the people, to clericalize the Eucharist, and to create a church within the church. The Eucharist became remote and awesome, a matter to be feared and held at a distance, no longer to be taken by the people, except once or twice a year.[11]

Later Medieval Churches

The movement toward the clericalization of worship in the early medieval period became solidified in the later medieval period as the theology of worship continued to change. Of particular interest is the Roman tendency to fill a church with altars (see Figure 4).[12]

Medieval Church

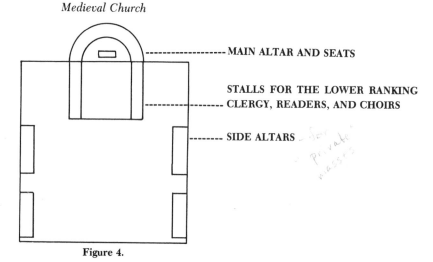

Figure 4.

The existence of the side altars resulted from the growing conviction that the mass was a sacrifice offered for the benefit of the living or the dead. Liturgist William D. Maxwell puts it this way:

> As each mass was held to have value as an act of merit, it was now seriously computed how many were required to bring a soul through purgatory to paradise, and to what extent a mass could alleviate the pangs of a soul condemned to eternal punishment. There were masses for success in temporal affairs: for one going on a journey, for recovery from sickness, for the capture of thieves and the return of stolen goods, for rain or fair weather, for the release of captives; and here again the number required to achieve the object was solemnly determined. Masses were said even to bring about the death of persons; these were condemned and forbidden by the Synod of Toledo in 694. Private masses became, as Heiler says, a cancer feeding upon the soul of the Church.[13]

Again, the relationship between theology and space in worship was evident. The time for reform was ripe in the sixteenth century.

The Protestant Church

Protestants continued to worship in the cathedrals and churches that had belonged to the Roman church. Therefore, their first impulse toward changing the use of space in worship was limited to the alteration of the building in which they worshiped. Here is an example from the reformer Zwingli:

> In the summer of 1524, the "cleansing" of the churches began. Zwingli and his colleagues, accompanied by all manner of craftsmen, entered the churches and set to work. They disposed of the relics, raised their ladders against the walls and whitewashed the paintings and decorations, carted away the statues and ornaments, the gold and silver equipment, the costly vestments and splendidly bound service-books. They closed the organs in token that no music of any kind would resound in the churches again: *the people were to give ear to the Word of God alone* [emphasis added].[14]

The use of space in Protestants' buildings was especially marked by the centrality of the pulpit. The pulpit was either raised high above the people where it could be easily seen (on one side of the sanctuary) or placed in the middle of the front on a raised platform. The symbolic location of the pulpit communicated the Protestant renewal of the Word and emphasis on preaching. This became the single most powerful symbolic use of space in the Protestant church.[15] A second feature of the Protestant use of space was to place the communion table under the pulpit or in a less central place. Symbolically, this makes communion less important than preaching.[16]

These alterations were both an expression of the changed view of worship and a vehicle through which the changed view of worship became more solidified. Today many American Protestants are offended by a centralized raised communion table. Unfortunately, the emphasis on the Word preached has led Protestants into a one-sided and clergy-centered worship. The mistake of the medieval period was that the congregation *watched* worship. In the modern Protestant church the mistake is that the congregation tends to *listen* to worship. We must return to worship that is the work of the congregation and to a use of space that permits and encourages the people to do worship.[17]

Conclusion

This brief overview of the biblical, theological, and historical understanding of the relationship between worship and space can be summarized in the following principles:

1. Because of creation and even more because of the Incarnation space cannot be regarded as profane.
2. In worship we are given the opportunity to incarnate the meaning of redemption through the forms that signify the victory of Christ over the dominion of Satan in this world.
3. The sanctification of our creative impulses results in the transfiguration of wood and stone and other earthly elements that image the meaning of our worship.
4. When the meaning of worship is lost, the misunderstandings that we adopt will be expressed in our use of space.
5. When the meaning of worship is recovered, the renewed internal perception of worship should be expressed in the external use of space.

Chapter 13

Worship
and Time

AChristian understanding of time proclaims the historic event of Christ as it relates to everyday existence.[1] If the Christian world is to break from secularism, it must examine the unthinking way it has adopted a secular way of reckoning time in worship. Instead of shaping worship around the saving events of the life of Jesus, many churches have allowed worship to revolve around days such as Mother's Day, Father's Day, Children's Day, Thanksgiving, and other national holidays.

In order to correct this problem we must understand the Christian view of time, and apply the Christian view of time to the yearly, weekly, and daily cycle of worship.

THE CHRISTIAN UNDERSTANDING OF TIME

The Christian concept of time is most clearly understood against the background of the Greek and Old Testament views of time.

The Greek View of Time

The two most important words used in the Greek language to describe time are *kairos* and *chronos*. *Kairos* designates a moment of importance and may refer to special times such as the time of birth, the time of marriage, the time of death. *Chronos*, on the

161

other hand, refers to the time between special events and may be appropriately designated as the time of sequence or chronology. For this reason *kairos* is always looked upon as the better time, the time of a special or significant event.[2]

From a more philosophical point of view, there were two distinguishing characteristics of time among the Greeks. In the first place, Greek philosophers separated time (as bound to creation) from timelessness (as above creation). Because of this separation, that which is eternal or above time cannot enter into time. Thus, time has no eternal or ontological meaning; it is a prison in which man is held.

The second emphasis among the Greeks was the notion that time is cyclical. It has no goal. It is not proceeding toward a final moment *(kairos)* that will give meaning and purpose to the chronology of time. Thus, history and man are doomed to an eternal recurrence of time. This pessimistic view sees time as without meaning outside of those existential events that a particular person may find meaningful for his or her existence.

The Hebraic Concept of Time

The ancient Hebrew people also had a sense of time characterized by *chronos* and *kairos*. However, their view differed significantly from that of the Greeks because Hebrews held a theological world view. They were committed to the existence of a transcendent God who makes Himself present in time through historical action.

Therefore, the first mark of Hebraic time is that it is defined by historical events. These events are a series of special moments *(kairoi)* that represent the saving acts of Yahweh. For example, great attention is given to the time of Moses and the Exodus out of Egypt (Deut. 1:9, 16, 18; 2:33–34; 3:3–4; 4:4; 6:6; 9:19). Other significant events include the reign of David (1 Chron. 21:28–29) and the building of Solomon's temple (2 Chron. 7:8). Throughout the Old Testament a strong interest is shown in history, especially the details of those events that mark the action of Yahweh on behalf of the people of Israel (see Neh. 1:5–9; Ps. 78; Jer. 11:1–5). For the Hebrews time was not empty of meaning, for it was in the time-oriented events of history that God was at work accomplishing His will and purposes through the people of Israel. Time for Israel was linear, moving in a particular direction.

Consequently, the second mark of Hebraic time is its emphasis on prophecy. Time is rooted not only in the past events, such as the Exodus, but also in the future events toward which it is moving. The events that have already occurred in time contain an element of expectation, of hope, of fulfillment, and even judgment. The prophets especially foretell the impending eschatological judgment of God against the nations and against Israel for her unfaithfulness to God (Isa. 18:1; Jer. 4:11–12; 8:1; Dan. 12:1; Joel 3:1–2; Mic. 3:4).

Nevertheless, beyond judgment is the hope of a new age. Zion and those who remain faithful (Ps. 81:13–16) and practice righteousness (Ps. 106:3) will achieve everlasting salvation (Isa. 60:20–22; Dan. 12:1–3; Zeph. 3:16–20).

A number of significant features of Hebraic time result from the emphasis on historical events and prophecy. In the first place, unlike the Greek concept of time, the Hebraic approach recognizes the presence of the eternal in time. Time and eternity are not antithetical concepts. Rather, God, who created time, is active in time, moving it toward the fulfillment that He intends. Consequently, time is an integral structure of God's reality. For this reason events in time have real and ultimate meaning. They are not the result of chance but an evidence of God's benevolent care and purpose for His creation.

One implication of the Hebraic concept of time is seen in the Old Testament view of worship. Because worship enacted the past events *(kairoi)* and made them present, the marking of time in worship was an indispensable feature of Old Testament faith: in the yearly cycle the festivals of Passover, the Feast of Weeks, the Feast of Tabernacles, as well as the lesser feasts; in the weekly cycle the Sabbath; and in the daily cycle the prayers of morning and evening all celebrated the action of God in history. The enactment of these historic events sanctified the present moment, gathering it up in the eternal meaning of that event which represented the presence of the transcendent and eternal God in time. Furthermore, in worship Israel anticipated the fulfillment of worship in the dawning of the new age.[3]

The Christian Synthesis

The Christian understanding of time also uses the concepts of *chronos* and *kairos*, maintaining the distinction given to them in

Greek, but viewing them in a manner similar to the Hebraic usage.

The unique feature of the Christian conception of time is the major moment *(kairos)* through which all other *kairoi* and *chronoi* find their meaning. This unique moment is the incarnation, death, and resurrection of Christ. Thus, in Christianity, all time has a *center*. Paul developed this notion in his epistle to the Colossians declaring that Christ is the creator of all things (1:16), the one in whom all things hold together (1:17), and the one through whom all things are reconciled (1:20). Christ is the cosmic center of all history. Everything before Christ finds fulfillment in Christ. Everything since Christ finds its meaning by pointing back to Christ.

From Christ the center three kinds of time are discerned. First, there is fulfilled time. The incarnation of God in Christ represented the fulfillment of the Old Testament messianic longings. Here, in this event, all the Hebraic hopes rooted in the sequence of significant historical moments of the Old Testament were completed. For in Christ the new time *(kairos)* had arrived as Jesus Himself announced: "'The time has come,' he said. 'The kingdom of God is near. Repent and believe the good news!'" (Mark 1:15).

Second, the coming of Christ is the time of salvation. The death of Christ came at the appointed time as Paul wrote to the Romans: "You see, at just the right time, when we were still powerless, Christ died for the ungodly" (Rom. 5:6; see also Matt. 26:18; John 7:6). Jesus' death was the moment of victory over sin: "Having disarmed the powers and authorities, he made a public spectacle of them, triumphing over them by the cross" (Col. 2:15). Consequently, the death of Christ introduced the time of salvation: "I tell you, now is the time of God's favor, now is the day of salvation" (2 Chron. 6:2).

Third, the Christ-event introduces the Christian anticipatory time. This aspect of time is based on the resurrection, the ascension, and the promise of Christ's coming again. Consequently, the church, like the Old Testament people of God, lives in anticipation of the future. Now, however, it is understood christologically as the time of Christ's glory (1 Tim. 6:14) and as the time of the final judgment (John 5:28–30; 1 Cor. 4:5; 1 Peter 4:17; Rev. 11:18).

This Christian conception of time is important because, it plays a significant role in the worship of the church. The historic and unrepeatable Christ-event is the content which informs and gives meaning to all of time.[4] Therefore, in worship we sanctify present time by enacting the past event of Jesus in time which transforms the present and gives shape to the future.[5] The church celebrates the Christ-event in a yearly, weekly, and daily manner.

THE YEARLY, WEEKLY, AND DAILY CELEBRATION OF TIME

The Yearly Celebration of Time

The most common term for the yearly celebration of time is the church year. The church year, developed in antiquity, was a vital part of worship until the Reformation.[6] The Reformers dropped it because of the abuses attached to it in the late medieval period: every day of the year had been named after a saint. The emphasis on these saints and the feasts connected with their lives overshadowed the celebration of the Christ-event and the sanctification of time because of Jesus' death and resurrection. The Reformers laid the knife to the entire church year and lost the good with the bad. A return to the church year among Evangelicals ought to advocate a very simple and unadorned year that accents the major events of Christ, a church year similar to that of the early church.

The ultimate source of the church year is not paganism as some have supposed, but the life, death, resurrection, ascension, and second coming of the Lord Jesus Christ. The understanding of time was immediately a part of Christian consciousness in the recognition that the death and resurrection of Jesus began the "new time." The fact that two major events of the church took place during Jewish celebrations—Passover and Pentecost—helped the early Christians to associate themselves with the Jewish reckoning of time and yet dissociate themselves by recognizing that a new time had begun. Thus, like the Jews, the early Christians marked time but, unlike the Jews, they marked their time now by the events of the new age.[7]

The oldest evidence of a primitive church year is found in Paul's first letter to the Corinthian Christians in A.D. 57. Here Paul refers to "Christ our Passover lamb" and urges the people to "keep the Festival" (1 Cor. 5:7–8). This reference seems to suggest that the early Christians celebrated the death and resurrection of Christ during the Jewish Passover.

There is considerable information from the second and third centuries to describe the significance of Easter. It became the major day of the year for baptism, which was preceded by a time of prayer and fasting. However, we do not have evidence of a fully developed church year until the fourth century.[8] Because space does not permit a full treatment of the origins and development of the church year, the following summary will do no more than outline the church year and touch on the origin and meaning of each part.[9]

Advent. The word *advent* means "coming."[10] It signifies the period preceding the birth of Christ when the church anticipates the coming of the Messiah. Although it signals the beginning of the church year, it appears that Advent was established after other parts of the year as a means of completing the cycle. Its purpose was to prepare for the birth of our Lord. The Roman church adopted a four-week season before Christmas, a practice that became universally accepted.

Epiphany. The word *epiphany* means "manifestation."[11] It was first used to refer to the manifestation of God's glory in Jesus Christ (see John 2:11) in His birth, His baptism, and His first miracle. Although the origins of the Epiphany are obscure, it is generally thought to have originated among the Christians in Egypt as a way of counteracting a pagan winter festival held on January 6. Originally it probably included *Christmas* (celebrated on December 25 to replace the pagan festival of the Sun). In the fourth century Christmas became part of Advent, and the beginning of Epiphany on January 6 became associated with the manifestation of Jesus to the wise men (i.e., the Gentile world). The celebration of Epiphany is older than that of Christmas and testifies to the whole purpose of the Incarnation. Therefore the emphasis in worship during Epiphany is on the various ways Jesus was manifested to the world as the incarnate Son of God. This period ends with the Transfiguration.

Lent. *Lent* signifies a period of preparation before Easter.[12] The origins of Lent lie in the preparation of the catechumen before baptism. The setting aside of a time of preparation for baptism goes back as early as the *Didache* and is attested to in Justin Martyr and detailed in *The Apostolic Tradition* of Hippolytus. Gradually the time of preparation was associated with the number forty: Moses spent forty years preparing for his mission; the Israelites wandered in the wilderness for forty years; Jesus spent forty days in the wilderness. In addition, the congregation joined the catechumenate in preparation, making it a special time for the whole church.

Scriptural readings and sermons during this period highlight the ministry of Jesus, especially His teaching in parables and His miracles. Special emphasis is given to the growing conflict of Jesus with His opposition and the preparation He Himself made for His death. The church joins Jesus in the recalling of this significant period of His life.

The period of Lent was gradually marked off by *Ash Wednesday*[13] at its beginning and *Holy Week*[14] at its ending. The beginnings of Ash Wednesday lie in obscurity. It was in use by the fifth century, and the meaning of it was derived from the use of ashes, a penitential symbol originating in the Old Testament and used in the church as early as the second century to symbolize repentance. The formula used for the imposition of ashes is based on Genesis 3:19: "Remember man, that you are dust and into dust you shall return." These words signal the beginning of a time dedicated to prayer, repentance, self-examination, and renewal. It ends in the celebration of the Easter resurrection when the minister cries, "Christ is risen!"

Before Easter, however, the church enacts the final week of Jesus. Although traces of a special emphasis during this week can be found in the third century, Holy Week was developed in the fourth century by the Christians of Jerusalem. The essential feature of Holy Week was to link the final events of Jesus' life with the days and the places where they occurred. Jerusalem, of course, was the one place in the world where this could actually happen. For here were the very sites of His last days. As pilgrims poured into Jerusalem, the church of Jerusalem evolved this structure to provide them with a meaningful cycle of worship. The worship services that were developed during this time are still used today in some churches. The use of the ancient Maundy Thursday service, the Good Friday veneration of the cross, and the Saturday night vigil make Holy Week the most special time of worship in the entire Christian calendar.

The aim of Holy Week was to make the life of Christ real for the worshiper. Enacting His last days and entering into His experience was a way of offering worship to Him. This liturgical realism made a significant impact on the Christian world. It served as a primary impetus toward the development of the church year as a way of manifesting the entire life of Christ in the life of the worshiper throughout the year.

Easter. The Easter season stands out as the time of joy and celebration.[15] Unlike Lent, which is sober in tone, Easter is the time to focus on resurrection joy. Augustine said:

> These days after the Lord's Resurrection form a period, not of labor, but of peace and joy. That is why there is no fasting and we pray standing, which is a sign of resurrection. This practice is observed at the altar on all Sundays, and the Alleluia is sung, to indicate that our future occupation is to be no other than the praise of God.[16]

The preaching of this period calls attention to the postresurrection appearances of Jesus and the preparation of His disciples to witness to the kingdom. It is fifty days in length.

Pentecost. The term *Pentecost* means fifty, referring now to the fifty days after Passover when the Jews celebrated the Feast of Weeks, the agricultural festival that celebrated the end of the barley harvest and the beginning of the wheat harvest.[17] In the Christian calendar the term is associated with the coming of the Holy Spirit and the beginning of the early church. Possible evidence of Pentecost in the Christian church goes back to Tertullian and Eusebius in the beginning of the third century. More dateable, however, are the references mady by Etheria to the celebration of Pentecost in Jerusalem during the latter part of the fourth century. Liturgist A. A. McArthur describes the event in these words:

> Just after midday the people gathered at the sanctuary on the traditional site of the ascension, and the passages about the ascension from the gospel and Acts were read. A great candlelight procession came to the city in the darkness, and it was eventually about midnight when the people returned to their homes.[18]

Pentecost is the longest season in the church, having twenty-seven or twenty-eight Sundays, lasting until Advent. Preaching during this time should concentrate on the development of the early church with an emphasis on the power of the Holy Spirit in the ministry of the apostles and the writing of the New Testament literature.

The Weekly Cycle of Time

The weekly cycle of time, based on the church's observance of Sunday, is a highly complicated and somewhat controversial subject. Consequently, little more than the major outline of the relationship of Sunday to a Christian understanding of time can be given here. We will note the relationship between the Sabbath and Sunday and summarize the major interpretation of Sunday by the early Christians.

To begin, we ask how Sunday is related to the Sabbath. The biblical answer to this question is that the Sabbath is an Old Testament institution that, like the temple, pointed to Jesus Christ. This was the conviction of the early church. Therefore, Paul included the Sabbath day as "a shadow of the things that were to come; the reality . . . is found in Christ" (Col. 2:16–17).

In the Old Testament the Sabbath was a day of rest and it was the seventh day (Exod. 16:23, 26). In this sense the Sabbath was related to time. It was the symbol of sacred time as it looked to the future and to its fulfillment in something far greater than itself.

Christ, of course, was the fulfillment of the Sabbath (Matt. 12:1–13). He, himself, brought the rest that the Sabbath anticipated: "Come to me, all you who are weary and burdened, and I will give you rest" (Matt. 11:28). This was the theme of the seventh day that the author to Hebrews so eloquently developed (Heb. 4:1–11). He saw three "rests" in the economy of God: the rest after creation; the rest that Israel sought in the Promised Land; and the rest that is Jesus Christ. The Sabbath, therefore, had an eschatological character. It pointed to the future, to Jesus Christ its fulfillment. The Christian now lives in the Sabbath rest found in Jesus Christ.

Consequently, the Sabbath, like the temple, is an institution that was abolished. But the principle of rest, like the principle of God's presence in the temple, remains. The exterior practice of rest is now fulfilled in the interior rest in Jesus Christ. The Christian lives in the age of rest. Nevertheless, the Christian also has an external expression of inner rest, and this is manifested in Sunday observance.

Nevertheless, the primary reason for worship on Sunday is that Sunday is the day of the Resurrection. The early church gathered on this day, the Lord's day as they called it, in remembrance of Christ's resurrection. Every Sunday was Easter Day. On the other hand this day contained the potential for additional interpretations for three reasons: it was the first day of the Jewish week; it fell on the day of the sun; and it was the eighth day. An examination of the symbolic meaning attached to these three less obvious meanings shows how Sunday was related to the concept of time by the early Christians.[19]

Sunday was the first day of the Jewish week. Consequently, the early Christians regarded it as the anniversary of the creation of the world.[20] But Sunday was more than an anniversary because it represented the day that God began to create again—the beginning of the new creation. For that reason Sunday was also seen as a figure for the end of the first creation. As liturgist Jean Daniélou puts it: "On the sixth day creation was finished; on the seventh, God rested from all his works. But in the Gospel, the Word says: I have come to finish the work."[21] Consequently, Sunday also symbolizes the generation of the Word. All these concepts cluster around the notion of Sunday, the beginning and the end of the first creation. All these notions have to do with time and the meaning time has because of these events.

Second, Sunday was the day of the sun in the astrological calendar. The ancient Christians made no attempt to synthesize Sunday with the day of the sun. However, they did seize it as an opportunity to Christianize the pagans through a reinterpretation of the day of the sun in keeping with the motif of a new creation. Regarding this, Jerome wrote, "The day of the Lord, the day of the Resurrection, the day of the Christians is our day. And if it is called the day of the sun by the pagans, we willingly accept this name. For on this day arose the light, on this day shone forth the sun of justice."[22]

More important, however, is the notion of Sunday as the eighth day.[23] Although the origins of this notion are somewhat obscure, it appears to be of Christian origin, being found among the early church fathers. The meaning of the term appears to have an eschatological flavor. While the seventh day is a figure of rest, and the symbol of the first day is that of re-creation, the eighth day is the figure of the future world. It preserves the eschatological expectation of the early church, looking to the end of the present age and the beginning of the eternal age.

Even if one does not accept all the interpretations given to Sunday by the early church, the implication is obvious. It is a day that *marks time.* It is the end of one age, the beginning of the new, and an expectation of the eternal future. Consequently, worshiping on Sunday is not a mere coincidence; on this day the church enacts the Resurrection and thus reaffirms the meaning of the history of the world.

The Daily Cycle of Time

The daily cycle of prayer is rooted in the worship practices of the Old Testament where prayers were said at various times throughout the day.[24] We know that prayer at certain times was observed in the temple (1 Chron. 23:30) and that Daniel prayed three times a day (Dan. 6:10). The sense of marking the day with times of prayer was carried over into the early Christian community. Luke, in the book of Acts, informs us that "Peter and John were going up to the temple at the time of prayer—at three in the afternoon" (Acts 3:1), presumably to pray. Peter, Luke tells us later, "about noon . . . went up to pray" (Acts 10:9). Luke also emphasizes the occurrence of the coming of the Holy Spirit at the third hour (9 A.M.): "These men are not drunk, as you suppose. It's only nine in the morning" (Acts 2:15). The time orientation of these important events at nine, noon, and three in the afternoon must be more than a mere coincidence—they have to do with marking time in a religious way.

There is, however, no direct evidence in the New Testament of a community-oriented, organized daily worship. Nevertheless, it is plausible that early Christians, particularly Jewish Christians who were accustomed to the habit of daily prayer, continued the practice of prayer at particular times of the day.

The most significant evidence of times for prayer in the pre-Nicene church comes from *The Apostolic Tradition* of Hippolytus. Because of allusions to times of prayer in the early fathers, we may assume the practice detailed by Hippolytus precedes his description and dates back perhaps to the middle of the second century. Here is the description of prayer from Hippolytus:

> If at the *third hour* thou art at home, pray then and give thanks to God; but if thou chance to be abroad at that hour, make thy prayer to God in thy heart. For *at that hour Christ was nailed to the tree;* therefore in the old (covenant) the law

commanded the showbread to be offered continually for a type of the body and blood of Christ, and commanded the sacrifice of the dumb lamb, which was a type of the perfect Lamb; for Christ is the Shepherd, and he is also the Bread that came down from heaven.

At the sixth hour likewise pray also, for, after Christ was nailed to the wood of the cross, *the day was divided* and there was a great darkness; wherefore let (the faithful) pray at that hour with an effectual prayer, likening themselves to the voice of him who prayed (and) caused all creation to become dark for the unbelieving Jews.

And at the *ninth hour* let a great prayer and a great thanksgiving be made, such as made the souls of the righteous ones, blessing the Lord, the God who does not lie, who was mindful of his saints and sent forth his Word to enlighten them. At that hour, therefore, *Christ poured forth from his pierced side water and blood,* and brought the rest of the time of that day with light to evening; so, when he fell asleep, by making the beginning of another day he completed the pattern of his resurrection.

Pray again before thy body rests on thy bed [emphases added].[25]

The unique feature of the prescription for prayer set forth by Hippolytus is *the interpretation of time through the events of Jesus' death.* He gives insight into the concept of time held by the ancient Christians. Time, this approach suggests, finds meaning through Jesus Christ, the center of all time.

This concept of time was the basis of later development in the noneucharistic prayer life of the church. This is especially seen in the development of matins and vespers and the more complicated series of daily prayers that characterized the monastic movement. This approach to prayer was used by the Christian community (with some modifications) for centuries.[26] After the Reformation, particularly through the influence of the Pietists, the concept of hours of prayer (especially morning and evening prayer) shifted into the home. More recently the same notion is stressed in the idea of daily devotions, morning and evening. Unfortunately, however, we have lost the sense of marking time Christianly through our prayer.

Conclusion

Time, like space and sound, can play a vital part in worship. Here are the principles of time that need to be kept in mind:

1. The Christian understanding of time has a *center*. The center from which all time is understood is the Christ-event.
2. Center time is marked by special *kairos* events—Christ's birth, manifestation, death, and resurrection; Pentecost; and Christ's coming again. These events give meaning to all of time.
3. We also live in *chronos* time—the sequence of time between the resurrection and the consummation. This time is characterized by fulfillment and anticipation.
4. The application of *kairos* time to *chronos* time in worship gives all time a transcendent meaning and brings every moment of life into relationship with Christ, the center of meaning.
5. The application of *kairos* time to *chronos* time in our day-to-day living is also expressed in the meaning of daily hours, the significance of the weekly cycle, and the importance of the yearly marking of time.

Chapter 14

Worship
and Sound

The theological principle for sound in worship is the same that governs the use of space and time: All creation was made to praise God, but because all of creation was subjected to futility by the fall, creation may be used as the instrument of Satan. However, because of the redemption in Christ all creation may be employed in the service of praise to the Father. So it is with sound. It is a legitimate and desirable way to express praise to God. Sound belongs to God by way of redemption.

This chapter will discuss the various types of sound used in Christian worship; it also surveys the use of sound and music throughout church history.

THE ROLE OF SOUND IN WORSHIP

No apology needs to be set forth for the use of sound in the church. Nevertheless, a few words about the significance of sound in worship are in order.

The Purpose of Sound in Worship

First, sound witnesses to the transcendence of God and to His work of salvation hymned in the heavens. The apostle John describes this sound as a new song (Rev. 5:9–13).

175

Second, sound in worship draws the earthly worshiper into the heavens to stand with the heavenly throng as they offer praise to the Father. This posture of worship was recognized by the early church especially in the singing of the *Sanctus*.

Third, sound induces an attitude of worship. It elicits from deep within a person the sense of awe and mystery that accompanies a meeting with God. In this way sound releases an inner nonrational part of our being that words with their more rational and discursive meanings cannot unearth and set free to utter praise.[1]

Fourth, sound in worship affirms the corporate unity of the body of Christ because it is something that the entire congregation does together. Ignatius, in one of his many musical metaphors, left the following image of the church unified in song:

> Wherefore your accord and harmonious love is a hymn to Jesus Christ. Yes, one and all, you should form yourself into a choir, so that, in perfect harmony and taking your pitch from God, you may sing in unison and with one voice to the Father through Jesus Christ.[2]

Singing together brings out the essential mystery of the church as a *fellowship*. The unity and diversity of the church are brought together in a unique way through song as noted by John Chrysostom (A.D. 380):

> The psalm which occurred just now in the office blended all voices together, and caused one single fully harmonious chant to arise; young and old, rich and poor, women and men, slaves and free, all sang one single melody. . . . All the inequalities of social life are here banished. Together we make up a single choir in perfect equality of rights and of expression whereby earth imitates heaven. Such is the noble character of the Church.[3]

Purposes That Various Kinds of Sound Fulfill

We sometimes fail to recognize that there are a variety of sounds (and silence) in the course of a service of worship. Each of these sounds may be looked on as a means of support for the words or actions that are a vital part of worship. Because worship is an action, it takes on the dimension of a congregational performance. Consequently, the moods and meaning of each part of worship are conveyed in the sound made as well as in the words spoken or the actions carried out by the congregation.

Following the sound of ordinary speech, the next type of "rhythmo-musical recitation" is called "proclamation." By this means a message is conveyed to God by the congregation or from God through the designated member of the congregation. These tones occur in prayer, in the reading of Scripture, in prefaces, blessings, benedictions, and the sermon. Although everyday speech is used, elements of rhythm and melody are present as a way of proclaiming the meaning and urgency of the words.[4] Tones that betray listlessness and apathy convey a sense of tedium and boredom. On the other hand a tone of enthusiasm and clarity creates a sense of excitement, importance, and relevance.

Second, rhythmic cadences with a formalized tone pattern aid the spirit of meditation. The sound itself allows the worshiper to savor the meaning of the text. This is the sound used in singing the Lord's Prayer, singing responses to the intercessions, and especially in singing the psalms. Here the sound fits the words in such a way that one worships in the unity of word and sound. For example, in the early church, psalms were sung in a responsorial manner so that the congregation repeated the refrain (and sound) of the cantor, allowing the psalm in an antiphonal manner to be sung twice.[5]

A third sound is known as "chant." In this musical expression the shape of the sound evolves from the words and refrains. Chant is a natural way to pronounce the words musically. In this way the full meaning of the text is always the focal point of interest, not the sound itself. This musical expression is highly conducive to Christian worship.[6] It was derived from the Old Testament and was used in the early Christian congregations in the reading of Scripture and singing of responses.

The acclamation is a fourth kind of sound. In this action the vocal activity itself is of final importance. For this reason acclamations are generally retained in their original language of Hebrew, Greek, or Latin. The acclamation is like the cry of help (e.g., Maranatha, Hosanna), the prayer recognizing one's sinfulness (*Kyrie eleison*), the heartfelt response affirming the Word of God or the action of prayer (Amen) or the joyous response of a people to salvation (Alleluia).[7]

In the hymn the musical element becomes extremely important. Here the melody, because of its rhythm and cadences, leads the worshiper. In the hymn the worshiper is drawn into a unified act of offering vocal praise to the Father.

Finally, there is sound without words, what was known as *jubilus* in the early church.[8] Initially this was developed from the last vowel of the alleluia that was continued spontaneously by the worshiping community. In our time the *jubilus* is fulfilled by charismatic singing in the spirit or by the more formal sound of organ music or that of instruments played by musicians and offered to God as an act of worship.

A HISTORY OF SOUND IN WORSHIP

A brief survey of sound in the church will demonstrate how sound has been offered to God as an act of worship and serves as an aid in the application of sound to the contemporary church.

The New Testament Church

In the New Testament the distinction between speaking and singing was far less pronounced than it is today. Neither Hebrew nor Greek had a separate word for singing in distinction from speaking. (Nevertheless the early foundations of what later came to be known as singing are clearly evident in the New Testament church.)

The roots of sound in the early church are found in the Old Testament heritage. Among these are (1) the monodic system of chanting with cadences, (2) congregational song with repetition as in the antiphon and responsory, and (3) elaborate melodies on a single vowel (as in the Alleluia). In the Jewish synagogue these styles of sound were used in the scriptural readings, the *shema*, the prayers, and the psalms.[9]

The New Testament provides ample evidence of sound in worship. Paul admonished the Ephesians: "Speak to one another with psalms, hymns and spiritual songs. Sing and make music in your heart to the Lord" (5:19; see also 1 Cor. 14:15; Acts 16:25; Col. 3:16; James 5:13). In the New Testament itself there are a number of identifiable lyrics such as the *Amen*, the *Alleluia*, the *Holy, Holy, Holy*, and other hymns to the Lamb in Revelation. There are also a number of canticles in Luke that have become major musical statements in Christian worship. See Luke 1:28–29, 42–45 *(Ave Maria)*; Luke 1:46–55 *(Magnificat)*; Luke 1:68–79 *(Benedictus)*; Luke 2:14 *(Gloria in excelsis)*; Luke 2:29–32 *(Nunc*

Dimittis). Besides these, other passages such as John 1:14 and Philippians 2:6–11 have been identified as hymns of the early church.[10]

The Ancient Church

During this period there were frequent references to music in the church as well as a number of hymn texts. The most interesting feature of this period is the rise of syllabic tendencies of hymnody. This gave music a more popular character and emphasized the text rather than the sound itself. As a result, many hymns were written to spread teaching, both heretical and orthodox. This was particularly true of Arianism (the denial of the diety of Christ) that spread its heresy by marching through the streets singing its viewpoint in a popularized form of music.

During the fourth and fifth centuries, when the liturgy was developing along a more elaborate Roman and Byzantine style, music in the church became more highly developed. The most important development during this period was the spread of the responsorial psalm. A soloist sang the psalm and the congregation responded at the end of each verse with a refrain chosen from the psalm. The psalms, and this way of singing them, became exceedingly popular throughout the Christian world. They were sung not only between Scripture readings but also at the Eucharist, during vigils, and in morning and evening prayer. They were also sung in the home and fields. These psalms became a vital spiritual force in the lives of many Christians.[11]

Another important development was the rise of hymnody encouraged by Ambrose, bishop of Milan. Ambrose, known as the "father of hymnody in the Western church" developed a large body of church music based on four scales that became known as the Ambrosian chant. Two centuries later, Gregory the Great added four more scales to the Ambrosian system, creating what came to be known as the Gregorian chant.[12]

In the meantime the responsorial psalm underwent significant changes: the assembly was divided into two choirs or choruses that repeated the refrains. Eventually the refrain was no longer repeated after each verse. Rather, the verses were recited alternately by two choirs so that singing became the privilege of the monks and clerics, and the congregation was put in the position of watching and listening.

The Medieval Church

The musical developments of the ancient church were expanded and became more sophisticated in the medieval church. This was particularly true of the chant and overall hymnology.[13]

The medieval church produced a number of hymns that are still used today: Gregory the Great (540–604), "Father We Praise Thee"; Theodulph of Orleans (ca. 750–821), "All Glory, Laud, and Honor"; Bernard of Clairvaux (1090–1153), "Jesus, the Very Thought of Thee" and "O Sacred Head, Now Wounded"; an anonymous twelfth-century writer, "O Come, O Come, Emmanuel." The blot on the medieval record is that the singing of hymns in the church by the lay person was banned. The Council of Constance in 1415, which ordered the burning of the Bohemian reformer John Hus at the stake, also decreed: If laymen are forbidden to preach and interpret the scripture, much more are they forbidden to sing publicly in the church.[14]

The most important contribution to church music in the medieval period is the development of the Gregorian chant. Formed by the chanters of the eighth century, Gregorian chant has been called "the greatest revolution in the history of Christian singing."[15] It spread rapidly throughout the entire West and gave a beauty, dignity, and solemnity to the liturgy of the church.

The value of medieval music is, of course, in its professionalism. The music was indeed beautiful and inspiring to listen to, but the fact that it was taken away from the people and put into the category of performance was undesirable for worshp. Worship was no longer the action of the congregation. It was now the work of a privileged few.

The Reformation

One of the most important contributions made by the Reformers in worship was the restoration of congregational music. The earliest Protestant hymnbooks were two that were published by the Bohemian Brethren (later known as the Moravians), one in 1501 (containing eighty hymns) and the other in 1505 (containing four hundred hymns). In 1522 these Brethren contacted Luther, who received them warmly and later used some of their hymns in his own hymnbook.[16]

Luther's influence on music in worship was revolutionary. He himself was a music lover and well trained in music. He also had the gift of writing clearly and creating a music close to the hearts of the common people. His work was so effective that one of his enemies wrote, "Luther's songs have damned more souls than all his books and speeches."[17]

Luther's contribution was in the area of chorale music. His hymns were characterized by "a plain melody, a strong harmony and a stately rhythm."[18] This type of music continued to develop in the church and was perfected by Johann Sebastian Bach (1685–1750).[19]

Calvin's contribution to music in the church was the restoration of psalm singing. For him hymns were man-made, whereas the psalms were the inspired Word of God. At first Calvin permitted only unison singing (as opposed to Luther's advocation of singing in parts) and rejected the use of accompanying instruments as worldly (he later changed his mind). Calvinists produced a number of psalm books. The best known work is *The Genevan Psalter* (1562). It was the major psalm book of the Reformation and regarded by many as the most famous book of praise produced by the church. There were at least 1,000 editions and it was translated into many languages. Other well-known books include the *Bay Psalm Book* (Boston, 1640) in America and the *Scottish Psalter* (1650) used by the Scottish Presbyterian churches.[20]

The Modern Period

The birth of modern hymnody is associated with the genius and influence of Isaac Watts (1674–1748). He reacted against the limited use of psalm singing, which he believed had grown cold and lifeless. Furthermore, he was convinced that the slavish reproduction of psalms was frequently not in the spirit of the gospel. So he set out to write hymns that reflected the devotion and encouragement of the Psalms combined with the New Testament fulfillment and joy of the resurrection.[21] He wrote:

> It is necessary to divest *David* and *Asaph* etc. of every other character but that of a *psalmist* and a *saint*, and to make them *Always speak the common sense of a Christian*. When the Psalmist describes Religion by the *Fear* of God, I have often joined *Faith and Love* to it. Where he talks of sacrificing *Goats and Bullocks*, I rather chuse to mention the sacrifice of *Christ*,

the Lamb of God. When he *attends the Ark with shouting in Zion,* I sing the *Ascension of my Saviour into heaven,* or *His presence in His Church on earth* (italics his).[22]

An example of this method is found in his use of Psalm 72:

> *Jesus shall reign where'er the sun*
> *Doth his successive journeys run.*

Through the influence of Isaac Watts, who wrote more than six hundred hymns, the eighteenth century became the first age of hymn singing in England. Watts was followed by the work of John and Charles Wesley, two of the most prolific hymn writers of all time. With the Wesleys, however, there came a noticeable shift toward the subjective. For the most part, singing in the church had been God-centered. The emphasis was on the perfection of God, the glory of His works, the graciousness of His acts in Jesus Christ. Now, however, with the whole tenor of Christianity in revivalism shifting toward subjective experience, the use of sound was put to the service of personal experience and evangelism. This shift is clearly discernable in the second preface to the *Collection of Hymns for the Use of the People Called Methodists* (1780). Here Wesley wrote:

> The hymns are not carelessly jumbled together, but carefully ranged under proper heads, according to the experience of real Christians. So that the book is, in effect, a little body of experimental and practical divinity.[23]

Although the revival songs of the eighteenth century were concerned with personal experience, they still retained a healthy objective emphasis on God. Many hymns such as "Love Divine All Loves Excelling" (Charles Wesley), "The God of Abraham Praise" (Thomas Olivers), "All Hail the Power of Jesus' Name" (Edward Perronet), and "Glorious Things of Thee Are Spoken" (John Newton) exhibit a good balance between the subjective and the objective.[24]

The trend toward a preoccupation with the subjective experience is exhibited in many (not all) of the gospel songs that came into use in the late nineteenth century. These songs have a great popular appeal and have been widely used in revival meetings. They frequently contain references to "I" and "me" and dwell on the state of personal feeling. Fanny Crosby is probably the best-known author of gospel songs with her "Rescue the Perishing" and many others. Other well-known gospel songs include "Just As I Am Without One Plea" (Charlotte Elliott), "Take My Life and Let It Be" (Frances Ridley Havergal), and "Jesus Loves Me, This I Know" (Anna B. Warner).[25]

Conclusion

This brief survey of the theological meaning of sound and its use in history may be summarized in the following principles:

1. Sound is a means through which the church in worship joins the heavenly song, offers otherwise unutterable praises, and experiences the unity of the body of Christ.
2. Sound expresses the worship of proclamation, meditation, and praise and thus affects the attitude of the worshiper.
3. The use of music has undergone a number of significant changes throughout history. Consequently there are a variety of musical sounds in the church, many of which are reflective of particular historical periods or ethnic groups. Thus, the church has a rich depository of music from which to draw on for worship renewal.

Chapter 15

Worship
and the World

Worship practices must relate to the individual and corporate responsibility of Christians in the world. Worship is not to be regarded as an end in itself. The author of Hebrews made this clear by placing the following admonition in the context of worship: "Let us consider how we may spur one another on toward love and good deeds. Let us not give up meeting together, as some are in the habit of doing, but let us encourage one another—and all the more as you see the Day approaching" (Heb. 10:24-25). This same theme was expressed by Hippolytus in the concluding portion of his eucharistic liturgy when he added this terse but powerful admonition to a life of holiness and good works:

> And when these things are completed, let each one hasten
> to do good works, and to please God and to live aright, devoting
> himself to the church, practicing the things he has learned,
> advancing in the service of God.[1]

The point being made by both writers is that the church is to be "formed" by her worship. Because worship is an offering of self to God, worship demands commitment to a life lived according to the content and vision of worship.

In order to understand how worship relates to life in the

185

world, we must first understand the meaning of the word *world*. New Testament usages fall into two categories: (1) the world as a natural or physical sphere; and (2) the world as the powers of evil.[2] The former refers to creation and recognizes the inherent goodness of the world. The latter speaks of the power of evil that exercises its influence in the world. Paul identified this evil world in the following statement: "For our struggle is not against flesh and blood, but against the rulers, against the authorities, against the powers of this dark world and against the spiritual forces of evil in heavenly realms" (Eph. 6:12).

A discussion of the relationship that worship sustains to the world must take into account these two levels of meaning. With this in mind I wish to argue for a threefold relationship between worship and the world: (1) worship identifies with the world; (2) worship is against the world; and (3) worship transforms the world.

WORSHIP IDENTIFIES WITH THE WORLD

To suggest that worship is identified with the world is to speak of the world in terms of the natural creation. There are a number of ways in which this is true.

First, worship occurs in a particular time and place. There is a paradox that lies at the very heart of worship—the paradox between the temporal and the eternal. Worship has to do with the eternal, the transcendent, the other world. In worship we are like John—momentarily transferred into the heavens. We join the eternal throng of worshipers and offer with them our songs of praise and adoration. But this takes place in the body, in the world, the arena of God's saving activity. Thus, as God entered the historical sphere to work out our salvation and yet remained in the heavens, so we enter into the eternal sphere to worship and yet remain on earth.

Second, this worship is acted out in a physical way. It is people who worship. We act out our worship according to a certain order or ritual. Our senses of sight, hearing, touch, taste, and smell are engaged in what we do.

Third, earthly worship is a meal (the Lord's Supper). The meal belongs to the realm of spoken and acted-out imagery. It is a sign of the relationship that exists between man and God. Furthermore the meal points to the dependence of creation on God. Man thanks God in the context of the meal for food and drink. Also, the meal expresses the positive relationship that exists between the worshiper and the material creation. It contains and fosters no dichotomy between something as mundane as eating and drinking and the high and lofty spiritual meaning of that physical act.

Fourth, worship heightens the Christian's consciousness of the problems of the world. This is particularly true in the area of prayer. The church prays not only for the needs of its members but also for global needs. Prayer for the hungry, needy, orphaned, widowed, deprived, and displaced as well as for minorities and those against whom injustices are perpetrated are forever on the lips of the church. But to be effective, these prayers must be translated into action!

WORSHIP IS AGAINST THE WORLD

To suggest that worship is against the world is to refer to the world as the powers of spiritual wickedness.

In the first place, worship expresses a transcendent allegiance. The recurring references to the Father, Son, and Holy Spirit that appear in the doxologies, benedictions, prayers of the people, and eucharistic prayer acknowledge God as transcendent and beyond His created order. This allegiance is further expressed in the Lord's Prayer: "Our Father in heaven." In worship we proclaim that this world is not all that is. There is another realm to which this world is subject. We worship the triune God who has authority over the realm in which we live.

Second, worship celebrates Christ's victory over the world of sin and death. Paul teaches us that Christ has "disarmed the powers and authorities, he made a public spectacle of them, triumphing over them by the cross" (Col. 2:15). Worship enacts this victory and celebrates it. Consequently, all the liturgical prayers of the early church are careful to include the prayer of thanksgiving and its specific mention of Christ's victory over evil. This motif is clearly set forth in the eucharistic prayer of Hippolytus:

> And when he was betrayed to voluntary suffering that he might destroy death, and break the bonds of the devil, and tread down hell, and shine upon the righteous, and fix the limit, and manifest the resurrection. . . .[3]

Third, worship anticipates the judgment of evil. This motif is already indicated in the words of Jesus, "I will not drink of this fruit of the vine from now on until that day when I drink it anew with you in my Father's kingdom" (Matt. 26:29). The future judgment against sin is already present in every celebration of the Eucharist. Paul was clear about this in his letter to the Corinthians. Their sins of division and gluttony had already been judged in the Eucharist. For by eating unworthily they were eating and drinking judgment on themselves (see 1 Cor. 11:27–34). But each Eucharist antici- pates the future and points to the end of the world as well. In this way the Eucharist foreshadows the complete destruction of evil (Rev. 20) and the new heavens and the new earth (Rev. 21–22). This motif is also seen in the liturgical prayer of the early church, *Maranatha* (Our Lord, come).

WORSHIP TRANSFORMS THE WORLD

The consideration that worship transforms the world has to do with both usages of the word *world*. Worship is a vision of what the world will be without the influence of evil. As a projection of the application of Christ's work to the entire creation, it summons up images of the world to come.

In the first place, worship is a vision of the new creation. This dimension of worship is already indicated in Revelation 4 and 5. Here, in this imagery is the stuff of eternity, the ongoing worship of God's creation. This is emphasized on earth through the sanctifica- tion of nature: the use of space, the stained-glass windows, the stuff of the building (wood, brick, stone, mortar, etc.)—all represent the creation set aside for worship, transforming the present into an image of the future. Here nature is doing what it was created to do—give glory to God. Man too is employed in service, doing what he was created to do. This image of man and nature expressing the transformation of the world in worship is expressed in these words of Norman Pittenger in his work *Life as Eucharist:*

> In worship the right relationship between God and his creation is manifested. The Eucharist shows us the utter dependence of all things on God, the adoration of God through the created order (as in the *Sanctus*), where through men's lips and by their lives they are ready to kneel in his presence, to sing his praise, and to offer to him their oblation of love and service. The created order is here doing what it is meant to do; for heaven and earth are united, living and departed are at one, and the creation is ordered for its own great good and for God's great glory. Man is

in his place, nourished by the life that comes from God; he is man as God means him to be, the crown of the creation and the image and likeness of God himself. All that he does is related to God as he meets men in Christ and unites them with himself. Sin and failure are forgiven, strength is imparted, a redeemed and transfigured cosmos is both signified and present. Whenever the Body of Christ gathers its members for eucharistic worship, all this is seen, as men worship God the Father through Christ the Son in the power of the Holy Spirit.[4]

Second, worship reveals the action that the body of Christ must take to participate in the transformation of the world. This action is hinted at in the Lord's Prayer: "Your will be done on earth as it is in heaven." There is a place where God's will is fully carried out—heaven. The radical side of worship is clearly indicated as the worshiper prays that the earth may become a place where the will of God is also fulfilled.

In this sense the Eucharist contains a radical side. The Old Testament roots of the Eucharist lie in the liberation of the people of Israel from Egypt. This sense of liberation is also carried through in the Eucharist. For the Eucharist is the symbol of the potential liberation of the whole creation in Christ.[5]

Paul tells us that the entire creation (man as well) "was subjected to frustration, not by its own choice, but by the will of the one who subjected it, in hope that the creation itself will be liberated from its bondage to decay and brought into the glorious freedom of the children of God" (Rom. 8:20–21). The Eucharist is the sign of this liberation. The elements have a twofold reference. Both bread and wine represent redemption in Christ. When these two images are brought together, the relationship between redemption and creation are clearly seen in worship. The redemption accomplished by Christ transforms the entire creation.

This transformation first takes effect within the worshiping community, which may be called the eucharistic community. The vision of the earliest Christian community is one of a people who take the social implication of the Eucharist seriously. Theologian Tissa Balasuriya comments on that early Christian community in these words:

> The early Christians thus understood the deep meaning of the symbol instituted by Jesus. Its social impact was the main

criterion of its value and credibility. That is why the early Christians were so acceptable to many, especially the poor, and so detested by some of the powerful, particularly the exploiters. Christianity was then a dynamic movement of human liberation from selfishness and exploitation. All were to be equal in the believing community and this was symbolized by the eucharistic meal.[6]

The question for us, of course, is a recovery of the social implication of the Eucharist. It was lost in the medieval period when the Eucharist was turned into an action to be observed. The reformers tended to interpret the Eucharist in terms of personal devotion, a tradition still found among many Protestants (and also Catholics) today. More recently, in the modern era the social and eschatological dimensions of the Eucharist have been lost in the notion of the Eucharist as a memorial. Contemporary liturgical scholarship, however, is helping today's church return to the full implications of the Eucharist through the study of ancient practices.

Conclusion

The point that we must always keep before us is that worship has a horizontal as well as a vertical dimension. It is important for us to enact the work of Christ as an offering of praise and thanksgiving to the Father. But it is equally important that we *act on* what we have enacted. If we really praise God for the redemption of the world through Jesus Christ, then we must do as Paul instructs: "Offer your bodies as living sacrifices, holy and pleasing to God—which is your spiritual worship. Do not conform any longer to the pattern of the world, but be transformed by the renewing of your mind" (Rom. 12:1–2). The pattern of this world is one of injustice, inequality, discrimination, war, hate, immorality, and all those human abuses that the New Testament and the early church fathers describe as the way of death (see Rom. 1:21–32; Gal. 5:19–21; Col. 3:5–9; *Didache*, 5–6). The true worship of God inevitably leads the people of God into positive social action. Our calling is to worship God not only with our lips but also with our lives.

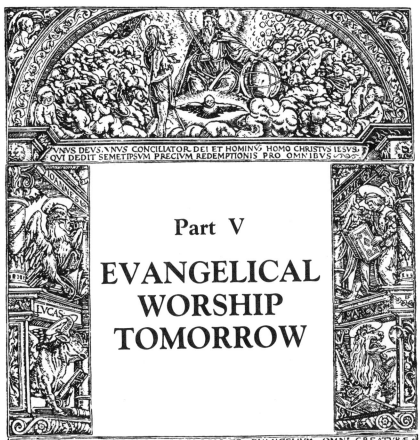

Part V

EVANGELICAL WORSHIP TOMORROW

Chapter 16

Nine Proposals

I have presented the material of the preceding sections to my students at Wheaton College in a course entitled "The History and Theology of Worship." This past year I asked the seventy students enrolled in the course to suggest how this material might be useful to evangelical Christians. Representing many different worship traditions including Bible churches, free churches, and independent churches, as well as Baptists, Presbyterians, Lutherans, Reformed, Brethren, Methodists, Episcopalians, and Charismatics, they made a number of suggestions, which I have summarized in the following proposals and pass on to evangelical worshipers.

1. *Educate the people.* There was a complete consensus that very little is known about worship in many of our evangelical churches. For this reason, it was regarded as a matter of priority that Evangelicals study the biblical, historical, and theological sources of Christian worship. Churches should sponsor lectures and discussion on worship and should bring pastors from other traditions to share their understanding of worship. Christians should visit other congregations from time to time. A genuine renewal of worship cannot proceed out of guess work, but must be accompanied by the labor of study and constant prayer for God's direction.

193

2. *Acknowledge the distinction between services for worship and services for teaching.* It was agreed that the sermon held the prominent place in evangelical churches and that its thrust was either for teaching or evangelism. Very few students felt that their home church actually experienced the enactment of Christ's work or had a sense of worship as an offering of praise. It was suggested, therefore, that evangelical churches choose one weekly time of meeting to concentrate on worship. Some thought this should be on Sunday morning, others on Sunday night, and a few suggested a week-day evening. Other meeting times could therefore be set aside especially for teaching or evangelism. This approach has the advantage of achieving balance.

3. *Do not disregard the tradition of your denomination.* The students generally recognized that each denomination retained the most basic elements of ancient worship: Scripture, sermon, prayer, music, and the Lord's Supper. Consequently, most agreed that a satisfactory worship could be attained without doing violence to the currently accepted structures. By understanding worship, each congregation would be free to develop existing forms to a more heightened communal experience of praise.

4. *Orient worship toward God rather than human beings.* Many students felt that the worship of their church was more oriented toward human beings and their experience than toward God. They pointed to the current trend in Christian music that emphasizes a near narcissistic self-interest and to the entertainment approach in worship that attracts the crowds but fails to lead them into the praise of God's person and work. For this reason more care should be given to the planning of the service so that a vertical focus be regained. This could be accomplished by the use of more God-oriented hymns, the singing of the psalms, an acknowledgment of sin, a confession of faith, and the use of the Lord's Prayer.

5. *Restore a sense of awe and reverence, mystery and transcendence.* It was agreed that a frivolous attitude too frequently appears in the social chit-chat before the service, in overextended announcements, and in too casual an atmosphere projected by the minister. The key to changing this lies in the attitude and actions of the minister. The demeanor of his voice and body language can create a sense of the holy. The congregation must then follow his lead and act with a sense of hushed silence, a reverential awe, an

appropriate fear. The sense of mystery can also be communicated in the design of the worship space, the location of the people, the use of lighting, the sense of time (use of the church year), and the proper use of music.

6. *Recover a christocentric focus through enactment.* Man-centered worship not only fails to focus on God but also fails to reenact the Christ-event as an offering of praise and thanksgiving to the Father. This christocentric focus of worship may be recovered through a recognition that God's work through Christ is proclaimed through recitation (reading of Scripture and preaching) and drama (the Lord's Supper). A focus on Christ may also be made more prominent in the prayers and music. It is important that the worshipers leave worship with a sense of having been confronted again with the work of Christ on their behalf as well as the claim of Christ on their entire life. In this sense worship as an encounter with the person and work of Jesus Christ is accomplished. The most strategic way to accomplish this is through Christ-centered sermons and a more frequent use of the Lord's Supper.

7. *Restore congregational involvement in worship.* It is a matter of concern that worship in many places does not engage the full congregation. Rather, it is something that the pastor and the choir do while the "audience" watches and listens, occasionally standing and singing. If worship is an action done by the entire congregation and is offered to God as a communal act, then more attention must be given to the involvement of the entire congregation in worship. There are a number of ways congregational action can be restored. For example, the leader or the worship committee should consider reintroducing some of the following: the salutation, the use of lay readers for the Scripture lessons, the congregational response to Scripture, the congregational prayers of intercession, the kiss of peace, the *Sursum corda*, the *Sanctus*, antiphonal singing, and varied ways of serving communion (e.g., have the people walk to the communion table to receive). All of this ought to be done, of course, in the full knowledge that these are signs of congregational action.

8. *Attain spontaneity with the proper balance on form and freedom.* Congregational worship implies a degree of spontaneity rather than a wooden ritualistic response. An overemphasis on form or spontaneity can lead either to the error of ritualism or to chaos. A balance is needed. Form is maintained through a pre-

determined structure that guides the experience of the worshiper from the invocation to the benediction. Spontaneity is accomplished by allowing for the freedom to offer praise or prayer in the context of the form. Exactly how this is done ought to be left to each congregation and will more than likely depend on the particular tradition of the church. A time for praise, if handled well, can be a lifting experience. A time for brief statements of personal prayer can be easily worked into the congregational prayer. The point that needs to be made as these details are worked out by each congregation is that order ought to be the servant of spontaneity, not its enemy. The worshipers who learn and practice this principle will recover a dynamic sense of worship as an offering of praise and thanksgiving by the community of God's people.

9. *Restore the relationship of worship to all of life.* Worship is not an isolated aspect of the Christian life, but the center from which all of life is understood and experienced. For this reason Evangelicals ought to give careful consideration to the recovery of the church year (i.e., the most basic seasons of the year), to a more thoughtful use of space (e.g., the location of the pulpit, table, and the arrangement of the people), to a full range of music (i.e., draw from the tradition of the entire church), and to a more concentrated effort to engage the senses of sight, sound, taste, smell, and hearing. They should try to make people more conscious of their social responsibility. In these ways the redemption of creation, the history of God's people, and the role of the church in the world are made more clear in and through worship.

Conclusion

Clearly worship renewal does not consist of moving chairs in a circle, rearranging the order of worship, or finding new gimmicks. The heart of worship renewal is a recovery of the power of the Holy Spirit who enables the congregation to offer praise and thanksgiving to God. The value of studying the history and theology of worship is that it provides us with insights into the work of the Holy Spirit in the past and allows us to be open to His work in the present. In this way the Holy Spirit may lead us into ways of worship that are continuous with the historic witness of worship given to the church throughout its history in the world, and at the same time He may lead us into the discovery of new forms and patterns that meet the needs of people in our day.

Chapter 17

Three Models

Throughout its history Christianity has been in the process of spreading from one culture to another. This pattern of growth and development has not been without its problems. One of the major issues that has confronted the church again and again is that of contextualization. To what extent, one must ask, does the theology, worship, and practice of the church accommodate itself to the prevailing culture?

In an attempt such as this to relate the history of Christian worship to the contemporary evangelical culture, we face the problem of contextualization. What from the past is indispensable to worship? What in the present may be legitimately used in worship? The following are four basic principles that may be used to regulate our approach to contemporary worship renewal.

BASIC PRINCIPLES OF WORSHIP RENEWAL

1. *Christian worship must be rooted in the Scripture.* The Scripture of the Old and New Testament is the major source and final authority for matters of worship. Within its pages, as we have seen, the early patterns of Christian worship that emphasize the Word, the Lord's Supper, hymns, benedictions, and doxologies are found.

2. *The central focus of Christian worship is the work of Jesus Christ.* The event that informs and gives shape to the content and form of Christian worship is the birth, life, death, resurrection, and consummation of Jesus Christ. Worship praises the Father for the work of redemption accomplished by the Son and reenacts this work through the Word and the Lord's Supper.

3. *The church has established the basic theology and practice of worship.* The Holy Spirit has given the church the gift of understanding and has led the church into the development of universally accepted elements of worship that are rooted in the biblical and theological understanding of worship. The fixed content of Christian worship is:

a. the structure of Word and Lord's Supper,
b. the adornment of doxologies, benedictions, prayers, confessions of faith, and acclamations of praise, and
c. a sense of time, space, sound, and relationship to the world.

The church contains a rich deposit of worship resources that can be translated into all new cultural situations as the church grows and spreads.

4. *The manner in which the fixed content of worship is translated into a given situation is relative.* Many variables of worship are determined by the cultural context. How one sits, what kind of music is played, and whether the service is spontaneous or highly formal are of secondary importance. Therefore, though worship always expresses the fixed content, it will vary from place to place.

MODELS OF WORSHIP

In view of the above four principles as well as the nine proposals suggested in the previous chapter, my students proposed three basic models of worship suitable to evangelical Christians. These suggestions are only illustrations and are offered as guides that congregations may wish to use. Each congregation may want to modify or change these models. For lack of better terms they will be called free worship, planned worship, and formal worship. In each one the Lord's Supper has been included.

Free Worship

Free worship is most applicable for small groups (perhaps the house-church movement; small rural churches; small congregations that meet in firehalls, restored garages, etc.) in which the accent is on the church as a community of pilgrim people. It can also be adaptable to larger groups or to weekday house gatherings of a larger church.

ORDER OF SERVICE

Preparation
Hymns of Praise
Prayers of Intercession
Scripture Reading
Sermon
Response of Accountability
Communion
Benediction

Preparation. There is a definite desire among Christians to have a time of quietness and personal preparation before public worship begins. This may be a time for prayer, reading of Scripture, or personal confession.

Hymns of Praise. This could be a time of hymn-sermons similar to the Moravian approach where hymns were sung in continuity without announcement. This approach allows for a degree of spontaneity, as any person may choose to begin a hymn.

At this time the congregation could also learn some of the ancient hymns such as the *Magnificat* and the *Gloria in excelsis Deo,* as well as some of the majestic hymns of Thomas Aquinas, Bernard of Clairvaux, and hymns of the English revival. There is also a renewed emphasis on psalm singing, with many new arrangements of the Psalms and other portions of Scripture. Congregations should avoid gospel songs and music that emphasizes "me and my experience" and should use those hymns that glorify God for His person and work.

Prayers of Intercession. The time of prayer in this approach can also be spontaneous. The pastor or worship leader could announce the topics of prayer and allow people to pray spontaneously for the announced need. Also, in this situation it is not necessary for only one person to pray at a time. The entire congregation can pray aloud at the same time if they are so agreed.

Scripture Reading. Scripture readings may be read by a number of people in the congregation. There may be assigned readings as well as spontaneous readings. Readings should include selections from the Old Testament, the Psalms, and the Epistles, and end with the Gospels. The congregation could agree on their response, such as an "Amen," sung "alleluias," "thanks be to God," or some other appropriate way of acknowledging the importance of Scripture.

Sermon. In a worship service such as this the sermon ought to be short, calling attention to one or more points that can be understood and applied.

Response of Accountability. In a period of response to the sermon people can comment on how God spoke to them through the sermon, how it helped and encouraged them, and what they can do as a result of what they have heard. Accountability should not only be personal, but should also extend to one's life in the world—the world of work and social responsibility. This is also a time when well-prepared dramatic vignettes could be used to illustrate the point of the sermon.

Communion. Communion in such a service could be reverently informal. Chairs could be placed in a circle around the communion table and the people could receive the communion by coming forward to the table or by having one person passing the communion to another. Care should be taken by the celebrant to include a prayer of thanksgiving, an invocation of the Holy Spirit, and the words of remembrance. The congregation may use the kiss of peace either at the beginning or the end, say the *Sursum corda* at the beginning, use the *Sanctus,* and conclude with a hymn of joyful resurrection and a benediction.

Benediction. Benedictions may vary from week to week, reflecting the particular emphasis of the service. They may be composed by the person who pronounces them or they may be taken from Scripture passages such as the Aaronic blessing (Num. 6:23–26) mentioned earlier, or some other (e.g., Rom. 15:5; 2 Cor. 13:14; Eph. 6:23–24; Heb. 13:20; 1 Peter 5:10–11; Jude 24–25). Such benedictions are fitting conclusions to worship as they emphasize the blessings that come to the believer from Almighty God.

This type of service can be a very meaningful time of offering praise to God through enacting the work of the Son in recitation and drama. It also has the advantage of creating an intimate sense of community in which people share each other's lives and achieve a sense of responsibility toward each other.

Planned Worship
Call to Worship
 Choral
 Pastoral
 Response
Hymn of Praise
Ascription(s) of Praise*
Gloria
Prayer for Illumination (or Collect for the Day)
Old Testament Lesson (lay persons may read)
New Testament Lesson (lay persons may read)
Sermon
 Invitation to Response
Hymn (or Psalm or Chorus)
Confession of Sin (Hymn or Brief Statement)
Declaration of Pardon (Hymn or 1 John 1:9)
Response (of the People)
Affirmation of Faith (Creed)
Concerns of the Church (Prayer Needs)
The Prayers of the People (or Pastoral Prayer or Litany)
Testimony(ies) to God's Faithfulness* (Short Acclamations)
The Peace
Offering
 Collection
  Anthem or Special Music
 Presentation†
 Doxology
Invitation to the Lord's Table
Thanksgiving
Lord's Prayer
Communion (Hymns may be sung)
Response*
Charge (Dismissal)
Benediction

---

*At these times there may be individual and corporate expressions of praise and thanksgiving, either spoken or sung.
†The presentation consists of the gifts of the congregation and the elements of communion.

The planned service will be more useful for a congregation of several hundred people where the sense of a small intimate group is no longer present. This service of worship contains all the elements of the free worship but is designed to emphasize the flow of events, to set the fixed elements of worship in a more specific way, and to limit the spontaneity to specific places within the service. Nevertheless, the sense of the congregation *doing* the worship can be easily attained as the people become used to their responsive role.

Planned worship represents a good balance between the fixed elements and the contextual. Hymns as well as prayers, ascriptions of praise, and responses will reflect community commitments and needs. As the people become accustomed to this approach to worship, they will gain more and more freedom to enter into the spirit of it with enthusiasm and a great measure of spontaneity. This service provides a good balance for a congregation using a fixed location for worship with relatively little freedom to move the pews and other furniture. It should proceed without announcement, allowing the natural flow of the service to be characterized by a sense of congregational action that accents lay participation instead of a clericalized form of worship.

Formal Worship

GOD CALLS HIS PEOPLE TO WORSHIP
    Processional Hymn
    Greeting (a call to worship)
    Invocation
    Acknowledgment of God's Character (*Gloria* or some other
        appropriate hymn)
    Recognition of Sinfulness (*Kyrie eleison* or appropriate confession)

GOD SPEAKS THROUGH HIS WORD
    Old Testament Lesson (read by a lay person)
    Psalm (sung or read responsively)
    Epistle (read by a lay person)
    Psalm or Alleluia
    Gospel (standing; minister may walk into the midst of the
        congregation to read)
    Sermon

THE PEOPLE SPEAK TO GOD

Offering of Faith (a confessional statement, e.g., Apostles' Creed)

Offering of Petitions (may be congregational prayer rather than pastoral prayer)

The Kiss of Peace

THE PEOPLE GIVE THANKS TO GOD

He Took

Bread and wine are brought to the table, where they are prepared.

The minister washes his hands.

The minister places his hands on the bread and wine.

He Blessed

The Salutation

the *Sursum corda*

The Preface

The *Sanctus*

The Prayer of Thanksgiving

The Preliminary Epiclesis

At first the salutation, the *Sursum corda*, and the *Sanctus* may be written out but should soon be memorized by the congregation to encourage spontaneity.

He Broke

The Narrative of Institution

The Anamnesis (remembrance)

The Prayer of Intercession (Lord's Prayer)

The Epiclesis (invocation over bread and wine and the people)

The Fraction

He Gave

Distribution (with proper words and response; during the communion the choir may sing and congregational hymns may be sung as well)

Prayer

Benediction

Dismissal

At first glance the formal approach to worship appears to stifle spontaneity and involvement by the congregation. Although this is a danger of formal worship, it is not an inevitable result.

Formal worship can be an exhilarating experience when the

congregation knows what to do and does it with intention and enthusiasm. This kind of worship requires a great deal of preparation on the part of the pastor and congregation. It has the character of a play enacted by a group of players, each one having his or her part and doing it in the conscious effort of making a communal offering of praise and thanksgiving to God the Father through our Lord Jesus Christ. The congregation must *intentionally* incarnate the spirit of worship through the forms, transfiguring the forms into a living expression of faith.

This is an action of the whole community, the pastor playing the role of leader, and the members of the congregation filling in their parts to make worship into the unified action of all who are gathered. The congregational role is particularly expressed in the singing (*Gloria, Kyrie*, hymns, psalms, *Sanctus*, Lord's Prayer), in the responses (salutation, *Sursum corda*, acclamation to the Scripture [e.g., Thanks be to God]), in the offering and prayer (especially if the intercessions provide, as they should, for congregational participation), and in the Eucharist, during which the congregation goes to the table to receive the bread and wine.

A real sense of having reenacted the life, death, and resurrection of Christ, as well as expressing hope for His consummation, occurs when the people worship in faith. This service can also help the people achieve a sense of community (having done something together) and can be done with a well-thought-out use of space along with an accent on the time of the church year.

Conclusion

These three services are only examples of what may be done with the fixed elements of worship and the particular context most adaptable to a specific congregation. They should be treated as guides, and each congregation should take the time to carefully work through the biblical, historical, and theological meaning of worship before adopting one of them or adjusting one or more of them to suit its own needs.

Worship, like everything else in life, is something that we must *learn* to do. It has been neglected for too long by too many evangelical congregations. We should no longer miss out on the personal and corporate spiritual value of worship. Now is the time to reverse the trend toward the further reduction and misunderstanding of worship. Let us give time to the restoration of the ministry of worship that we offer to God the Father in praise and thanksgiving for His Son in and through the power of the Holy Spirit. The road to worship renewal is long and tedious and may be fraught with difficulties, misunderstanding, and resistance. But there are no shortcuts, no instant success stories, no proven gimmicks. *Dominus Vobiscum* (The Lord be with you).

Appendix 1

An Annotated Bibliography for Church Leaders

The purpose of this brief annotated bibliography is to suggest a basic beginning library for pastors, church librarians, and beginners in the academic field of liturgies. In developing this list I have attempted to keep three concerns in mind. First, I have been careful to choose the books most useful to Evangelicals. There is, of course, a considerable amount of material on the market. For that reason I have attempted to select neutral rather than denominational material. Second, I am concerned about the availibility of the books. Most of the material I have listed is in print at this time. And finally, I have attempted to keep the cost in mind. At present prices, these books will cost a total of approximately $300. I consider their purchase a good investment.

General Introduction. To begin with, most people will find a liturgical dictionary to be useful. The only one in print, and happily a good work, is J. G. Davies, ed., *Westminster Dictionary of Worship* (Philadelphia: Westminster, 1979). This work was formerly entitled *A Dictionary of Liturgy and Worship.* Second, in the area of philosophy I suggest Ninian Smart, *The Concept of Worship* (New York: Macmillan, 1972), and Rudolf Otto, *The Idea of the Holy* (New York: Oxford, 1977). Neither of these books concentrates on Christianity exclusively, though that is their major concern. Both are interested in how the transcendent God is communicated within the creation through worship. Third, a thoroughly biblical concern for worship is taken up by Jean Daniélou, *The Bible and the Liturgy* (Notre Dame: University of Notre Dame Press, 1956). His concern is with the types and figures of worship in both Testaments. His treatments on baptism, the Eucharist, Easter, etc., are classics. Fourth, for a general overview of the history of worship I suggest Gregory Dix, *The Shape of the Liturgy* (London: Dacre, 1945), a classic in twentieth-century liturgical scholarship, and a more recent work edited by Cheslyn Jones, Geoffrey Wainwright, and Edward Yarnold: *The Study of Liturgy* (New York: Oxford, 1978). The last-named work is the most up-to-date single volume on liturgical studies available. Fifth, in regard to theology, I suggest Alexander Schmemann, *Introduction to Liturgical Theology* (Tuckahoe, N.Y.: St. Vladimir's, 1978). Although this work is geared toward an evaluation of Eastern worship, his chapters on the development of the order of worship in the early church (more than half the book) are priceless. I also recommend Jean-J. von Allmen, *Worship: Its Theology and Practice* (New York: Oxford, 1965). Allmen writes from the Reformed point of view and distills the major European works of this century in the field of liturgies. He covers the entire gamut of theological issues and provides much stimulating food for thought.

Primary Sources. Until recently not many primary sources were available to the general reading public. However, recent translation and publication of primary sources have been on the increase. These valuable works allow the nonscholar to have a chance to read, ponder, and interpret for himself. However, the material for the most part is from the early church. It is there, of course, that we must begin our study. Three works that concentrate on the early period of church development are Lucien Deiss, *Early Sources of the Liturgy* (Collegeville: Liturgical Press, 1975); Hippolytus, *The Apostolic Tradition*, edited by Burton Scott Easton (Hamden, Conn.: Archon, 1962); and Willy Rordorf et al., *The Eucharist of the Early Christians* (New York: Pueblo, 1978). Hippolytus, or course, is the document that revolutionized our understanding of Christian worship. Although the work has been known since 1691, it was the German publication of Hippolytus in 1891 that opened up the more recent critical scholarship. Easton's edition provides a helpful commentary. Rordorf's work is especially helpful because he and other liturgical scholars have commented on the liturgical writings of the *Didache*, Tertullian, the *Didascalia*, and others. I also suggest R. C. D. Jasper and G. C. Cuming, *Prayers of the Eucharist: Early and Reformed*, 2nd ed. (New York: Oxford, 1980). This brief work is most helpful because its forty selections and brief introductions range from Jewish prayers to the 1662 *Book of Common Prayer*. It is most helpful to compare the selections of Luther, Calvin, Zwingli, and other Protestants with the early church fathers. The full text of some of these liturgies is found in Bard Thompson, *Liturgies of the Western Church* (1961; reprint, New York: Fortress, 1980). Most of the liturgies are Protestant, including those of Luther, Zwingli, Bucer, Calvin, Baxter, Wesley, and others.

Old and New Testament Worship. In the study of Old Testament worship, I suggest concentrating on works by Jewish scholars. The most helpful work I have come across is Abraham Millgram, *Jewish Worship* (Philadelphia: The Jewish Publication Society of America, 1971). This work covers every aspect of Jewish worship in detail and is clearly written. For Christians the major interest is the relationship of the Old Testament worship to the development of worship in the New Testament. In liturgical scholarship this field of inquiry is receiving increasing attention. A recent work written by a Jewish scholar who explores the relationship between synagogue and church is Eric Werner, *The Sacred Bridge: Liturgical Parallels in Synagogue and Early Church* (New York: Schocken, 1970). Two equally important, but older, works that explore this same area are C. W. Dugmore, *The Influence of the Synagogue Upon the Divine Office* (Westminster: Faith, 1964) and W. O. E. Oesterley, *The Jewish Background of the Christian Liturgy* (Gloucester, Mass.: Peter Smith, 1965). All these works point to a significant relationship of continuity, especially between the synagogue and the early church.

Although the books described above also treat the New Testament, I suggest several additional works. Ralph Martin, *Worship in the Early Church* (Grand Rapids: Eerdmans, 1964), provides us with the basic issues and facts pertaining to New Testament worship, although he offers very little analysis. More analytical and interpretive is Oscar Cullmann, *Early Christian Worship* (London: SCM, 1953), Charles Moule, *Worship in the New Testament* (Richmond: John Knox, 1961) and Ferdinand Hahn, *The Worship of the Early Church* (Philadelphia: Fortress, 1977). Hahn has done a very detailed work of scholarship, and the average reader may find the book difficult reading. For a scholarly but much easier work to read I suggest Werner Elert, *The Lord's Supper Today* (St. Louis: Concordia, 1973).

Historical Periods. The *Ancient Church* (100–600) is, in my estimation, one of the most exciting sources for the study of worship. The question that comes up repeatedly here deals with the relationship between the New Testament and the vast amount of liturgical literature of the Fathers. One of the most scholarly inquiries is that of Hans Leitzmann, *Mass and the Lord's Supper* (Leiden: Brill, 1953). A more recent work, not as detailed but very helpful, is Joseph A. Jungmann, *The Early Liturgy: To the Time of Gregory the Great* (Notre Dame: University of Notre Dame Press, 1959). These works are very helpful, but above all, one should study the primary sources already mentioned above.

Studies of changes and developments in the ancient church inevitably lead to an examination of those changes and developments in the *Medieval Period.* The most thorough treatment of this period is Joseph A. Jungmann, *The Mass of the Roman Rite* (New York: Benziger, 1959). It covers every aspect of medieval liturgy in significant detail and is easy to read. I also recommend the shorter but highly acclaimed work of Theodor Klausser, *A Short History of the Western Liturgy* (New York: Oxford, 1979). This work offers a penetrating analysis and interpretation of the changes in Western worship.

Next, we turn to the *Reformation.* First, I suggest an acquaintance with the Reformers' actual liturgies. This can be obtained through the primary sources listed above. For an examination of how these liturgies may be rooted in the early church I suggest the excellent and thorough work of Hughes Oliphant Old, *The Patristic Roots of Reformed Worship* (Zurich: Theologischer Verlag Zurich, 1975). The next question, then, is to ask how worship changed in the succeeding centuries. In addition to the primary source material, I have found James Hasting Nichols, *Corporate Worship in the Reformed Tradition* (Philadelphia: Westminster, 1968) to be most helpful. He offers an interpretation of the general developments in Protestant worship through the nineteenth century. Unfortunately there are not many books written about worship in those years. There seemed to be very little interest in liturgies until the twentieth century. For an examination of worship in the various denominations I suggest the article on "Liturgies" in the *Westminster Dictionary of Worship* mentioned above as well as the articles on specific denominational approaches to worship in the same book.

Special Areas. A great number of works have been written about *music*, but two that I think are most useful for a local church are Erik Routley, *Church Music and the Christian Faith* (Carol Stream, Ill.: Agape, 1978) and Donald P. Ellsworth, *Christian Music in Contemporary Witness* (Grand Rapids: Baker, 1979). In the study of *church architecture* I suggest Edward A. Sovik, *Architecture for Worship* (Minneapolis: Augsburg, 1973); Louis Bouyer, *Liturgy and Architecture* (Notre Dame: University of Notre Dame Press, 1967); and James F. White, *Protestant Worship and Church Architecture* (New York: Oxford, 1964). These works are concerned with the development of architecture in history and the contemporary relationship between worship renewal and the use of space. Concerning the *church year* two helpful works are H. Boone Porter, *Keeping the Church Year* (New York: Seabury, 1977), and Patricia B. Buckland, *Advent to Pentecost: A History of the Church Year* (Wilton, Conn.: Morehouse-Barlow, 1979). Both offer useful suggestions for texts and emphasis for preaching. For *worship and the world* I suggest Norman Pittenger, *Life as Eucharist* (Grand Rapids: Eerdmans, 1973).

Those who are interested in knowing more about the art of contextualizing worship into new forms should read the works of James F. White. His books, *New Forms of Worship* (New York: Abingdon, 1971); *Christian Worship in Transition* (New York: Abingdon, 1976); and *An Introduction to Christian Worship* (New York: Abingdon, 1980) are all most helpful for Evangelicals.

Appendix 2

Preaching
the Church Year

The following texts are arranged for a three-year cycle for Scripture readings and preaching.

SEASON OF ADVENT

1st Sunday in Advent

A	B	C
Psalm 122	Psalm 80:1–7	Psalm 25:1–9
Isaiah 2:1–5	Isaiah 63:16b–17; 64:1–8	Jeremiah 33:14–16
Romans 13:11–14	1 Corinthians 1:3–9	1 Thessalonians 3:9–13
Matthew 24:37–44	Mark 13:33–37	Luke 21:25–36
or Matthew 21:1–11	or Mark 11:1–10	or Luke 19:28–40

2nd Sunday in Advent

Psalm 72:1–14 (15–19)	Psalm 85	Psalm 126
Isaiah 11:1–10	Isaiah 40:1–11	Malachi 3:1–4
Romans 15:4–13	2 Peter 3:8–14	Philippians 1:3–11
Matthew 3:1–12	Mark 1:1–8	Luke 3:1–6

3rd Sunday in Advent

Psalm 146	Luke 1:45b–55	Isaiah 12:2–6
Isaiah 35:1–10	Isaiah 61:1–3, 10–11	Zephaniah 3:14–18a
James 5:7–10	1 Thessalonians 5:16–24	Philippians 4:4–7 (8–9)
Matthew 11:2–11	John 1:6–8, 19–28	Luke 3:7–18

213

4th Sunday in Advent

Psalm 24	Psalm 89:1–4, 14–18	Psalm 80:1–7
Isaiah 7:10–14 (15–17)	2 Samuel 7:(1–7) 8–11, 16	Micah 5:2–4
Romans 1:1–7	Romans 16:25–27	Hebrews 10:5–10
Matthew 1:18–25	Luke 1:26–38	Luke 1:39–45 (46–55)

SEASON OF CHRISTMAS

Christmas Day

Psalm 96	Psalm 97	Psalm 98
Isaiah 9:2–7	Isaiah 52:7–10	Isaiah 62:10–12
Titus 2:11–14	Hebrews 1:1–9	Titus 3:4–7
Luke 2:1–20	John 1:1–14	Luke 2:1–20

1st Sunday after Christmas

Psalm 111	Psalm 111	Psalm 111
Isaiah 63:7–9	Isaiah 45:22–25	Jeremiah 31:10–13
Galatians 4:4–7	Colossians 3:12–17	Hebrews 2:10–18
Matthew 2:13–15, 19–23	Luke 2:25–40	Luke 2:41–52

2nd Sunday after Christmas

A, B, C

Psalm 147:12–20
Isaiah 61:10–62:3
Ephesians 1:3–6, 15–18
John 1:1–18

SEASON OF EPIPHANY

January 6 (Epiphany Day) (Epiphany enacts the visit to the magi)

Psalm 72
Isaiah 60:1–6
Ephesians 3:2–12
Matthew 2:1–12

1st Sunday after Epiphany (always enacts the baptism of our Lord)

Psalm 45:7–9	Psalm 45:7–9	Psalm 45:7–9
Isaiah 42:1–7	Isaiah 42:1–7	Isaiah 42:1–7
Acts 10:34–38	Acts 10:34–38	Acts 10:34–38
Matthew 3:13–17	Mark 1:4–11	Luke 3:15–17, 21–22

2nd Sunday after Epiphany

Psalm 40:1–12	Psalm 67	Psalm 36:5–10
Isaiah 49:1–6	1 Samuel 3:1–10	Isaiah 62:1–5
1 Corinthians 1:1–9	1 Corinthians 6:12–20	1 Corinthians 12:1–11
John 1:29–41	John 1:43–51	John 2:1–11

3rd Sunday after Epiphany

Psalm 27:1–9	Psalm 62:6–14	Psalm 113
Isaiah 9:1b–4	Jonah 3:1–5, 10	Isaiah 61:1–6
or Amos 3:1–8		
1 Corinthians 1:10–17	1 Corinthians 7:29–31	1 Corinthians 12:12–21, 26–27
Matthew 4:12–23	Mark 1:14–20	Luke 4:14–21

4th Sunday after Epiphany

Psalm 1	Psalm 1	Psalm 71:1–6, 15–17
Micah 6:1–8	Deuteronomy 18:15–20	Jeremiah 1:4–10
1 Corinthians 1:26–31	1 Corinthians 8:1–13	1 Corinthians 12:27–13:13
Matthew 5:1–12	Mark 1:21–28	Luke 4:21–32

5th Sunday after Epiphany

Psalm 112	Psalm 147:1–13	Psalm 85:8–13
Isaiah 58:5–9a	Job 7:1–7	Isaiah 6:1–8 (9–13)
1 Corinthians 2:1–5	1 Corinthians 9:16–23	1 Corinthians 14:12b–20
Matthew 5:13–20	Mark 1:29–39	Luke 5:1–11

6th Sunday after Epiphany

Psalm 119:1–16	Psalm 32	Psalm 1
Deuteronomy 30:15–20	2 Kings 5:1–14	Jeremiah 17:5–8
1 Corinthians 2:6–13	1 Corinthians 9:24–27	1 Corinthians 15:12, 16–20
Matthew 5:20–37	Mark 1:40–45	Luke 6:17–26

7th Sunday after Epiphany

Psalm 103:1–13	Psalm 41	Psalm 103:1–13
Leviticus 19:1–2, 17–18	Isaiah 43:18–25	Genesis 45:3–8a, 15
1 Corinthians 3:10–11, 16–23	2 Corinthians 1:18–22	1 Corinthians 15:35–38a, 42–50
Matthew 5:38–48	Mark 2:1–12	Luke 6:27–38

8th Sunday after Epiphany

Psalm 62	Psalm 103:1–13	Psalm 92
Isaiah 49:13–18	Hosea 2:14–16 (17–18) 19–20	Jeremiah 7:1–7 (8–15)
1 Corinthians 4:1–13	2 Corinthians 3:1b–6	1 Corinthians 15:51–58
Matthew 6:24–34	Mark 2:18–22	Luke 6:39–49

Last Sunday after Epiphany (Epiphany ends with Transfiguration of our Lord)

Psalm 2:6–13	Psalm 50:1–6	Psalm 99:1–5
Exodus 24:12, 15–18	2 Kings 2:1–12a	Deuteronomy 34:1–12
2 Peter 1:16–19 (20–21)	2 Corinthians 3:12, 4:2	2 Corinthians 4:3–6
Matthew 17:1–9	Mark 9:2–9	Luke 9:28–36

SEASON OF LENT

Ash Wednesday

Psalm 51:1-13
Joel 2:12-19
2 Corinthians 5:20b-6:2
Matthew 6:1-6, 16-21

1st Sunday in Lent

Psalm 130	Psalm 6	Psalm 91
Genesis 2:7-9, 15-17; 3:1-7	Genesis 22:1-18	Deuteronomy 26:5-10
Romans 5:12 (13-16), 17-19	Romans 8:31-39	Romans 10:8b-13
Matthew 4:1-11	Mark 1:12-15	Luke 4:1-13

2nd Sunday in Lent

Psalm 105:4-11	Psalm 115:9-18	Psalm 42:1-7, 11-15
Genesis 12:1-8	Genesis 28:10-17 (18-22)	Jeremiah 26:8-15
Romans 4:1-5, 13-17	Romans 5:1-11	Philippians 3:17-4:1
John 4:5-26 (27-30, 39-42)	Mark 8:31-38	Luke 13:31-35

3rd Sunday in Lent

Psalm 142	Psalm 19:7-14	Psalm 126
Isaiah 42:14-21	Exodus 20:1-17	Exodus 3:1-8b, 10-15
Ephesians 5:8-14	1 Corinthians 1:22-25	1 Corinthians 10:1-13
John 9:1-41 or John 9:13-17, 34-39	John 2:13-22	Luke 13:1-9

4th Sunday in Lent

Psalm 43	Psalm 27:1-9 (10-18)	Psalm 32
Hosea 5:15-6:2	Numbers 21:4-9	Isaiah 12:1-6
Romans 8:1-10	Ephesians 2:4-10	1 Corinthians 1:18-31 or 1 Corinthians 1:18, 22-25
Matthew 20:17-28	John 3:14-21	Luke 15:1-3, 11-32

5th Sunday in Lent

Psalm 116:1-8	Psalm 51:11-16	Psalm 28:1-3, 7-11
Ezekiel 37:1-3 (4-10), 11-14	Jeremiah 31:31-34	Isaiah 43:16-21
Romans 8:11-19	Hebrews 5:7-9	Philippians 3:8-14
John 11:1-53 or John 11:47-53	John 12:20-33	Luke 20:9-19

Sunday of the Passion—Psalm Sunday

Psalm 31:1–5, 9–16	Psalm 31:1–5, 9–16	Psalm 31:1–5, 9–16
Isaiah 50:4–9a	Zechariah 9:9–10	Deuteronomy 32:36–39
Philippians 2:5–11	Philippians 2:5–11	Philippians 2:5–11
Matthew 26:1–27:66	Mark 14:1–15:47	Luke 22:1–23:56
or Matthew 27:11–54	or Mark 15:1–39	or Luke 23:1–49

Monday in Holy Week

Psalm 36:5–10
Isaiah 42:1–9
Hebrews 9:11–15
John 12:1–11

Tuesday in Holy Week

Psalm 71:1–12
Isaiah 49:1–6
1 Corinthians 1:18–25
John 12:20–36

Wednesday in Holy Week

Psalm 70:1–2, 4–6
Isaiah 50:4–9a
Romans 5:6–11
Matthew 26:14–25

Maundy Thursday

Psalm 116:10–17	Psalm 116:10–17	Psalm 116:10–17
Exodus 12:1–14	Exodus 24:3–11	Jeremiah 31:31–34
1 Corinthians 11:17–32	1 Corinthians 10:16–17	Hebrews 10:15–39
or 11:23–26	(18–21)	
John 13:1–17, 34	Mark 14:12–26	Luke 22:7–20

Good Friday

Psalm 22:1–23
Isaiah 52:13–53:12
or Hosea 6:1–6
Hebrews 4:14–16; 5:7–9
John 18:1–19:42
or John 19:17–30

SEASON OF EASTER

The Resurrection of our Lord—Easter Day

Psalm 118:1–2, 15–24	Psalm 118:1–2, 15–24	Psalm 118:1–2, 15–24
Acts 10:34–43	Isaiah 25:6–9	Exodus 15:1–11
		or Psalm 118:14–24
Colossians 3:1–4	1 Corinthians 15:19–28	1 Corinthians 15:1–11
John 20:1–9 (10–18)	Mark 16:1–8	Luke 24:1–11
or Matthew 28:1–10	or John 20:1–9	or John 20:1–9
	(10–18)	(10–18)

The Resurrection of our Lord—Easter Evening
Psalm 150
Daniel 12:1c–3
or Jonah 2:2–9
1 Corinthians 5:6–8
Luke 24:13–49

2nd Sunday of Easter

Psalm 105:1–7	Psalm 148	Psalm 149
Acts 2:14a, 22–32	Acts 3:13–15, 17–26	Acts 5:12, 17–32
1 Peter 1:3–9	I John 5:1–6	Revelation 1:4–18
John 20:19–31	John 20:19–31	John 20:19–31

3rd Sunday of Easter

Psalm 16	Psalm 139:1–11	Psalm 30
Acts 2:14a, 36–47	Acts 4:8–12	Acts 9:1–20
1 Peter 1:17–21	1 John 1:1–2:2	Revelation 5:11–14
Luke 24:13–35	Luke 24:36–49	John 21:1–14

4th Sunday of Easter

Psalm 23	Psalm 23	Psalm 23
Acts 6:1–9; 7:2a, 51–60	Acts 4:23–33	Acts 13:15–16a, 26–33
1 Peter 2:19–25	1 John 3:1–2	Revelation 7:9–17
John 10:1–10	John 10:11–18	John 10:22–30

5th Sunday of Easter

Psalm 33:1–11	Psalm 22:24–30	Psalm 145:1–13
Acts 17:1–15	Acts 8:26–40	Acts 13:44–52
1 Peter 2:4–10	1 John 3:18–24	Revelation 21:1–5
John 14:1–12	John 15:1–8	John 13:31–35

6th Sunday of Easter

Psalm 66:1–6, 14–18	Psalm 98	Psalm 67
Acts 17:22–31	Acts 11:19–30	Acts 14:8–18
1 Peter 3:15–22	1 John 4:1–11	Revelation 21:10–14, 22–23
John 14:15–21	John 15:9–17	John 14:23–29

The Ascension of our Lord
Psalm 110
Acts 1:1–11
Ephesians 1:16–23
Luke 24:44–53

7th Sunday of Easter

Psalm 47	Psalm 47	Psalm 47
Acts 1: (1–7) 8–14	Acts 1:15–26	Acts 16:6–10
1 Peter 4:12–17; 5:6–11	1 John 4:13–21	Revelation 22:12–17, 20
John 17:1–11	John 17:11b–19	John 17:20–26

SEASON OF PENTECOST

The Day of Pentecost

Psalm 104:25–34	Psalm 104:25–34	Psalm 104:25–34
Joel 2:28–29	Ezekiel 37:1–14	Genesis 11:1–9
Acts 2:1–21	Acts 2:1–21	Acts 2:1–21
John 20:19–23	John 7:37–37a	John 15:26–27; 16:4b–11

The Holy Trinity—First Sunday after Pentecost

Psalm 29	Psalm 149	Psalm 8

Genesis 1:1–2:3
  or Deuteronomy 4:
  32–34, 39–40
	Deuteronomy 6:4–9	Proverbs 8:22–31

2 Corinthians 13:11–14	Romans 8:14–17	Romans 5:1–5
Matthew 28:16–20	John 3:1–17	John 16:12–15

2nd Sunday after Pentecost

Psalm 31:1–5 (6–18) 19–24	Psalm 81:1–10	Psalm 117

Deuteronomy 11:18–21,
  26–28
	Deuteronomy 5:12–15	1 Kings 8:(22–23, 27–30)
		  41–43

Romans 3:21–25a, 27–28	2 Corinthians 4:5–12	Galatians 1:1–10
Matthew 7:(15–20) 21–29	Mark 2:23–28	Luke 7:1–10

3rd Sunday after Pentecost

Psalm 50:1–15	Psalm 61:1–5, 8	Psalm 30
Hosea 5:15–6:6	Genesis 3:9–15	1 Kings 17:17–24
Romans 4:18–25	2 Corinthians 4:13–18	Galatians 1:11–24
Matthew 9:9–13	Mark 3:20–35	Luke 7:11–17

4th Sunday after Pentecost

Psalm 100	Psalm 92:1–5 (6–10), 11–14	Psalm 32
Exodus 19:2–8a	Exekiel 17:22–24	2 Samuel 11:26–12:10, 13–15
Romans 5:6–11	2 Corinthians 5:1–10	Galatians 2:11–21
Matthew 9:35–10:8	Mark 4:26–34	Luke 7:36–50

5th Sunday after Pentecost

Psalm 69:1–20	Psalm 107:1–3, 23–32	Psalm 63:1–8
Jeremiah 20:7–13	Job 38:1–11	Zechariah 12:7–10
Romans 5:12–15	2 Corinthians 5:14–21	Galatians 3:23–29
Matthew 10:24–33	Mark 4:35–41	Luke 9:18–24

6th Sunday after Pentecost

Psalm 89:1–4, 15–18	Psalm 30	Psalm 16
Jeremiah 28:5–9	Lamentations 3:22–23	1 Kings 19:14–21
Romans 6:1b–11	2 Corinthians 8:1–9, 13–14	Galatians 5:1, 13–25
Matthew 10:34–42	Mark 5:21–24a, 35–43 or Mark 5:24b–34	Luke 9:51–62

7th Sunday after Pentecost

Psalm 145:1–2 (3–13), 14–22	Psalm 143:1–2, 5–8	Psalm 66:1–11, 14–18
Zechariah 9:9–12	Ezekiel 2:1–5	Isaiah 66:10–14
Romans 7:15–25a	2 Corinthians 12:7–10	Galatians 6:1–10, 14–16
Matthew 11:25–30	Mark 6:1–6	Luke 10:1–12, 16 (17–20)

8th Sunday after pentecost

Psalm 65	Psalm 85:8–13	Psalm 25:1–9
Isaiah 55:10–11	Amos 7:10–15	Deuteronomy 30:9–14
Romans 8:18–25	Ephesians 1:3–14	Colossians 1:1–14
Matthew 13:1–9 (18–23)	Mark 6:7–13	Luke 10:25–37

9th Sunday after Pentecost

Psalm 86:11–17	Psalm 23	Psalm 15
Isaiah 44:6–8	Jeremiah 23:1–6	Genesis 18:1–10a (10b–14)
Romans 8:26–27	Ephesians 2:13–22	Colossians 1:21–28
Matthew 13:24–30 (36–43)	Mark 6:30–34	Luke 10:38–42

10th Sunday after Pentecost

Psalm 119:129–136	Psalm 145	Psalm 138
1 Kings 3:5–12	Exodus 24:3–11	Genesis 18:20–32
Romans 8:28–30	Ephesians 4:1–7, 11–16	Colossians 2:6–15
Matthew 13:44–52	John 6:1–15	Luke 11:1–13

11th Sunday after Pentecost

Psalm 104:25–31	Psalm 78:23–29	Psalm 49:1–11
Isaiah 55:1–5	Exodus 16:2–15	Ecclesiastes 1:2; 2:18–26
Romans 8:35–39	Ephesians 4:17–24	Colossians 3:1–11
Matthew 14:13–21	John 6:24–35	Luke 12:13–21

12th Sunday after Pentecost

Psalm 85:8–13	Psalm 34:1–8	Psalm 33
1 Kings 19:9–18	1 Kings 19:4–8	Genesis 15:1–6
Romans 9:1–5	Ephesians 4:30–5:2	Hebrews 11:1–3, 8–16
Matthew 14:22–33	John 6:41–51	Luke 12:32–40

13th Sunday after Pentecost

Psalm 67	Psalm 34:9–14	Psalm 82
Isaiah 56:1, 6–8	Proverbs 9:1–6	Jeremiah 23:23–29
Romans 11:13–15, 29–32	Ephesians 5:15–20	Hebrews 12:1–13
Matthew 15:21–28	John 6:51–58	Luke 12:49–53

14th Sunday after Pentecost

Psalm 138	Psalm 34:15–22	Psalm 117
Exodus 6:2–8	Joshua 24:1–2a, 14–18	Isaiah 66:18–23
Romans 11:33–36	Ephesians 5:21–31	Hebrews 12:18–24
Matthew 16:13–20	John 6:60–69	Luke 13:22–30

16th Sunday after Pentecost

Psalm 119:33–40	Psalm 146	Psalm 10:12–15, 17–19
Ezekiel 33:7–9	Isaiah 35:4–7a	Proverbs 9:8–12
Romans 13:1–10	James 1:17–22 (23–25), 26–27	Philemon 1 (2–9), 10–21
Matthew 18:15–20	Mark 7:31–37	Luke 14:25–33

17th Sunday after Pentecost

Psalm 103:1–13	Psalm 116:1–8	Psalm 51:1–18
Genesis 50:15–21	Isaiah 50:4–10	Exodus 32:7–14
Romans 14:5–9	James 2:1–5, 8–10, 14–18	1 Timothy 1:12–17
Matthew 18:21–35	Mark 8:27–35	Luke 15:1–10

18th Sunday after Pentecost

Psalm 27:1–13	Psalm 54:1–4, 6–7a	Psalm 113
Isaiah 55:6–9	Jeremiah 11:18–20	Amos 8:4–7
Philippians 1:1–5 (6–11), 19–27	James 3:16–4:6	1 Timothy 2:1–8
Matthew 20:1–16	Mark 9:30–37	Luke 16:1–13

19th Sunday after Pentecost

Psalm 25:1–9	Psalm 135:1–7, 13–14	Psalm 146
Ezekiel 18:1–4, 25–32	Numbers 11:4–6, 10–16, 24–29	Amos 6:1–7
Philippians 2:1–5 (6–11)	James 4:7–12 (13–5:6)	1 Timothy 6:6–16
Matthew 21:28–32	Mark 9:38–50	Luke 16:19–31

20th Sunday after Pentecost

Psalm 80:7–14	Psalm 128	Psalm 95:6–11
Isaiah 5:1–7	Genesis 2:18–24	Habakkuk 1:1–3; 2:1–4
Philippians 3:12–21	Hebrews 2:9–11 (12–18)	2 Timothy 1:3–14
Matthew 21:33–43	Mark 10:2–16	Luke 17:1–10

21st Sunday after Pentecost

Psalm 23	Psalm 90:12–17	Psalm 111
Isaiah 25:6–9	Amos 5:6–7, 10–15	Ruth 1:1–19a
Philippians 4:4–13	Hebrews 3:1–6	2 Timothy 2:8–13
Matthew 22:1–10 (11–14)	Mark 10:17–27 (28–30)	Luke 17:11–19

22nd Sunday after Pentecost

Psalm 96	Psalm 91:9–16	Psalm 121
Isaiah 45:1–7	Isaiah 53:10–12	Genesis 32:22–30
1 Thessalonians 1:1–5a	Hebrews 4:9–16	2 Timothy 3:14–4:5
Matthew 22:15–21	Mark 10:35–45	Luke 18:1–8a

23rd Sunday after Pentecost

Psalm 1	Psalm 126	Psalm 34
Leviticus 19:1–2, 15–18	Jeremiah 31:7–9	Deuteronomy 10:12–22
1 Thessalonians 1:5b–10	Hebrews 5:1–10	2 Timothy 4:6–8, 16–18
Matthew 22:34–40 (41–46)	Mark 10:46–52	Luke 18:9–14

24th Sunday after Pentecost

Psalm 63:1–8	Psalm 119:1–16	Psalm 145
Amos 5:18–24	Deuteronomy 6:1–9	Exodus 34:5–9
1 Thessalonians 4:13–14 (15–18)	Hebrews 7:23–28	2 Thessalonians 1:1–5, 11–12
Matthew 25:1–13	Mark 12:28–34 (35–37)	Luke 19:1–10

25th Sunday after Pentecost

Psalm 90:12–17	Psalm 107:1–3, 33–43	Psalm 148
Hosea 11:1–4, 8–9	1 Kings 17:8–16	1 Chronicles 29:10–13
1 Thessalonians 5:1–11	Hebrews 9:24–28	2 Thessalonians 2:13–3:5
Matthew 25:14–30	Mark 12:41–44	Luke 20:27–28

26th Sunday after Pentecost

Psalm 131	Psalm 16	Psalm 98
Malachi 2:1–2, 4–10	Daniel 12:1–3	Malachi 4:1–2a
1 Thessalonians 2:8–13	Hebrews 10:11–18	2 Thessalonians 3:6–13
Matthew 23:1–12	Mark 13:1–13	Luke 21:5–19

27th Sunday after Pentecost

Psalm 105:1–7	Psalm 111	Psalm 68:1–4
Jeremiah 26:1–6	Daniel 7:9–10	Isaiah 52:1–6
1 Thessalonians 3:7–13	Hebrews 13:20–21	1 Corinthians 15:54–58
Matthew 24:1–14	Mark 13:24–31	Luke 19:11–27

Christ the King—Last Sunday of Pentecost

Psalm 95:1–7a	Psalm 93	Psalm 95:1–7a
Ezekiel 34:11–16, 23–24	Daniel 7:13–14	Jeremiah 23:2–6
1 Corinthians 15:20–28	Revelation 1:4b–8	Colossians 1:13–20
Matthew 25:31–46	John 18:33–37	Luke 23:35–43

Notes

CHAPTER 1—INTRODUCTION

[1]See "The Constitution on the Sacred Liturgy" in Austin P. Flannery, ed., *Documents of Vatican II* (Grand Rapids: Eerdmans, 1975); Michael J. Taylor, *The Protestant Liturgical Renewal* (Westminster: Newman, 1963); Kenneth G. Phifer, *A Protestant Case for Liturgical Renewal* (Philadelphia: Westminster, 1965).

[2]See David R. Mains, *Full Circle: The Creative Church for Today's Society* (Waco: Word, 1971); James L. Christensen, *Don't Waste Your Time in Worship* (Old Tappan: Revell, 1978), chaps. 1 and 2.

[3]This attitude is quite prevalent in recent books on worship by evangelical authors. The inaccurate treatment of ancient and medieval worship by Paul E. Engle, *Discovering the Fullness of Worship* (Philadelphia: Great Commission, 1978), ch. 10, and the total disregard of the history of worship by Robert G. Rayburn, *O Come, Let Us Worship* (Grand Rapids: Baker, 1980) betray a lack of historical concern.

[4]See the discussion of this point in James Hitchcock, *The Recovery of the Sacred* (New York: Seabury, 1974), pp. 54–73.

[5]Hughes Oliphant Old in *The Patristic Roots of Reformed Worship* (Zurich: Theologischer Verlag Zurich, 1975) has effectively shown the indebtedness of the Reformers to the ancient liturgy. However, the shift toward the subjective is clearly set forth in the eucharistic prayers of John Calvin. See "John Calvin: Form of Church Prayers," in R. C. D. Jasper and G. Cuming, eds., *Prayers of the Eucharist*, 2nd ed. (New York: Oxford, 1980), pp. 153ff.

[6]For a good account of mistaken expectations in worship see Christensen, *Don't Waste Your Time in Worship*, pp. 11–20.

[7]See the discussion of God's holiness in worship in A. Verheul and

H. Winstone, *Introduction to the Liturgy* (Collegeville: Liturgical, 1968), pp. 22ff.

[8]See the discussion on this point by J. D. Crichton, "A Theology of Worship," in Cheslyn Jones, Geoffrey Wainwright, and Edward Yarnold, eds., *The Study of Liturgy* (New York: Oxford, 1978), pp. 3–29.

[9]See "The Place of Christ in the Liturgy" in Verheul and Winstone, *Introduction to the Liturgy*, pp. 35–50.

[10]This prayer is taken from the ancient Liturgy of St. Mark. For this and other ancient liturgies see *The Ante-Nicene Fathers* (Grand Rapids: Eerdmans, 1970), 7:529ff.

[11]An excellent discussion of Christ as mediator in worship is found in Geoffrey Wainwright, *Doxology* (New York: Oxford, 1980), pp. 68ff.

[12]See ibid., pp. 118ff.

[13]See ibid., pp. 90–95.

[14]See the discussion on "Sign Character of the Liturgy" in Verheul and Winstone, *Introduction to the Liturgy*, chap. 5.

[15]See the discussion on "The Physical Side of Worship," in Peter Gillquist, *The Physical Side of Being Spiritual* (Grand Rapids: Zondervan, 1979), pp. 115ff.

[16]See Norman Pittenger, *Life as Eucharist* (Grand Rapids: Eerdmans, 1973).

CHAPTER 2—OLD TESTAMENT SOURCES

[1]See "The Task and Method of Liturgical Theology" in Alexander Schmemann, *Introduction to Liturgical Theology* (Bangor: American Orthodox, 1967), pp. 9–27. See also "The Jewish Background to Christian Worship," in Cheslyn Jones, Geoffrey Wainwright, and Edward Yarnold, eds., *The Study of Liturgy* (New York: Oxford, 1978), pp. 39–51. A solid case for the Jewish origins of Christian worship is also made by Frank Gavin, *The Jewish Antecedents of the Christian Sacraments* (New York: Ktav, 1969).

[2]For a survey of the study of Old Testament worship see "Historical Survey of the Study of Old Testament Worship," in Hans-Joachim Kraus, *Worship in Israel*, trans. Geoffrey Buswell, (Richmond: John Knox, 1966), pp. 1–25. The best work by a Jewish scholar on Old Testament worship is Abraham Millgram, *Jewish Worship* (Philadelphia: The Jewish Publication Society of America, 1971). I also recommend Abraham L. Idelsohn, *Jewish Liturgy and Its Development* (New York: Schocken, 1975). An excellent overview by a Protestant scholar is H. H. Rowley, *Worship in Ancient Israel* (Philadelphia: Fortress, 1967).

[3]See Conrad Antonsen, "Jewish Sources of Christian Worship," *Modern Liturgy* 3, no. 4 (April 1976): 4ff.

[4]For a scholarly discussion of the temple see Abraham Idelsohn, *Jewish Liturgy and Its Development* (New York: Schocken, 1967), pp. 10–26. See also Andre Parrot, *The Temple of Jerusalem*, trans. B. E. Hooke (London: SCM, 1957); G. H. Box, "The Temple Service," in *Encyclopaedia Biblica*.

[5]William Dyrness in *Themes in Old Testament Theology* (Downers Grove: InterVarsity, 1979), chap. 8, makes pertinent and important comments on the notion of sacred place, time, and action.

[6]See W. O. E. Oesterley, *Sacrifices in Ancient Israel: Their Origin, Purposes, and Development* (London: Hodder and Stoughton, 1937); George Buchanan Gray, *Sacrifice in the Old Testament: Its Theory and Practice* (Oxford: Clarendon, 1925).

[7]See Lewis Finkelstein, "The Origin of the Synagogue," *Proceedings of the American Academy for Jewish Research* 1 (1928-30): 49-59; 2 (1931): 69-81.

[8]For a good description of synagogue worship see "The Framework of Jewish Worship," in Millgram, *Jewish Worship*, p.89-120.

[9]Ibid., p. 102.

[10]Ibid., p. 103.

[11]See Jacob Mann, *The Bible as Read and Preached in the Old Synagogue* 2 vols. (New York: Ktav, 1971).

[12]Quoted by Millgram in *Jewish Worship*, p. 113.

[13]See Israel Bettan, "Early Preaching in the Synagogue," in *Studies in Jewish Preaching* (Cincinnati: Hebrew Union College, 1939).

[14]See Hoyyim Schauss, *The Jewish Festivals* (New York: Union of American Hebrew Congregations, 1938).

[15]See Isaac Levy, *A Guide to Passover* (London: Jewish Chronicle, 1959); T. H. Gastor, *Passover: Its History and Tradition* (New York: Schuman, 1949).

CHAPTER 3—NEW TESTAMENT DEVELOPMENTS

[1]For a brief but comprehensive view of the various approaches to worship in the New Testament see Ferdinand Hahn, *The Worship of the Early Church* (Philadelphia: Fortress, 1973).

[2]See Ralph P. Martin, *Worship in the Early Church* (Grand Rapids: Eerdmans, 1974), chap. 2; Eric Werner, *The Sacred Bridge: Liturgical Parallels in Synagogue and Early Church* (New York: Schocken, 1970).

[3]See Hahn, *Worship of the Early Church*, chap. 3.

[4]See C. F. D. Moule, *Worship in the New Testament* (Bramcote: Grove, 1977), 1:9-10.

[5]See Hahn, *Worship of the Early Church*, chap. 4.

[6]See "Hymns and Spiritual Songs," in Martin, *Worship in the Early Church*, pp. 43-45.

[7]For an example see John C. Kirby, *Ephesians Baptism and Pentecost* (Montreal: McGill University Press, 1968).

[8]James D. G. Dunn, *Unity and Diversity in the New Testament* (Philadelphia: Westminster, 1977), p. 141. Dunn argues against this position; see pp. 141-49.

[9]Hahn, *Worship of the Early Church*, chap. 5.

[10]See Ernst Haenchen, *The Acts of the Apostles: A Commentary*, trans. R. McL. Wilson et al. from the 14th German ed. (1965), (Philadelphia: Westminster, 1971).

[11]See Rudolf Schnackenburg, *The Church in the New Testament* (New York: Herder and Herder, 1965), pp. 40ff.

[12]See C. F. D. Moule, *Worship in the New Testament*, 1:10-12.

[13]Oscar Cullmann, *Early Christian Worship* (London: SCM, 1973), pp. 9-10.

[14]See Hahn, *Worship of the Early Church*, chap. 6.

[15]Ibid., chap. 7.

[16]Ibid., chap. 8.

[17]Cullmann, *Early Christian Worship*, p. 37. The presentation of this point continues from p. 31 through p. 119.

[18]See Massey H. Shepherd, *The Paschal Liturgy and the Apocalypse* (Richmond: John Knox, 1960).

CHAPTER 4—EARLY CHRISTIAN WORSHIP

[1]Joachim Jeremias, *The Eucharistic Words of Jesus* (Philadelphia: Fortress, 1977), pp. 132ff.

[2]See Henry Bettenson, *Documents of the Christian Church*, 2nd ed. (New York: Oxford, 1963), pp. 5–6.

[3]Joseph A. Jungmann, *The Mass of the Roman Rite*, trans. Francis A. Brunner, Rev. Charles K, Riepe (New York: Benziger Brothers, 1959), p. 4.

[4]Ibid., pp. 10–11.

[5]J. A. Kleist, trans., *The Didache*, Ancient Christian Writers, vol. 6 (Westminster, Md.: Newman, 1948), pp. 20–21.

[6]For a detailed discussion of this matter see Willy Rordorf et al., *The Eucharist of the Early Christians* (New York: Pueblo, 1978), pp. 1–23.

[7]See Jeremias, *Eucharistic Words*, p. 110.

[8]See L. W. Bernard, *Justin Martyr: His Life and Thought* (Cambridge: Cambridge University Press, 1967).

[9]Justin Martyr, *First Apology*, chap. 67 in Cyril Richardson, ed., *Early Christian Fathers* (Philadelphia: Westminster, 1953), pp. 287–88.

[10]See Jeremias, *Eucharistic Words*, p. 119.

[11]Quoted by Ralph Martin, "Approaches to New Testament Exegesis" in Howard Marshall, ed., *New Testament Interpretation* (Grand Rapids: Eerdmans, 1977), p. 231.

[12]See also Oscar Cullmann, *Early Christian Worship* (London: SCM, 1973), pp. 12–20.

[13]The best discussions of the relationship between the synagogue and the church are found in the following books: W. O. E. Oesterley, *The Jewish Background of the Christian Liturgy* (Gloucester: Peter Smith, 1965); C. W. Dugmore, *The Influence of the Synagogue Upon the Divine Office* (Westminster: Faith, 1964); Eric Werner, *The Sacred Bridge: Liturgical Parallels in Synagogue and Early Church* (New York: Schocken, 1970).

[14]Dugmore, *Influence of the Synagogue*, p. 2.

[15]Ibid., pp. 13–14.

[16]See Oesterley, *Jewish Background*, chap. 5.

[17]See Werner, *Sacred Bridge*, chap. 8.

[18]See Oesterley, *Jewish Background*, pp. 54, 125.

[19]*Didache*, chap. 8.

[20]Oesterley, *Jewish Background*, p. 127.

[21]Ibid., pp. 129–50.

[22]There are numerous discussions of the origins and development of the Lord's Supper. Among them I suggest Hans Lietzmann, *Mass and the Lord's Supper*, trans. Dorothea H. G. Reeve (Leiden: Brill, n.d.); A. J. B. Higgins, *The Lord's Supper in the New Testament* (Chicago: Regnery, 1952); Max Thurian, *The Eucharistic Memorial*, 2 parts (Richmond: John Knox, 1963).

[23]Jungmann, *Mass of the Roman Rite*, p. 8.

[24]See Jeremias, *Eucharistic Words*, pp. 103–5.

[25]Ibid., p. 121.

[26]Ibid., pp. 117–19.

CHAPTER 5—ANCIENT AND MEDIEVAL WORSHIP

[1]A great deal of historical material is contained in Cheslyn Jones, Geoffrey Wainwright, and Edward Yarnold, eds., *The Study of Liturgy* (New York: Oxford University Press, 1978); and Joseph Jungmann, *The Mass of the Roman Rite,* trans., Francis A. Brunner, Rev. Charles H. Riepe (New York: Benziger Brothers, 1959). Two shorter but highly valuable works are Theodor Klauser, *A Short History of the Western Liturgy,* 2nd ed. (New York: Oxford University Press, 1979), and William D. Maxwell, *An Outline of Christian Worship* (London: Oxford University Press, 1939). For primary sources of liturgy see Bard Thompson, *Liturgies of the Western Church* (New York: New American Library, 1974).

[2]See Lucien Deiss, *Early Sources of the Liturgy,* trans. Benet Weatherhead (Collegeville: Liturgical Press, 1975) and Willy Rordorf et al., *The Eucharist of the Early Christians* (New York: Pueblo, 1978).

[3]Maxwell, *Outline of Christian Worship,* p. 17.

[4]For evidence of the widespread usage of these forms in the early liturgies of the church see R. C. D. Jasper and G. C. Cuming, eds., *Prayers of the Eucharist: Early and Reformed* 2nd ed. (New York: Oxford University Press, 1980); see also Maxwell, *Outline of Christian Worship,* pp. 15–16.

[5]For a good description of congregational action in early worship see Gregory Dix, *The Shape of the Liturgy* (London: Dacre, 1975), chap. 2.

[6]An excellent interpretation of this era is provided by Alexander Schmemann, *Introduction to Liturgical Theology* (Bangor: American Orthodox, 1967), chap. 3.

[7]See Nikolaus Liesel and Tibor Makula, *The Eucharistic Liturgies of the Eastern Church* (Collegeville: Liturgical Press, 1963). This work contains the text, together with pictures, of the Coptic, Ethiopic, Syrian, Malankarese, Maronite, Greek, Melkite, Russian, Ruthenian, Chaldean, Malabarese, and Armenian rites.

[8]Maxwell, *Outline of Christian Worship,* pp. 40–41.

[9]See Timothy Ware, *The Orthodox Church* (Baltimore: Penguin, 1963), p. 269.

[10]For an interpretation of the Orthodox liturgy see Alexander Schmemann, *For the Life of the World* (Crestwood, N.Y.: St. Vladimir's Press, 1973).

[11]See Jungmann, *The Mass of the Roman Rite,* pp. 37ff.

[12]See Jasper and Cuming, *Prayers of the Eucharist,* pp. 105ff.

[13]See Thompson, *Liturgies of the Western Church,* pp. 41–42.

[14]For an excellent interpretation of this process see Alexander Schmemann, *Introduction to Liturgical Theology,* pp. 72ff.

[15]Ibid., p. 98.

[16]For an evaluation of the influence of mystery cults on ancient Christian worship see Joseph A. Jungmann, *The Early Liturgy to the Time of Gregory the Great* (Notre Dame: University of Notre Dame Press, 1959), pp. 122ff.

[17]See Thompson, *Liturgies of the Western Church,* p. 42.

[18]Quoted by Jungmann, *Mass of the Roman Rite,* pp. 67–68.

[19]Ibid., pp. 97ff.

[20]See Schmemann, *Introduction to Liturgical Theology,* pp. 105ff.

CHAPTER 6—REFORMATION AND MODERN PROTESTANT WORSHIP

[1]A good comparison of Protestant liturgies is found in Bard Thompson, *Liturgies of the Western Church* (New York: New American Library, 1961).

[2]William D. Maxwell, *An Outline of Christian Worship*, (London: Oxford University Press, 1939), p. 72.

[3]See "The Babylonian Captivity of the Church," in Robert Ferm, *Readings in the History of Christian Thought* (New York: Holt, Rinehart, and Winston, 1964), p. 500.

[4]Thompson, *Liturgies of the Western Church*, p. 98.

[5]The most thorough work on the relationship between Reformation worship and the ancient church is detailed in Hughes Oliphant Old, *The Patristic Roots of Reformed Worship* (Zurich: Theologischer Verlag Zurich, 1975).

[6]Augsburg Confession, 24.

[7]See Thompson, *Liturgies of the Western Church*, pp. 231–32.

[8]See Riedemann's Confession quoted in "Worship, Public," in *The Mennonite Encyclopedia* (Hillsboro, Kansas: Mennonite Brethren Publishing House, 1955), 4:984–85.

[9]For information about Bucer's liturgy see Thompson, *Liturgies of the Western Church*, pp. 159–66; Old, *The Patristic Roots of Reformed Worship*, pp. 119ff.

[10]See R. C. D. Jasper and G. J. Cuming, *Prayers of the Eucharist, Early and Reformed* (New York: Oxford, 1980) 2nd ed., pp. 153ff.

[11]For a description of Calvin's service see Maxwell, *Outline of Christian Worship*, p. 115.

[12]Quoted in Maxwell, *Outline of Christian Worship*, p. 118.

[13]See James Hastings Nichols, *Corporate Worship in the Reformed Tradition* (Philadelphia: Westminster, 1968), pp. 90ff.

[14]Quoted in "Baptist Worship," in *Westminster Dictionary of Worship*, edited by J. G. Davies. (Philadelphia: Westminster, 1972), p. 65.

[15]"Congregationalist Worship," Davies, *Dictionary*, p. 149.

[16]See "Quaker Worship," Davies, *Dictionary*, pp. 328–29.

[17]Nichols, *Corporate Worship*, p. 96.

[18]See "Reformed Worship," Davies, *Dictionary*, pp. 331ff.

[19]See Nichols, *Corporate Worship*, pp. 111ff.

[20]Ibid, p. 122.

[21]For further discussion see "Methodist Worship," Davies, *Dictionary*, pp. 269ff.

CHAPTER 7—A CHRISTOCENTRIC FOCUS

[1]Support for relationship of these six doctrines to Christ and worship may be drawn from a study of the eucharistic prayers of the early church. See R. C. D. Jasper and G. J. Cuming, *Prayers of the Eucharist: Early and Reformed* (New York: Oxford, 1980).

[2]For a thorough treatment of the doctrine of creation see Langdon B. Gilksey, *Maker of Heaven and Earth: A Study of the Christian Doctrine of Creation* (Garden City, N.J.: Doubleday, 1959).

[3]See George Florosky, *Creation and Redemption* (Belmont, Mass.: Nordland, 1976).

[4]See Irenaeus, "Against Heresies," in Cyril C. Richardson, *Early Christian Fathers* (Philadelphia: Westminster, 1953), p. 389.

[5]For a discussion of this notion in the early church see Gustav Aulin, *Christus Victor* (New York: Macmillan, 1953).

[6]See Florosky, *Creation and Redemption.*

[7]For a detailed discussion of this point see Geoffrey Wainwright, *Eucharist and Eschatology* (London: Epworth, 1971).

[8]For a detailed discussion of this point see Jean-Jacques von Allmen, *Worship: Its Theology and Practice* (New York: Oxford, 1965), pp. 21ff.

[9]See Massey H. Shepherd, *The Paschal Liturgy and the Apocalypse* (Richmond: John Knox Press, 1960).

[10]Allmen, *Worship*, pp. 42–43.

[11]Ibid., p. 57ff. and Wainwright, *Eucharist and Eschatology*, pp. 110ff.

CHAPTER 8—A THEOLOGY OF ENACTMENT

[1]See Thomas Howard, "Imagination, Rites, and Mystery," *Reformed Journal* 29 (March 1979): 15–19; see also "The Order of Worship," in Jean-J. von Allmen, *Worship: Its Theology and Practice* (New York: Oxford, 1965), pp. 283–311.

[2]See "The Church as a Cult Community," in A. Verheul and H. Winstone, *Introduction to the Liturgy* (Collegeville: Liturgical Press, 1968), pp. 75ff.

[3]See Donald L. Williams, "The Israelite Cult and Christian Worship," in James M. Efird, ed., *The Use of the Old Testament in the New and Other Essays* (Durham: Duke University Press, 1972), pp. 110ff.

[4]See "'The Pattern of Sound Words'—Early Creeds and Confessions of Faith," in Ralph P. Martin, *Worship in the Early Church* (Grand Rapids: Eerdmans, 1974), pp. 53–65.

[5]See "Hymns and Spiritual Songs," in Martin, *Worship in the Early Church*, pp. 39–52; "Early Christian Hymns," in James D. G. Dunn, *Unity and Diversity in the New Testament* (Philadelphia: Westminster, 1977), pp. 132ff.; "Psalmody and Hymnody," in Hughes Oliphant Old, *The Patristic Roots of Reformed Worship* (Zurich: Theologischer Verlag Zurich, 1975), pp. 251ff.

[6]See "The Ministry of the Word," in Martin, *Worship in the Early Church*, pp. 66–76; and "The Decline of Preaching," in Abraham Millgram, *Jewish Worship* (Philadelphia: The Jewish Publication Society of America, 1971), pp. 530ff.

[7]See Douglas Shand Tucci, "The High Mass as Sacred Dance," *Theology Today* 34 (April 1972): 58–72.

[8]Abraham Idelsohn, *Jewish Liturgy and Its Development* (New York: Schocken, 1960), p. 177.

[9]Ibid., p. 173.

[10]See James F. White, *Introduction to Christian Worship* (Nashville: Abingdon, 1980), pp. 145ff.

[11]See *Anamnesis*, Gerhard Kittel, ed., *Theological Dictionary of the New Testament*, trans. Geoffrey Bromiley (Grand Rapids: Eerdmans, 1964), 1:348–49.

[12]See Robert Howard Clausen, "Using Drama in Worship," *Concordia Journal*, (November 1977), pp. 246–54.

CHAPTER 9—A THEOLOGY OF FORM AND SIGN

[1]See Everett M. Stowe, *Communicating Reality Through Symbols* (Philadephia: Westminster, 1966).

[2]See Robert Webber, *God Still Speaks* (Nashville: Nelson, 1980), esp. chaps. 4–6, 9.

[3]See Langdon Gilkey, *Maker of Heaven and Earth: A Study of the Christian Doctrine of Creation* (Garden City, N.J.: Doubleday, 1959).

[4]Tertullian, *On Baptism,* 11.

[5]*To the Smyrnaeans,* 7:1.

[6]See William Dyrness, *Themes in Old Testament Theology* (Downers Grove: InterVarsity, 1979), pp. 143–60.

[7]The misunderstanding of this point by Evangelicals has produced a negative attitude toward symbolic communication. See for example, Paul E. Engle, *Discovering the Fullness of Worship* (Philadelphia: Great Commission Publications, 1978), esp. pp. 20, 31, 65–73.

[8]See James F. White, *Introduction to Christian Worship* (Nashville: Abingdon, 1980), pp. 145ff.

[9]See Peter Roche de Coppens, *The Nature and Use of Ritual* (Washington, D.C.: University Press of America, 1979), pp. 137ff.

[10]See James Hastings Nichols, *Corporate Worship in the Reformed Tradition* (Philadelphia: Westminster, 1968), esp. chaps. 5–7.

[11]See "Gesture," edited by J. G. Davies, in *Westminster Dictionary of Worship,* (Philadelphia: Westminster, 1972), pp. 185ff.

[12]See Geoffrey Wainwright, *Doxology: The Praise of God in Worship, Doctrine, and Life* (New York: Oxford, 1980), pp. 119–22.

CHAPTER 10—A THEOLOGY OF ORDER (THE WORD)

[1](New York: Oxford, 1958), pp. 211–12.

[2]See "Procession," in *Westminster Dictionary of Worship,* edited by J. G. Davies (Philadelphia: Westminster, 1972), pp. 323ff.

[3]Abraham Millgram, *Jewish Worship* (Philadelphia: The Jewish Publication Society of America, 1971), pp. 98–99.

[4]Bard Thompson, *Liturgies of the Western Church* (New York: New American Library, 1961), p. 197.

[5]Ibid., p. 357.

[6]Ibid., p. 417.

[7]See "Gloria in Excelsis Deo," in *New Catholic Encyclopedia* (New York: McGraw, 1967), 7:510–11.

[8]See Joseph A. Jungmann, *The Mass of the Roman Rite* (New York: Benziger, 1959), pp. 222ff.

[9]See Cyril Richardson, *Early Christian Fathers* (Philadelphia: Westminster, 1953), p. 287; William D. Maxwell, *An Outline of Christian Worship* (London: Oxford, 1939), pp. 14ff.

[10]See Jungmann, *Mass,* pp. 260ff.

[11]Quoted in "Psalmody," Davies, *Dictionary,* p. 326.

[12]Quoted in Psalmody," p. 326.

[13]See Jungmann, *Mass,* pp. 284ff.

[14]See John Knox, *The Integrity of Preaching* (Nashville: Abingdon, 1967); Robert E. C. Browne, *The Ministry of the Word* (Philadelphia: Fortress, 1975).

[15]See Cyril Richardson, *Early Christian Fathers* (Philadelphia: Westminster, 1953), p. 287.

[16]See Donald Coggen, *The Prayers of the New Testament* (New York: Harper, 1967).

¹⁷See "General Intercessory Prayers," Jungmann, *Mass* (New York: Benziger, 1959), pp. 391ff. and "The Prayer of Intercession," Hughes Oliphant Old, *The Patristic Roots of Reformed Worship* (Zurich: Theologischer Verlag Zurich, 1975), pp. 240ff.

¹⁸See Eric Werner, *The Sacred Bridge: Liturgical Parallels in the Synagogue and Early Church* (New York: Schocken, 1970), pp. 3ff.

¹⁹Gregory Dix, *The Shape of the Liturgy* (London: Dacre, 1945), pp. 42–43.

²⁰See "Gestures," Davies, *Dictionary*, pp. 185ff.

²¹Richardson, *Early Christian Fathers*, pp. 285–86.

CHAPTER 11—A THEOLOGY OF ORDER (THE EUCHARIST)

¹See the discussion on this question in Gregory Dix, *The Shape of the Liturgy* (London: Dacre, 1945), pp. 48–102; see also "Was the Last Supper a Passover Meal?" in Joachim Jeremias, *The Eucharistic Words of Jesus* (Philadelphia: Fortress, 1977).

²See Dix, *Shape*, pp. 110–23.

³*Clement's First Letter*, chap. 36.

⁴Ibid., chap. 44.

⁵*Apology*, I, 65.

⁶*Apostolic Tradition*, IV, 2.

⁷*Didache*, 14.

⁸*Letter to the Ephesians*, 5, 2.

⁹*Apostolic Tradition*, 4, 12–13.

¹⁰For a history of eucharistic theology see Joseph M. Powers, *Eucharistic Theology* (New York: Seabury, 1967); see also Cheslyn Jones, Geoffrey Wainwright, and Edward Yarnold, eds., *The Study of Liturgy* (New York: Oxford, 1978), pp. 147–288.

¹¹See Hughes Oliphant Old, *The Patristic Roots of Reformed Worship* (Zurich: Theologischer Verlag Zurich, 1975), pp. 101ff.

¹²See the eucharistic prayers and teaching of the early church fathers in R. C. D. Jasper and G. J. Cuming, *Prayers of the Eucharist* (New York: Oxford, 1980), esp. Justin Martyr, pp. 17–20.

¹³See the comments on this by Dix, *Shape*, pp. 114ff.

¹⁴Ibid., pp. 48ff.

¹⁵See "Anaphora," in *Westminster Dictionary of Worship* edited by J. G. Davies (Philadelphia: Westminster, 1972), pp. 10ff.

¹⁶The basic sources for comparison are found in Jones et al., *The Study of Liturgy*; Old, *The Patristic Roots of Reformed Worship*; Jasper and Cuming, *Prayers of the Eucharist*; Thompson, *Liturgies of the Western Church*.

¹⁷*Shape*, p. 117.

¹⁸Ibid., pp. 124–25.

¹⁹Thompson, *Liturgies*, p. 204.

²⁰Ibid., p. 111.

²¹Ibid., p. 369.

²²*First Apology*, 67.

²³Dix, *Shape*, pp. 126ff.

²⁴*Apostolic Tradition*, I, 4, 3.

²⁵Ibid.

[26]See Jasper and Cumings, *Prayers of the Eucharist,* p. 89.

[27]*Apostolic Tradition,* I, 4, 4–8; to compare with the eucharistic prayer of the Reformers see Old, *Patristic Roots,* pp. 283ff.; Jasper and Cuming, *Prayers of the Eucharist,* pp. 130–92; Thompson, *Liturgies,* pp. 95–374.

[28]See Jasper and Cuming, *Prayers of the Eucharist,* pp. 130ff.

[29]Ibid., pp. 153ff.

[30]Thompson, *Liturgies,* p. 369.

[31]*Letter to the Ephesians,* 20:1.

[32]*Didache,* 9:4.

[33]*Apostolic Tradition,* 1, 4:9–10.

[34]*The Apostolic Constitutions,* Book 8, see Jasper and Cuming, *Prayers of the Eucharist,* p. 76.

[35]See Dix, *Shape,* p. 161.

[36]*Apostolic Tradition,* I, 4:12.

[37]*For the Life of the World* (Crestwood, N.Y.: St. Vladimir's Press, 1973), p. 44.

[38]Dix, *Shape,* pp. 130–32.

[39]Ibid., p. 131.

[40]See Thompson, *Liturgies,* pp. 95–104.

[41]*The Apostolic Constitution,* Book 8, pp. 78–79.

[42]See Henry Bettenson, *Later Church Fathers* (New York: Oxford, 1970), pp. 46–47.

[43]On the use of the benediction among the Reformers see Old, *Patristic Roots,* pp. 330ff.

CHAPTER 12—WORSHIP AND SPACE

[1]See "Architectural Setting," in *Westminster Dictionary of Worship,* edited by J. G. Davies (Philadelphia: Westminster, 1972), pp. 21ff.; "The Place of Worship," in Jean-J. von Allmen, *Worship: Its Theology and Practice* (New York: Oxford, 1965), pp. 240–82.

[2]See "The Language of Space," James F. White, *Introduction to Christian Worship* (Nashville: Abingdon, 1980), pp. 76ff.

[3]See "Dedication," Davies, *Dictionary,* p. 162.

[4]See "Means by Which the Numinous is Expressed in Art," Rudolf Otto, *The Idea of the Holy* (New York: Oxford, 1977), pp. 65ff.

[5]In medieval architecture the error of the mass as a sacrifice is expressed in the plurality of altars. Some Evangelicals on the other hand have made the Grecian urn and colonial architecture into the symbol of conservatism.

[6]See Louis Bouyer, *Liturgy and Architecture* (Notre Dame: University of Notre Dame Press, 1967), pp. 8–24.

[7]Ibid., p. 11.

[8]Ibid., pp. 24–39.

[9]Ibid., pp. 39–60.

[10]See "Iconostasis," Davies, *Dictionary,* p. 196.

[11]For an excellent critique of liturgical developments in the East see Alexander Schmemann, *Introduction to Liturgical Theology* (Bangor: American Orthodox Press, 1966).

[12]See Bouyer, *Liturgy and Architecture,* pp. 70–86.

[13]*An Outline of Christian Worship* (London: Oxford, 1939), p. 68.

NOTES

NOTES 233

[14]Bard Thompson, *Liturgies of the Western Church* (New York: New American Library, 1974), p. 142.
[15]See "Pulpit," Davies, *Dictionary*, p. 326.
[16]See "Communion Table," Davies, *Dictionary*, p. 144.
[17]The following contain helpful suggestions in guiding a congregation to the renewed understanding and use of space: Edward A. Sovik, *Architecture for Worship* (Minneapolis: Augsburg, 1973); Peter G. Cobb, "The Architectural Setting of the Liturgy," Cheslyn Jones, Geoffrey Wainwright, and Edward Yarnold, eds., *The Study of Liturgy* (New York: Oxford, 1978), pp. 473–87; for a Catholic view see Karl Borromaeus Frank, *Fundamental Questions on Ecclesiastical Art* (Collegeville: Liturgical Press, 1962), pp. 60ff.

CHAPTER 13—WORSHIP AND TIME

[1]See "The Language of Time," James F. White, *Introduction to Christian Worship* (Nashville: Abingdon, 1980), pp. 44ff.
[2]See "Kairos," Colin Brown, ed., *Dictionary of New Testament Theology* (Grand Rapids: Zondervan, 1971), 3:833ff.
[3]See Abraham Millgram, *Jewish Worship* (Philadelphia: Jewish Publication Society of America, 1971).
[4]Oscar Cullman, *Christ and Time: The Primitive Conception of Time and History* (Philadelphia: Westminster, 1964).
[5]Marion J. Hatchett, *Sanctifying Life, Time, and Space* (New York: Seabury, 1976), pp. 9ff.
[6]See Peter G. Cobb "The History of the Christian Year," Cheslyn Jones, Geoffrey Wainwright, and Edward Yarnold, eds., *The Study of Liturgy* (New York: Oxford, 1978), pp. 403–19.
[7]See the perceptive comments on this subject by Alexander Schmemann, *Introduction to Liturgical Theology* (Bangor: American Orthodox Press, 1970), pp. 34ff.
[8]See "The Liturgical Year," Jean-J. von Allmen, *Worship: Its Theology and Practice* (New York: Oxford, 1965), pp. 227–36.
[9]Some helpful books on the church year are: Patricia B. Buckland, *Advent to Pentecost: A History of the Christian Year* (Wilton, Conn.: Morehouse-Barlow, 1979); H. Boone Porter, *Keeping the Church Year* (New York: Seabury, 1977); Robert Wetzler and Helen Huntington, *Seasons and Symbols: A Handbook on the Church Year* (Minneapolis: Augsburg, 1962).
[10]See "Advent," in *Westminster Dictionary of Worship*, edited by J. G. Davies (Philadelphia: Westminster, 1972), pp. 1ff.
[11]See "Epiphany," Davies, *Dictionary*, pp. 170ff.
[12]See "Lent," Davies, *Dictionary*, pp. 212ff.
[13]See "Ash Wednesday," Davies, *Dictionary*, p. 41.
[14]See "Holy Week," Davies, *Dictionary*, pp. 193ff.
[15]See "Easter," Davies, *Dictionary*, pp. 166ff.
[16]Quoted by White, *Introduction*, p. 53.
[17]See "Pentecost," Davies, *Dictionary*, pp. 310ff.
[18]Quoted in "Pentecost," pp. 310–11.
[19]See "The Lord's Day," Jean Daniélou, *The Bible and the Liturgy* (Notre Dame: University of Notre Dame Press, 1956), pp. 242ff.

[20]Daniélou, *Bible and Liturgy*, p. 249.
[21]Ibid., p. 251.
[22]Quoted by Daniélou, *Bible and Liturgy*, p. 255.
[23]See "The eighth day," in Daniélou, *Bible and Liturgy*, pp. 262ff.
[24]See Millgram, *Jewish Worship*, pp. 143ff.
[25]*The Apostolic Tradition*, IV, 36.
[26]See Jones, et al., *The Study of Liturgy*, pp. 350–402.

CHAPTER 14—WORSHIP AND SOUND

[1]See "The Numinous in Poetry, Hymn, and Liturgy," Rudolf Otto, *The Idea of the Holy* (New York: Oxford, 1977), pp. 186ff.
[2]*Letter to the Ephesians*, 4.
[3]Hom, 5, quoted by J. Gelineau, "Music and Singing in the Liturgy," in Cheslyn Jones, Geoffrey Wainwright, and Edward Yarnold, eds., *The Study of Liturgy* (New York: Oxford, 1978), p. 442.
[4]Jones et al., *Study*, p. 451.
[5]Ibid., pp. 451–52.
[6]Ibid., p. 452.
[7]Ibid., pp. 452–53.
[8]Ibid., pp. 453–54; also see Eddie Ensley, *Sounds of Wonder* (New York: Paulist, 1977).
[9]For a discussion of the relationship between music in the Old Testament and the New see especially Eric Werner, *The Sacred Bridge: Liturgical Parallels in Synagogue and Early Church* (New York: Schocken, 1970).
[10]See "Hymns and Spiritual Songs," Ralph P. Martin, *Worship in the Early Church* (Grand Rapids: Eerdmans, 1976), pp. 39–52.
[11]See Donald P. Ellsworth, *Christian Music in Contemporary Witness* (Grand Rapids: Baker, 1979), pp. 32–34.
[12]See "Gregorian Chant," in Hugh Leichtentnitt, *Music History and Ideas* (Cambridge: Harvard University Press, 1961), pp. 22ff.
[13]See Ellsworth, *Christian Music in Contemporary Witness*, pp. 35–44.
[14]Quoted in Lester Hostetler, *Handbook to the Mennonite Hymnary* (Newton, Kas.: General Conference of the Mennonite Church of North America, 1949), p. xv.
[15]Jones et al., *The Study of Liturgy*, p. 444.
[16]Hostetler, *Handbook*, p. xv.
[17]Ibid., p. xvi.
[18]Ibid., p. xvii.
[19]See Erik Routley, *Church Music and the Christian Faith* (Carol Stream, Ill.: Agape, 1978), pp. 50ff.
[20]See "Psalmody and Hymnody," in Hughes Oliphant Old, *The Patristic Roots of Reformed Worship* (Zurich: Theologischer Verlag Zurich, 1975), pp. 251ff.
[21]For a brief but helpful survey of this period see Robert G. Rayburn, *O Come Let Us Worship* (Grand Rapids: Baker, 1980), pp. 223ff.
[22]Quoted by Alan Dunstan, "Hymnody in Christian Worship," in Jones et al., *Study*, p. 458.
[23]Quoted by Dunstan, "Hymnody," p. 460.

[24]See "Eighteenth Century Music," Ellsworth, *Christian Music in Contemporary Witness,* pp. 65ff.

[25]Ibid., p. 103ff.

CHAPTER 15—WORSHIP AND THE WORLD

[1]*The Apostolic Tradition,* II, 23:12.

[2]For a detailed examination of the word *kosmos* see Gerhard Kittel, ed., *Theological Dictionary of the New Testament,* vol. 3 (Grand Rapids: Eerdmans, 1965).

[3]*The Apostolic Tradition,* I, 4:8.

[4](Grand Rapids: Eerdmans, 1973), pp. 80–81.

[5]Tissa Balasuriya, *The Eucharist and Human Liberation* (Maryknoll: Orbis, 1979).

[6]Ibid., p. 25.

Bibliography

GENERAL INTRODUCTION

Bouyer, Louis. *Rite and Man: Natural Sacredness and Christian Liturgy.* Notre Dame: University of Notre Dame Press, 1967.

Christensen, James L. *Don't Waste Your Time in Worship.* Old Tappan: Revell, 1978.

Davies, J. G. *New Perspectives on Worship Today.* London: SCM, 1978.

Dix, Gregory. *The Shape of the Liturgy.* London: Dacre, 1945.

Eliade, Mircea. *The Sacred and the Profane.* Translated by William R. Trask. New York: Harcourt, Brace, and World, 1959.

Engle, Paul E. *Discovering the Fullness of Worship.* Philadelphia: Great Commission, 1978.

Garrett, Thomas S. *Christian Worship: An Introductory Outline.* New York: Oxford University Press, 1963.

Gaurdini, R. *The Spirit of the Liturgy.* London: Sheed and Ward, 1930.

Jones, Cheslyn; Geoffrey Wainwright; and Edward Yarnold, eds. *The Study of Liturgy.* New York: Oxford, 1978.

Micks, Marianne H. *The Future Present.* New York: Seabury, 1970.

Otto, Rudolf. *The Idea of the Holy.* Translated by John W. Harvey. New York: Oxford, 1958.

Phifer, Kenneth G. *A Protestant Case for Liturgical Renewal.* Philadelphia: Westminster, 1965.

Rayburn, Robert G. *O Come, Let Us Worship.* Grand Rapids: Baker, 1980.

Schmemann, Alexander. *Introduction to Liturgical Theology.* Bangor: American Orthodox, 1967.

Shaughnessy, James D. *The Roots of Ritual.* Grand Rapids: Eerdmans, 1973.

Smart, Ninian. *The Concept of Worship.* New York: Macmillan, 1972.

236

Underhill, Evelyn. *Worship*. London: Nisbet, 1936.
Verghese, Paul. *The Joy of Freedom: Eastern Worship and Modern Man*. Richmond: John Knox, 1967.
White, James F. *Introduction to Christian Worship*. Nashville: Abingdon, 1980.

PRIMARY SOURCES AND RESOURCE WORKS

Bibliotheca Ritualis. 3 vols. New York: Burt Franklin, originally published in Rome, 1776.
Book of Common Prayer. New York: The Church Hymnal Corporation, 1979.
Brightman, F. E. *Liturgies Eastern and Western*. Oxford: Clarendon, 1965.
Davies, J. G., ed. *Westminster Dictionary of Worship*. Philadelphia: Westminster, 1972. This work was formerly entitled *A Dictionary of Liturgy and Worship*.
Deiss, Lucien. *Early Sources of the Liturgy*. Collegeville: Liturgical Press, 1975.
Hänggi, A.; and Pahl, I., *Prex Eucharistica*. Fribourg: Fribourg University Press, 1968.
Hippolytus. *The Apostolic Tradition*. Edited by Burton Scott Easton. Hamden, Conn.: Archon, 1962.
Jasper, R. C. D.; and G. J. Cuming, ed. *Prayers of the Eucharist: Early and Reformed*. New York: Oxford, 1980.
Lutheran Book of Worship. Prepared by the churches participating in the Inter-Lutheran Commission on Worship. Minneapolis: Augsburg, 1978.
The New Catholic Encyclopedia. New York: McGraw, 1967.
Nicene and Post-Nicene Fathers. Series 1, 2, 3. Grand Rapids: Eerdmans, 1956.
The Book of Psalms for Singing. Pittsburgh: The Board of Education and Publication, Reformed Presbyterian Church of North America, 1973.
Rordorf, Willy et al. *The Eucharist of the Early Christians*. Translated by Matthew J. O'Connell. New York: Pueblo, 1978.
Swete, Henry B. *Church Services and Service-Books Before the Reformation*. London: SPCK, 1930.
Thompson, Bard, ed. *Liturgies of the Western Church*. Philadelphia: Fortress, 1980.
The Worship Book Services. Prepared by the Joint Committee on Worship for Cumberland Presbyterian Church, Presbyterian Church in the United States, and The United Presbyterian Church in the United States of America. Philadelphia: Westminster, 1970.

BIBLICAL

Old Testament

Box, G. H. "Worship, Hebrew." In *Encyclopedia of Religion and Ethics*, edited by James Hastings. 1918.
Eichrodt, Walter. *Theology of the Old Testament*. 2 vols. Philadelphia: Westminster, 1967.
Finkelstein, Lewis. "The Origin of the Synagogue." *Proceedings of the American Academy for Jewish Research* 1(1928–30): 49–59.
Gavin, Frank. *The Jewish Antecedents of the Christian Sacraments*. New York: Ktav, 1969.

Idelsohn, Abraham Z. *Jewish Liturgy and Its Development*. New York: Schocken, 1975.

Kaplan, Mordecai M. "The Future of Religious Symbolism—A Jewish View." In *Religious Symbolism*. Edited by F. Ernest Johnson. New York, 1955.

Keel, Othmar. *The Symbolism of the Biblical World: Ancient Near Eastern Iconography and the Book of the Psalms*. New York: Seabury, 1978.

Kraus, Hans-Joachim. *Worship in Israel: A Cultic History of the Old Testament*. Translated by Geoffrey Boswell. Richmond: John Knox, 1966.

Levy, Isaac. *A Guide to Passover*. London: Jewish Chronicle Publication, 1959.

Mann, Jacob. *The Bible as Read and Preached in the Old Synogogue*. Vol. 1: New York: Ktav, 1971; Vol. 2: Cincinnati: Hebrew Union College, 1966.

Millgram, Abraham. *Jewish Worship*. Philadelphia: Jewish Publication Society of America, 1971.

Mowinckel, Sigmund. *The Psalms in Israel's Worship*. Nashville: Abingdon, 1962.

Rad, Gerhard von. *Old Testament Theology*. 2 vols. New York: Harper, 1962.

Rowley, Harold H. *Worship in Ancient Israel: Its Forms and Meaning*. Philadelphia: Fortress, 1967.

Schauss, Hayyim. *The Jewish Festivals*. Cincinnati: Union of Hebrew Congregations, 1938.

Sonne, Isaiah. "The Paintings of the Dura Synagogue." *Hebrew Union College Annual* 20 (1947): 255–362.

Werner, Eric. *The Sacred Bridge: Liturgical Parallels in Synogogue and Early Church*. New York: Schocken, 1970.

Zeitlin, Solomon. "The Origin of the Synagogue." *Proceedings of the American Academy for Jewish Research* 2 (1931): 69–81.

_____. "An Historical Study of the First Canonization of the Hebrew Liturgy." *The Jewish Quarterly Review* 36 (1945–46): 211–29; 38 (1947–48): 289–316; 54 (1963–64): 208–40.

New Testament

Cranfield, C. E. B. "Divine and Human Action: The Biblical Concept of Worship." *Interpretation* 22 (1958): 387–98.

Cullmann, Oscar. *Early Christian Worship*. Translated by A. S. Todd and J. B. Torrence. London: SCM, 1953.

Delling, Gerhard. *Worship in the New Testament*. Translated by Percy Scott. Philadelphia: Westminster, 1962.

Dugmore, C. W. *The Influence of the Synagogue Upon the Divine Office*. Westminster, S. W.: Faith, 1964.

Elert, Werner. *The Lord's Supper Today*. Translated by Martin Bertram. St. Louis: Concordia, 1973.

Hamman, A. *Prayer—First Three Centuries of the Christian Church*. Translated by P. J. Oligny. Chicago: Franciscan Herald, 1971.

Jeremias, Joachim. *The Eucharistic Words of Jesus*. Philadelphia: Fortress, 1966.

Kirby, John C. *Ephesians: Baptism and Pentecost*. Montreal: McGill University Press, 1968.

Lohmeyer, Ernst. *Lord of the Temple*. Translated by S. Todd. Edinburgh: Oliver and Boyd, 1961.

MacDonald, Alexander B. *Christian Worship in the Primitive Church.* Edinburgh: Clark, 1934.

Martin, Ralph P. *Worship in the Early Church.* Grand Rapids: Eerdmans, 1975.

Marxsen, Willi. *The Lord's Supper as a Christological Problem.* Translated by Lorenz Nieting. Philadelphia: Fortress, 1970.

Moule, Charles Francis Digby. *Worship in the New Testament.* Richmond: John Knox, 1961.

Nielen, Josef M. *The Earliest Christian Liturgy.* Translated by P. Cummins. St. Louis: Herder, 1971.

Oesterley, W. O. E. *The Jewish Background of the Christian Liturgy.* Gloucester, Mass.: Peter Smith, 1965.

Parkes, James. *The Conflict of the Church and the Synagogue.* Cleveland: World, 1961.

Rordorf, Willy. *Sunday: The History of the Day of Rest and Worship in the Earliest Centuries of the Christian Church.* Translated by A. A. K. Graham. Philadelphia: Westminster, 1968.

Schweizer, Edward. *The Lord's Supper According to the New Tstament.* Translated by James M. Davis. Philadelphia: Fortress, 1971.

Williams, Donald L. "The Israelite Cult and Christian Worship." In *The Use of the Old Testament in the New and Other Essays,* edited by James M. Efird. Durham: Duke University Press, 1972.

HISTORICAL

General

Brunner, Peter. *Worship in the Name of Jesus.* Translated by M. H. Bertram. St. Louis: Concordia, 1968.

Clarke, William K. L. *Liturgy and Worship.* London: SPCK, 1932.

Duchesne, Louis M. O. *Christian Worship: Its Origin and Development.* Translated by M. L. McClure. London: SPCK, 1903.

Klauser, Theodor. *A Short History of the Western Liturgy.* Translated by John Halliburton. New York: Oxford, 1979.

Maxwell, William D. *An Outline of Christian Worship.* 1939. Reprint. London: Oxford, 1963.

Micklem, Nathaniel, ed. *Christian Worship: Studies in its History and Meaning.* Oxford: Oxford, 1936.

Srawley, J. H. *The Early History of the Liturgy.* 1913. Cambridge: Cambridge University Press, 1949.

Ancient and Medieval

Jones, B. H. "The Quest for the Origins of the Christian Liturgies," *Anglican Theological Review* 46 (1964): 5–21.

Jungmann, Joseph. *The Mass of the Roman Rite.* Translated by F. A. Brunner. 1951–55. 2nd ed., rev. and abridged. New York: Benziger, 1959. 1 vol.

Keating, J. F. *The Agape and the Eucharist in the Early Church.* London: Methuen, 1901.

Kraemer, C. J. "Pliny and the Early Church Service." *Journal of Classical Philology* 29 (1934).

Lietzmann, Hans. *Mass and the Lord's Supper.* Translated by D. H. G. Reeve. Leiden: Brill, 1953.

Mendenhall, George E. "Biblical Faith and Cultic Evolution." *The Lutheran Quarterly* 5 (1953): 235–58.

Warren, F. E. *The Liturgy and Ritual of the Ante-Nicene Church.* London: SPCK, 1912.

Woolley, R. M. *The Liturgy of the Primitive Church.* Cambridge: Cambridge University Press, 1910.

Reformation and Modern

Baird, Charles W. *Presbyterian Liturgies.* Grand Rapids: Baker, 1960.

Barkley, John M. *Worship of the Reformed Church.* Richmond: John Knox, 1967.

Barth, Karl. *The Knowledge of God and the Service of God According to the Teaching of the Reformation.* London: Hodder, 1938.

Macleod, Donald. *Presbyterian Worship: Its Meaning and Method.* Rev. ed. Richmond: John Knox, 1981.

Nichols, James Hastings. *Corporate Worship in the Reformed Tradition.* Philadelphia: Westminster, 1968.

Old, Hughes Oliphant. *The Patristic Roots of Reformed Worship.* Zurich: Theologischer Verlag Zurich, 1975.

Vajta, Vilnos. *Luther on Worship.* Philadelphia: Muhlenberg, 1958.

THEOLOGICAL THEMES AND ISSUES

General Theology

Allmen, Jean J. von. *Worship: Its Theology and Practice.* New York: Oxford, 1965.

――――. "Worship and the Holy Spirit." *Studia Liturgica* 2 (1963): 124–35.

Coppens, Peter Roche de. *The Nature and Use of Ritual.* Washington, D. C.: University Press of America, 1979.

Cox, Harvey. *The Feast of Fools.* New York: Harper, 1969.

Hitchcock, James. *The Recovery of the Sacred.* New York: Seabury, 1974.

Jungmann, Joseph A. *The Place of Christ in Liturgical Prayer.* London: Chapman, 1965.

――――. *The Liturgy of the Word.* Translated by H. E. Winstone. Collegeville: Liturgical Press, 1966.

Lamb, J. A. *The Psalms in Christian Worship.* London: Faith, 1962.

Mascall, E. L. *Theology and Images.* London: Mowbray, 1963.

Schmemann, Alexander. *For the Life of the World.* Crestwood, N.Y.: St. Vladimir's Press, 1973.

Vagaggini, C. *Theological Dimensions of the Liturgy.* Collegeville: Liturgical Press, 1976.

Vajta, V. "Creation and Worship." *Studia Liturgica* 2 (1963): 29–46.

Verheul, A.; and H. Winstone. *Introduction to the Liturgy.* Collegeville: Liturgical Press, 1968.

Wainwright, Geoffrey. *Doxology: The Praise of God in Worship, Doctrine, and Life.* New York: Oxford, 1980.

Church Year

Babin, David E. *Week In—Week Out: A New Look at Liturgical Preaching.* New York: Seabury, 1976.

Beckwith, R. T.; and W. Scott. *This is the Day: The Biblical Doctrine of the Christian Sunday in its Jewish and Early Christian Setting.* London: Marshall, Morgan, and Scott, 1978.

Browne, Robert E. C. *The Ministry of the Word.* Philadelphia: Fortress, 1976.

Buckland, Patricia B. *Advent to Pentecost.* Wilton, Conn.: Morehouse-Barlow, 1979.

Carrington, Philip. *The Primitive Christian Calendar.* Cambridge: Cambridge University Press, 1952.

Cowie, C.; and John Gummer. *The Christian Calendar.* Springfield, Mass.: Merriam, 1974.

Frank, B. Kare. *Fundamental Questions on Ecclesiastical Art.* Collegeville: Liturgical Press, 1962.

Fuller, R. H. *What Is Liturgical Preaching?* London: SCM, 1957.

Hatchett, Marion J. *Sanctifying Life, Time, and Space.* New York: Seabury, 1976.

Kleinhens, Theodore J. *The Year of the Lord: The Church Year—Its Customs, Growth, and Ceremonies.* St. Louis: Concordia, 1976.

McArthur, A. A. *The Evolution of the Christian Year.* London: SCM, 1953.

Morris, L. *The New Testament and Jewish Lectionaries.* London: Tyndale, 1964.

Porter, H. Boone. *Keeping the Church Year.* New York: Seabury, 1977.

Wetzler, Robert; and Helen Huntington. *Seasons and Symbols: A Handbook on the Church Year.* Minneapolis: Augsburg, 1962.

Architecture

Bruggink, Donald J.; and Carl H. Droppers. *Christ and Architecture.* Grand Rapids: Eerdmans, 1965.

Bouyer, Louis. *Liturgy and Architecture.* Notre Dame: University of Notre Dame Press, 1967.

Hammond, Peter, ed. *Towards a Church Architecture.* London: Architectural Press, 1962.

Sovik, E. A. *Architecture for Worship.* Minneapolis: Augsburg, 1973.

Eucharist

Balasuriya, Tissa. *The Eucharist and Human Liberation.* New York: Orbis, 1979.

Bouyer, Louis. *Eucharist: Theology and Spirituality of the Eucharistic Prayer.* Translated by Charles Underhill Quinn. Notre Dame: University of Notre Dame Press, 1968.

Cochrane, Arthur C. *Eating and Drinking With Jesus: An Ethical and Biblical Inquiry.* Philadelphia: Westminster, 1974.

Higgins, A. J. B. *The Lord's Supper in the New Testament.* Chicago: Regnery, 1952.

Powers, Joseph M. *Eucharistic Theology.* New York: Seabury, 1967.

Stone, D. *History of the Doctrine of the Holy Eucharist.* 2 vols. London: Longmans, 1909.

Thurian, Max. *The Eucharistic Memorial.* Translated by J. G. Davies. 2 vols. Richmond: John Knox, 1961.

Wainwright, Geoffrey. *Eucharist and Eschatology.* London: Epworth, 1971.
Watkins, Keith. *The Feast of Joy: The Lord's Supper in Free Churches.* St. Louis: Bethany, 1977.

Baptism

Aland, L. *Did the Early Church Baptize Infants?* London: SCM, 1963.
Bridge, Donald; and David Phypers. *The Water That Divides.* Downers Grove: Intervarsity, 1977.
Beasley-Murray, G. R. *Baptism in the New Testament.* London: Macmillan, 1962.
Cullmann, Oscar. *Baptism in the New Testament.* London: SCM, 1950.
Made, Not Born: New Perspectives on Christian Initiation and the Catechumenate. From the Murphy Center for Liturgical Research. Notre Dame: University of Notre Dame Press, 1976.

Music

Ellsworth, Donald P. *Christian Music in Contemporary Witness.* Grand Rapids: Baker, 1979.
Ensley, Eddie. *Sounds of Wonder.* New York: Paulist, 1977.
Leichtentritt, Hugo. *Music History and Ideas.* Cambridge, Mass.: Harvard University Press, 1961.
Northcott, Cecil. *Hymns in Christian Worship.* Richmond: John Knox, 1964.
Routley, Erik. *Church Music and the Christian Faith.* Carol Stream, Ill.: Agape, 1978.

The Christian Life and Worship

Bouyer, Louis. *Liturgical Piety.* Notre Dame: University of Notre Dame Press, 1955.
Braso, Gabriet M. *Liturgy and Spirituality.* Translated by Leonard J. Doyle. Collegeville: Liturgical, 1971.
Pittenger, Norman. *Life as Eucharist.* Grand Rapids: Eerdmans, 1973.

Index of Persons

Index of Subjects

Advent, 107, 166, 168

Aesthetic, the: in Eastern Christian worship, 63, 64, 65

Agape feast: in *Didache*, 46–49, 55; and the Lord's Supper, 48, 55–56, 132; origin of, 48; Pliny, 46, 48–49

Altars: proliferation of, in the Roman church, 158–59; replacement of, by Cranmer, 76

Anabaptists, 13, 76, 77

Ancient church: as source for modes of worship, 14–15; use of sound in, 179; worship in, 59–66, 71

Anglican, 76, 77, 81

Announcements: as an interruption of worship, 107

Apostles' Creed, 100–101

Apostolic tradition: importance of, 15

Aramaic Christian worship, 37

Ash Wednesday, 167

Baptism: Christ as the minister of, 17; as communicating spiritual reality, 94; as a dominical symbol, 114; on Easter, 166; established by Christ, 112; Gnostic denial of, 110; preparation for, in Lent, 166; and salvation, 110; and the sign character of worship, 18

Baptists, 76, 79

Basilica, Roman: use of space in, 156–57

Benediction, 33, 42, 56, 113, 146–47, 177, 187, 198, 199, 200, 201, 203

Bishop: increase of the power of, 156–57; in the third century, 62

Book of Common Prayer, 77, 81

Calvinism, 76

Ceremony: as means and end, 67; in medieval worship, 67, 71; Protestant attitudes toward, 76–77, 80–81

Chants, 70, 177, 179, 180

Charismatics, 13

Charismatic worship, 83–84

Christ: attitude of, toward worship, 34–35; as the content of worship, 56, 87–95; cosmic work of, 87–91; as the mediator of Christian worship, 16–17; Old Testament forms of worship fulfilled by, 14, 112; presence of, in worship, 94

Christ-event: as the center of time, 164–65, 172, 173; and enactment, 97–98, 107, 195; experienced by community in worship, 91; as the fulfillment of Old Testament worship, 30, 35–36, 43; gives meaning to worship, 91, 92; the nature of church, 93; recapitulation of, 91–93; as the root of Christian worship, 14, 30, 31, 33, 35–36, 43, 198

Christmas, 98, 166

Christocentric worship, 16–17, 61, 87–95

Church: actualized in worship, 93–94, 95; Anabaptist view of, 77; the beginning of, 30, 168; as the body of Christ, 19, 93–94, 95, 129, 137, 176; as the context of worship, 56; elements of worship developed by, 198; as the fulfillment of temple worship, 27, 39; as a hierarchical institution, 68; as an institution of power, 157; secularization of, 70; as a sign of Christ in the world, 19; as a sign of the new creation, 90; visible signs of, 94; as a worshiping community, 16, 17–18, 56, 93

Church history: as source for worship renewal, 14–15

Church year: as drama, 107; dropped by the Reformers, 165; medieval

245

Rituals, Jewish: fulfilled in Christ, 14, 112; relation of early Christians to, 37; in the temple, 26
Roman Catholic church, 11, 13, 73
Roman rite, 65–66

Sabbath: Jesus' interpretation of, 35; relation of, to Sunday worship, 169
Sacrament: Calvin's view of, 78; as a fixed part of worship, 15; as a proclamation of Christ's death, 78; rejected by Quakers, 80; as signs of the visible church, 94
Sacrifices: Old Testament, fulfilled in Christ, 38–39
Salutation: in the Eucharist, 138, 142; in evangelical worship, 195; origin of, 61; as a preparation for worship, 119–20; in the third century, 61; in worship models, 202, 204
Sanctus: dropped by Bucer, 77; in evangelical worship, 195; origin of, 61–62; in the third century, 61, 62; use of, in the Eucharist, 139–40, 141, 142; as a use of sound, 176; in worship models, 200–204 passim
Scripture: as the authoritative source for worship, 14, 197; centrality of, in worship, 51–52
Scripture reading: in evangelical worship, 195; history of, 122–24; as a sign of God speaking, 113; in the third century, 62; as a use of sound, 177; variety in the use of, 107; in worship models, 199–202 passim
Second-century worship, 45–50
Senses: use of, in worship, 108
Sermon: balance of preaching and teaching in, 125; in the early church, 102–3; in evangelical worship, 12–13; in modern Protestant worship, 80–81; prominence and use of, in evangelical worship, 194, 195; in the Reformed church, 78; as a sign of God speaking, 113; in the synagogue, 28–29; as use of

sound, 177; in worship models, 199, 200, 201, 202. See also Preaching.
Signs: and the character of worship, 18–19, 113–15; definition of, 113; make the church visible, 94; necessity of, 112. See also Symbol.
Silence: as preparation for worship, 118
Sinai-event: as an example of structural elements of worship, 24–25; recreated in Passover Seder, 104–5; as a revelatory act of God, 111; significance of, 24, 30, 35, 98; as a source of Christian worship, 23, 93
Singing: congregational, 176, 179, 180–81; of the gospel lesson, 64; of gospel songs, 182–83, 199. See also Hymns; Music; Psalms.
Social implications of worship, 19, 189–90
Sound: in the ancient church, 179; as an element of drama, 106; and the Fall, 88; as a fixed content of Christian worship, 198; in the medieval church, 180; in the modern period, 181–83; in the New Testament church, 178–79; purpose of, 175–76; in the Reformation, 180–81; variety of, 176–78
Space: as an element of drama, 106; evangelical use of, 153; and the Fall, 88, 151, 152; as a fixed content of Christian worship, 198; as a means of communication, 152; redemptive understanding of, 151–52; spiritual significance of, 152–53; use of, in the ancient Syrian church, 155–56; use of, in the late medieval period, 158–59; use of, in the Protestant church, 159–60; use of, in the Roman Basilica, 156–58; use of, in the synagogue, 154–55; use of, in the temple, 25–26
Spirit. See Holy Spirit.
Spiritual view of worship, 31, 79–80

Index of
Scripture References

256 INDEX